The Incarceration of Women

Palgrave Studies in Prisons and Penology

Edited by: **Ben Crewe**, University of Cambridge; **Yvonne Jewkes**, University of Leicester; and **Thomas Ugelvik**, University of Oslo

This is a unique and innovative series, the first of its kind dedicated entirely to prison scholarship. At a historical point in which the prison population has reached an all-time high, the series seeks to analyse the form, nature and consequences of incarceration and related forms of punishment. *Palgrave Studies in Prisons and Penology* provides an important forum for burgeoning prison research across the world.

Series Editors:

Ben Crewe is Deputy Director of the Prisons Research Centre at the Institute of Criminology, University of Cambridge, UK, and co-author of *The Prisoner*.

Yvonne Jewkes is Professor of Criminology, Leicester University, UK. She has authored numerous books and articles on the subject and is editor of the *Handbook on Prisons*.

Thomas Ugelvik is Senior Research Fellow in the Department of Criminology at the University of Oslo, Norway, and editor of *Penal Exceptionalism? Nordic Prison Policy and Practise*.

Advisory Board:

Anna Eriksson, Monash University, Australia
Andrew M. Jefferson, Rehabilitation and Research Centre for Torture Victims, Denmark
Shadd Maruna, Queen's University Belfast, Northern Ireland
Jonathon Simon, UC Berkely, California, USA
Michael Welch, Rutgers University, New Jersey, USA

Titles include:

Vincenzo Ruggiero and Mick Ryan
PUNISHMENT IN EUROPE
A Critical Anatomy of Penal Systems

Linda Moore and Phil Scraton
THE INCARCERATION OF WOMEN
Punishing Bodies, Breaking Spirits

Palgrave Studies in Prisons and Penology
Series Standing Order ISBN 978–1–137–27090–0 (hardback)
(*outside North America only*)

You can receive future titles in this series as they are published by placing a standing order. Please contact your bookseller or, in case of difficulty, write to us at the address below with your name and address, the title of the series and the ISBNs quoted above.

Customer Services Department, Macmillan Distribution Ltd, Houndmills, Basingstoke, Hampshire RG21 6XS, England

The Incarceration of Women

Punishing Bodies, Breaking Spirits

Linda Moore
School of Criminology, Politics and Social Policy, University of Ulster, UK

Phil Scraton
School of Law, Queen's University Belfast, UK

First published 2014 by
PALGRAVE MACMILLAN

Palgrave Macmillan in the UK is an imprint of Macmillan Publishers Limited,
registered in England, company number 785998, of Houndmills, Basingstoke,
Hampshire RG21 6XS.

Palgrave Macmillan in the US is a division of St Martin's Press LLC,
175 Fifth Avenue, New York, NY 10010.

Palgrave Macmillan is the global academic imprint of the above companies
and has companies and representatives throughout the world.

Palgrave® and Macmillan® are registered trademarks in the United States,
the United Kingdom, Europe and other countries.

ISBN 978-1-349-36661-3   ISBN 978-1-137-31784-1 (eBook)
DOI 10.1057/9781137317841

This book is printed on paper suitable for recycling and made from fully
managed and sustained forest sources. Logging, pulping and manufacturing
processes are expected to conform to the environmental regulations of the
country of origin.

A catalogue record for this book is available from the British Library.

A catalog record for this book is available from the Library of Congress.

Contents

Preface   vi

Acknowledgements   ix

1   Women behind Bars   1

2   Agency, Violence and Regulation in the Incarceration
    of Women   28

3   Researching Prison, Women's Voices   54

4   Women's Imprisonment, Conflict and Transition   72

5   Inside a Deteriorating Regime   98

6   Self-Harm and Suicide   120

7   Tale of Two Inquests   149

8   The Prison Within   172

9   The Pain of Confinement and Decarceration   203

*Appendix: Campaign Organizations against Women's
    Imprisonment*   235

Bibliography   238

Index   249

Preface

At a range of levels, the research process underpinning this book is unique. It spans a decade of in-depth, investigative enquiry and analysis during a defining period of political transition and conflict transformation in the North of Ireland – the discrete jurisdiction of Northern Ireland. Initiated and funded by the Northern Ireland Human Rights Commission following its serious concerns about the conditions under which women and girls were incarcerated, the research focused on potential breaches of Articles 2 (right to life) and 3 (inhuman and degrading treatment) of the European Convention on Human Rights. As girls were held in the women's prison, the research extended to cover potential breaches of the UN Convention on the Rights of the Child. We negotiated access to women incarcerated in the Mourne House Unit of the maximum-security and predominantly male jail at Maghaberry. Soon after completion of the first phase of the research, women and girl prisoners were transferred to the medium-security male Young Offenders' Centre at Hydebank Wood where the second phase was conducted.

In both jails, women and girl prisoners were held as a minority population within almost exclusively male environments. The independent, primary research conducted in both institutions over a three-year period is unprecedented, drawing on significant primary testimonies of women combined with close observation of the regimes in process. The story of the research, however, extends beyond the two phases of primary research. While methodology textbooks and ethical guidelines seek to establish clear boundaries between the researcher and 'subject' to establish and sustain 'distance', as if the place of study does not involve directly the 'presence' of the researcher, this is a false aspiration in the real world of conflicted interests and human tension. Prisons and the relationships within are not laboratories; they are closed institutions of volatility, unpredictability, discipline and control. As the research progressed we engaged, institutionally and publicly, in controversies regarding the deaths of women in custody, a hunger strike concerning the status of politically affiliated women prisoners, media revelations of inappropriate behaviour towards women by male prison guards, the use of punitive strip searches and punishment cells for vulnerable women and the debilitating and destructive force of a stagnating regime.

The boundaries we negotiated at the outset of the research dissolved as we took responsibility while the research was ongoing to reveal the harsh realities of the regime's operation not only to the funders, the Commission, but also to prisoners' lawyers and journalists. We understood that such a decision could compromise research access but the reality of 'bearing witness' to institutionalized neglect and, on occasion, cruelty transcends formalized agreements that reduce researchers to spectators. Thus a moral and political judgement has to be taken concerning when, how and in whose best interest researchers move from chronicling to intervening in events. We were well aware that previous researchers had heard disturbing testimonies from the women and girls inside and had chosen to remain silent. With the full support of the Commission, we chose a different path. Based on our research observations and interviews, our immediate interventions were as follows: writing affidavits; giving oral evidence at a judicial review hearing; writing statements and giving extensive oral evidence at two inquests; giving interviews for several television documentaries, radio debates and newspaper articles; and being interviewed by a Prison Review Team appointed by the Northern Ireland Assembly Department of Justice. This generated hostility from the Northern Ireland Prison Service, prison managers and guards and, inevitably, drew claims that the research was 'political' rather than 'academic'.

As this book demonstrates, the sustained impact of the primary research owes much to its access within the jail granted reluctantly via the powers of the Commission. It is also indebted to the openness and honesty of women in informal and formal interviews, focus groups, in prison meetings and in casual conversation. While the women's prison population in Northern Ireland is small, the number of women interviewed and involved in the research well exceeded the population on any given date. Freedom of movement within the prison allowed us to interact not only with women prisoners but also with the regime in operation. Despite an itinerary agreed daily with prison managers, we responded, often spontaneously, to events as they happened. Such rare access was complemented by disclosure of documents, including internal investigation reports on deaths in custody – the Commission was an agreed 'interested party' at the inquests – and the files of women considered 'at risk'. The longitudinal element of the research, although unintended, has enabled a systematic review of the impact of the research alongside the recording of the slow progress of a reform agenda delayed by defensive management and operational practices that should have been consigned to history. Their durability is a key feature of what regularly has been characterized a 'dinosaur mentality' within managerial and staff cultures.

Thus the research explores the dynamics of institutional denial and failure to reform, despite a series of critical inspection and independent monitoring reports, each of which has made recommendations founded on the urgent necessity of a small, discrete women's prison supported by appropriate and effective alternatives to punishment and custody which meet the complex needs of women. As the chapters that follow note, these are not 'new ideas' and have been the established priorities of penal reform and decarceration across democratic societies for half a century. In 2011 the recommendations were endorsed by an independent Prison Review Team established by the Department of Justice when its critical report called for the closure of the women's unit at Hydebank Wood and the creation of a small unit based on therapeutic principles. Subsequently, the Minister of Justice announced plans to progress the development of a discrete women's unit by 2018, 13 years after our first research report was published.

Our research has extended to include these developments, incorporating analysis of the consequences and aftermath of the 2010 devolution of policing and justice powers from the UK Government to the Northern Ireland Assembly. Women in prison in Northern Ireland comprise a small population in a small jurisdiction. Yet, the research and analysis is not limited to place. Clearly, the history of Ireland, the role of the British State, the legacy of the Conflict and the advent of the 'peace process' are each significant to establishing and interpreting the context and circumstances of incarceration during a period of political transition. The wider relevance of this research is its contribution, theoretically and politically, to the growth in international scholarship on the gendered politics, realities and resistances of women's incarceration. It is within that international context that our research and analysis is located.

Acknowledgements

The Incarceration of Women is the culmination of a decade's academic research, diverse publications and public engagement focusing on the lives and experiences of women and girls imprisoned and detained in the North of Ireland. While the research took place in the years following the advent of the Peace Process and the release of politically affiliated prisoners, as this book shows, the legacy of the Conflict has remained a dominant feature in the jails, their regimes and their culture. 'Ordinary' women prisoners have been caught in a double-bind of marginalization. First, they are women in a male penal estate that exudes masculinity in its patriarchal, deeply gendered custom and practice. Second, they are 'ordinary' prisoners in a context of resistance and reform that has prioritized the rights and interests of politically affiliated prisoners. It is instructive that while there are several organizations committed to supporting politically affiliated former prisoners, there have been no similar initiatives working on behalf of the majority prison population.

Research into the prevailing conditions under which women and girls were held in jail was initiated by the Northern Ireland Human Rights Commission. Two extensive research reports were published by the Commission and much of the evidence of the impact of incarceration on the lives of women and girls presented in the book is derived in that primary research. While acknowledging the support for the research from within the Commission, we are profoundly grateful for, and deeply respectful of, the commitment and trust shown to us by women and girl prisoners, former prisoners and prisoners' families whose personal experiences are presented in the core chapters of the book. Our work is predicated on the principle that critical research has a duty to enquire, investigate and bear witness to what happens behind the formidable walls, physical and psychological, of closed institutions. Historically, prisoners individually and collectively have formed alliances and movements demonstrating great strength and resilience in resisting the openly hostile and the quietly subtle manifestations of power in the routines of incarceration.

As the primary research chapters demonstrate, research in prison is contentious. Prison cells, access landings and recreation rooms are prisoners' 'homes'. Yet, there is no privacy. Under constant surveillance, intrusion into a prisoner's space by guards and their managers is forever a turning key. Every moment of 'agency' – the relative freedom of personal action – is also a moment of potential constraint. Every moment of resistance is also a moment of potential punishment. Researchers walk the landings not as guests of prisoners, their presence assumed to be an extension of prison's discretionary reach into the lives of the incarcerated. Critical researchers have a profound ethical responsibility to establish and maintain independence from the penal system, to show respect to all prisoners taking care not to intrude or enquire unless invited. Prisons are not zoos, prisoners are not exhibits, their lives defined solely by a criminal record and a sentence. The validity of research from the inside, the 'view from below', is that it gives the space and opportunity for silenced voices to be heard, it chronicles often contentious and punishing events and it informs public debates about what is done behind closely guarded walls 'in our name'.

* * *

We are grateful to all who informed the research over an extended period within Maghaberry and Hydebank Wood prisons including prison chaplains, volunteers, healthcare and education staff, Independent Monitoring Board members, prison managers and a small number of prison guards. Thank you also to the families' legal teams and lawyers with whom we engaged during the research. We are grateful to John Leckey, senior coroner for Northern Ireland; Kit Chivers, former chief inspector with the Criminal Justice Inspection (Northern Ireland) and the inspection team; Dame Anne Owers, former Chief Inspector for Prisons (England and Wales) and her inspection team; and former Prisoner Ombudsmen for Northern Ireland, Brian Coulter and Pauline McCabe.

The commissioners of the Northern Ireland Human Rights Commission contracted, endorsed and published the initial primary research on which this book is based (neither they nor the Commission are responsible for the contents of, or views expressed herein). The commissioners who initially visited Maghaberry Prison and identified the urgency for an investigation into the treatment of women prisoners showed considerable insight. Chief Commissioner, Professor Brice Dickson, was at all times supportive and his successor, Professor Monica McWilliams, continued to progress the issues and work for the rights of women in prison. Thank you to the staff who worked at the Human Rights Commission during the period of the research, especially Nadia Downing who worked technically to produce the primary research reports and who supported us in our media work. Thanks to our publishers, Palgrave Macmillan, especially Harriet Barker, Julia Willan and Rajeswari Balasubramanian for their patient support. Thank you to Agnieszka Martynowicz for compiling the index.

Finally, and most significantly, we pay tribute to the courage and trust shown by women prisoners in participating in this independent research, discussing often deeply personal issues. This extends to women in the community, including former prisoners, and their families who contributed to the research. We acknowledge particularly the resilience of the families of Annie Kelly and Roseanne Irvine for their openness before, during and after the inquests into the deaths of their loved ones.

Phil thanks his long-time collaborator researching deaths in custody, Kathryn Chadwick, and Anna Eggert, Bill Rolston, Barry Goldson, Janet Johnstone, Karen Lee, Sara Boyce, Laurence McKeown, Edel Quinn, Anne-Marie McAlinden, Faith Gordon, Chelsea Marshall, Bree Carlton, Sheri Chamberlain, Jude McCulloch, Kristin Bumiller, Scott Poynting, Lizzy Stanley, Lilly Artz, Siobhán McAlister, Tony Platt and Deb Coles and Helen Shaw at INQUEST. Thanks for the broader support of colleagues in the Institute of Criminology and Criminal Justice at Queen's University, and the Lowenstein Research Fellowship at Amherst College, Massachusetts, which enabled my contribution towards completion of the project. The support of fellow researchers in the European Group for the Study of Deviance and Social Control has been invaluable, and the annual conference has been a place in which critical scholarship has flourished – long may it continue! Finally, my partner Deena Haydon and sons Paul – partner Katrin Schoenig – and Sean, whose love and support have contributed immensely to my research and writing.

Linda thanks all colleagues in the criminology team and school office at the University of Ulster; Ruth Fee, Head of the School of Criminology, Politics and Social Policy; Cathy Gormley-Heenan, Director of the Institute for Research in Social Sciences; John Offer; Goretti Horgan and colleagues in the University and College Union. Thanks to Goretti Horgan and colleagues in UCU. Thanks for discussions on prison issues and for your support to: Una Convery, Elizabeth Craig, Paddy Kelly, Ann Jemphrey, Jackie Kerr, Agnieszka Martynowicz, Azrini Wahidin and Koulla Yiasouma. Thanks for your friendship and support to Deena Haydon; Tim, Paloma, Conor and Amaia; Malachy, Helen, Andy and Ada; Sam, Ying Ying and Carmel. Thanks to my parents, Alec and Libby Moore, for all their love and support, and to Henry, Alex and Annie with lots of love.

1
Women behind Bars

Introduction

Reflecting a growing literature on women's imprisonment, Diana
Medlicott (2007, p.246) notes that historically it has been a 'shadowy
phenomenon' as the discrete needs of women prisoners have remained
unidentified, institutionally subsumed within policies and practices that
prioritize a majority male prison population. Neglecting women's experiences, and written as if 'gender did not matter' (Bosworth, 2000,
p.266), traditional penal histories have ignored 'the physical presence
of women in prisons and the fact that prisons themselves are gendered
institutions, reflecting and reinforcing beliefs about sexual difference'
(Rafter, 1990, p.xii). Further, the experiences of Black and minority
ethnic women have been marginalized and largely absent from prison
histories.

More recently, feminist criminologists' research and women prisoners' testimonies have sought to redress these imbalances, challenging
established male-oriented interpretations of the penal system. Evidence from these accounts has focused on the gendered construction
of imprisonment, demonstrating that 'interpretive frameworks derived
from men's experience are insufficient' (Knepper and Scicluna, 2010,
p.408). Despite the recent identification of women prisoners' distinct,
gendered needs, at best they remain marginal to the study and practice
of imprisonment.

The genesis of contemporary penal policy and practice can be understood only against the backdrop of the inseparable histories of punishment and incarceration. This chapter explores key developments from
pre-modern punishments, through the emergence of separate prisons

1

for women, to the international rise in women's imprisonment in late 20th-century advanced democratic states. It also traces the origins and consolidation of recent 'gender-specific' initiatives.

Early developments in women's imprisonment

Michael Welch (1997, p.18) considers the 'prominent theme in the history of women and punishment' to be 'the persistent emphasis on regulating female morality'. In early modern European and colonial states, women were subject to extensive social control, punished for alleged witchcraft, adultery, disobedience, sexual deviance and for gossiping – or being 'scolds'. The physicality of punishments inflicted hurt and degradation on the body, including branding, whipping, burning, drowning, hanging and decapitation. A tangible social sanction, punishments were delivered regularly as a public spectacle. Thorsten Sellin (cited in Johnston, 2009, p.14S), for example, notes a woman executed in 1617 in Amsterdam 'had 21 prior arrests and had been exposed on the scaffold 11 times, whipped 8 times, branded with a hot iron 5 times, had her ears cut off, and had been banished for life 7 times'. While men and women were subject to extreme physical brutality, the punishment of women was influenced by social constructions of what constituted female 'decency'. Spierenburg (1998, p.49) notes an example of such ironic gentility in Amsterdam, where most condemned women were garrotted rather than hanged, the former considered as more 'acceptable' for females, despite prolonging the agonies of death.

Throughout the 16th century, changes in socio-economic conditions including mass migration from rural villages to developing urban areas resulted in the growth of begging, vagrancy, prostitution and petty crime. Responding to fears about the potential threat of social unrest, a range of institutions of confinement developed. The industrial revolution created a demand for increased factory labour. Women, children, the mentally ill, the homeless and prostitutes were significant sources of labour, as were those charged with criminal offences. Consequently, 'a merging of the criminal and welfare classes' developed in factories known as 'houses of correction' (O'Toole, 2006, p.9). Throughout Europe and the colonies, 'houses of correction' or 'bridewells' were established to confine those convicted of petty offences such as vagrancy or 'idleness'. Their objective was to reform through labour and women convicted of 'disorderly' conduct, acts involving prostitution, adultery and co-habitation, were committed to houses of correction (Shoemaker, 1991, p.173). From the 17th century, workhouses were built to reform vagrants, beggars and other petty offenders alongside accommodation and welfare relief for poor, old and sick people, orphans and widows.

Despite being centres of punishment and reform, by the 17th century many houses of correction had become corrupt and dangerous places. They included the London Bridewell, run by its governors as a 'highly profitable brothel' (Zedner, 1998, p.295). In contrast, opened in 1645, Amsterdam's Spinhuis was the first discrete women's prison, welcomed as a 'model institution... admired far and wide'. Initially housing only poor and 'disrespectful' women, its population expanded to include women who disobeyed husbands (a persistent theme in the incarceration of women) and parents, 'drunks' and prostitutes. Women were expected to work to 'instil habits of discipline'; the 'order, the systematic labor, and the segregation of the Dutch Spinhuis shone out against the dank, filthy disarray and corruption that overtook most early houses of correction' (p.295).

Prior to the 18th century, jails throughout Europe and the colonies functioned primarily as centres of detention, rather than as places of punishment. They prioritized the incarceration of debtors and those awaiting trial or the execution of a sentence. Women incarcerated in these filthy, disease-ridden and chaotic places were 'generally housed within male prisons and often herded alongside men' (Zedner, 1998, p.295). From the 17th to the 19th century, transportation from Great Britain and Ireland to the colonies of Australia and North America consolidated as an alternative form of punishment for convicted men, women and children. Conditions on convict ships were harsh and many prisoners failed to survive the passage. Women often endured extreme sexual violence from male convicts and sailors. Arriving in Australia, convict women who survived the passage were sent to 'female factories' where they worked at sewing, laundering and spinning. Often subjected to harsh treatment and punishment, many were forcibly separated from their children who were accommodated in orphanages. Over 12,000 women were transported to the female factories in Van Diemen's Land (Tasmania), designated a penal colony throughout the first half of the 19th century (O'Toole, 2006, p.171).

During the 18th century, institutions resembling the modern prison were founded in European cities and by the close of the century imprisonment had embarked on its 'triumphant rise' as the pre-eminent form of punishment (Spierenburg, 1998, p.55). Physical punishments, including execution, continued but were administered less frequently. By the close of the 19th century, many corporal punishments had been 'removed from the public realm'. No longer a public spectacle, executions were carried out 'within prison walls' (Spierenburg, 1998, p.55). Prison architecture developed, emphasizing regulation, order and surveillance, most notably adopting Jeremy Bentham's panoptical design (Hirst, 1998).

Michel Foucault (1979) dates the emergence of a modern, pan-European penal system between the mid-18th and early 19th centuries. McGowan (1998, p.71) notes that 'the contrast between a prison in 1780 and one in 1865 could scarcely have been greater'. The former was disorganized and arbitrary, housing a mixed population and demonstrating 'little evidence of authority'. This was replaced by 'quiet' incarceration, banning conversation under the 'silent system'. Increasingly, prisoners were confined to individual cells, their lives 'carefully regulated' by manifestations of a new 'culture' of imprisonment. Spierenburg (1998, p.58), however, argues that the use of confinement within workhouses as a form of punishment had consolidated and, 'far from representing radical change', the increased number of penitentiaries in the 18th century was a legacy left from the previous two centuries.

Mary Bosworth's (2000) history of female confinement in the Hôpital de la Salpêtrière, Paris, also challenges Foucault's claim of a decisive break between the *ancien* and modern regimes of punishment. She notes that early in the 17th century, Salpêtrière – a female house within the larger Hôpital Général – was shaped by the 'contradictory aims of punishment, welfare and charity' which eventually characterized the 19th-century penal system (Bosworth, 2000, p.269). Salpêtrière was built in response to 'civic concerns about mendacity and urban unrest'. For three decades it was a 'place of general confinement for women', and there were different routes through which women arrived within its walls. Some were sentenced by courts, given specific determinate sentences, while others were detained indefinitely on the demands of neighbours, relatives or husbands, particularly for alleged adultery.

Within the Salpêtrière regime, women were labelled as 'good', 'bad', 'poor' and 'mad' with 'ideas about femininity' determining their treatment (p.267). Bosworth notes an 'overlap of penal ideas' (p.270). For example, women were categorized differently and separated to prevent 'contagion', yet as many as six women shared a single bed. They were stigmatized, often physically branded, heads shaved, and compelled to make public confessions. Constructions of femininity prevailed and women were expected to perform traditionally female tasks such as embroidery and weaving. Although nominally a secular institution, religious services were central to the daily routine.

In the late 18th century the French Revolution, 'superficially at least', introduced an 'equitable, sanitary and universal standard for women's punishment'. By 1794 the women's prison at Salpêtrière was closed. Two years earlier, 35 female residents were killed and others raped by 'marauding' revolutionaries. Bosworth (2000, pp.274–275) concludes that 'female offenders, poor women and those who were mad were not to be suffered either in the old society or in the new'.

The impact of 19th century penal reform movements

As prison building intensified through the 19th century, reform movements developed in Europe, Australia and North America initiating campaigns to end overcrowding and ill-treatment of prisoners and to develop regimes based on rehabilitative ideals. Concerned about the dire conditions in English prisons, penal reformer John Howard travelled extensively, visiting houses of correction and prisons throughout Europe. Particularly impressed by the Dutch example (McGowan, 1998), Howard recommended the separation of male and female prisoners and segregation according to seriousness of criminal offence. He proposed cleanliness and quiet, individual cells for night-time solitude, purposeful work through the day and improvements in health and spiritual care. Gender segregation was also a key concern for other penal reformers, including English Quaker Elizabeth Fry, who established the Newgate-based Ladies' Association for the Reformation of Female Prisoners. Its mission was

> To provide for the clothing, the instruction and the employment of the women; to introduce them to a knowledge of the Holy Scriptures, and to form in them, as much as possible, those habits of order, sobriety and industry which may render them peaceable, whilst in prison, and respectable when they leave it.
>
> (Ryder, 1884 cited in Craig, 2009, p.38S)

Volunteer groups of 'Lady Visitors' were organized to supply food and clothing, befriend women prisoners and establish education for children imprisoned with their mothers. Fry considered that for propriety and to provide positive role models women should be supervised only by female wardens. She upheld the female warden as 'the representative and guardian of her sex' (cited in Zedner, 1998, p.35). In 1825 Fry published *Observations on the Siting, Superintendence, and*

Government of Female Prisoners, offering a vision significantly distinct from male regimes:

> Whereas proposals for male prison reform emphasized uniform treatment, formal direction, and rigid adherence to rules, Fry advocated that women be 'tenderly treated' with gentleness and sympathy so that they would submit cheerfully to the rules and cooperate willingly in their own reform.
>
> (Zedner, 1998, p.301)

While Fry's campaign was significant, in London's Newgate prison overcrowding and poor conditions persisted until its closure in 1828. In the 1820s, however, campaigns by middle-class women reformers contributed to the development of legislation requiring the separation of men and women prisoners in France, the United States and England. In England, legislative reform prohibited the flogging of women prisoners, and the 1823 Gaol Act required the separation of women from men under the supervision of women staff. Brixton prison opened in 1853 as England's first women-only convict prison. Gender segregation also suited the prison authorities as it alleviated concern about sexual abuse, assaults, corruption and prostitution in mixed-gender prisons. The imperative for separate prisons for women in the early 19th century was 'in large part disciplinary' (Zedner, 1998, p.297).

Despite the introduction of legislation requiring separation, 'in practice' implementation tended to be limited to accommodating women within rooms in the male prison. In Craig's (2009, p.385) assessment, however, Fry and her fellow reformers had identified 'humane ways to manage prisoners' in regimes through which 'incarcerated women and children could be rehabilitated'. Lucia Zedner (1998, p.298) agrees that despite limitations regarding its implementation, the principle of gender separation was 'one of the major achievements of nineteenth-century penal reform', sparing women from the 'degradation and exploitation of eighteenth-century prison life'.

Penal reform was not confined to English prisons. In the United States from the period of the American Revolution (1775–1783), the criminal justice system underwent profound change and 'the concept of prison reform seized the imaginations of many Americans' (Freedman, 1984, p.8). It was a politically vibrant period when 'democratic principles were receiving their most enthusiastic endorsement' and openness and opportunity emerged as symbolic ideals. Yet 'those convicted of crimes would be confined behind walls, in single cells, and would follow rigid and unyielding routines' (Rothman, 1998, p.100). In 1790 the first penitentiary was built in Philadelphia, designed as a place for penance where prisoners were expected to reflect in solitude and isolation to repent their sins.

Women prisoners constituted a small proportion of those held in state penitentiaries, less than in local jails. They were 'more closely regulated by... private institutions [the family and church]' and so 'less likely to become the subjects of new public agencies of punishment' (Freedman, 1984, p.10). Sentences, typically, were for 'petty street crimes' and, again reflecting patriarchal values, gender-specific offences that breached 'moral and sexual codes' (p.11). In her historical analysis of women's imprisonment in the United States, Nicole Rafter (1985, p.4) notes that the practice of holding female prisoners *'en masse* in old-fashioned large cells' in separate units within male institutions persisted into the 19th century. While men were closely supervised and regimented, women prisoners 'seldom had a matron' and 'idleness rather than hard labor was their curse'.

Estelle Freedman (1984, p.15) observes that the neglect of women prisoners in US prisons was 'rarely benevolent' and a predominant 'pattern of overcrowding, harsh treatment, and sexual abuse recurred throughout prison histories'. Freedman notes that the dire situation was well illustrated by the death in 1826 of Rachel Welch in New York's Auburn penitentiary. Auburn had no separate, individual cells for women and approximately 30 women were accommodated in an attic. The windows were sealed to prevent communication with men. While held in solitary confinement Rachel Welch became pregnant, was flogged during pregnancy and died in child-birth. In 1828 public concern about the circumstances of her death generated new legislation and the separation of male and female prisoners in county prisons. In 1839 Mount Pleasant Female Prison opened as a separate women's unit within Sing Sing penitentiary (Freedman, 1984).

Rafter (1985, p.10) identifies three phases in securing the separation of male and female prisoners in the United States. First, they were part of the general population, accommodated in separate cells or rooms. Then they were confined in separate sections within or attached to male penitentiaries. Finally, they were moved to discrete more isolated buildings within or outside the grounds of the main prison. Despite reformers' intentions to establish discrete prisons or units to identify and meet the needs of women prisoners, separation often resulted in their neglect as they constituted a small minority within the overall male prison population. Receiving less discipline and supervision than men, women prisoners also had greater opportunities for association, exposing them to higher levels of physical and emotional risk.

In the 1840s, a brief interlude of 'radical experimentation' occurred in Mount Pleasant, the women's unit in Sing Sing male penitentiary. It was initiated by matron Eliza Farnham who 'exhorted staff not to rely on punishment, and abolished the rule of silence' (Zedner, 1998, p.302). It was feared, however, that Farnham's reforms would create discontent among male prisoners and she was forced to resign. Despite such rare initiatives, brutal punishment and treatment persisted throughout US penal establishments. For example, in Ohio Penitentiary in the 1870s, women were not allowed to converse, were held in solitary confinement, beaten and forced to sit naked and blindfolded in tubs of water while electric currents were applied to their bodies (Rafter, 1985).

Throughout Europe, North America, Australia and UK colonies, gender separation became a core characteristic of penal regimes, often after scandals and inquiries regarding women's treatment in male regimes. However, the implementation of gender separation was often *ad hoc* and piecemeal, as evidenced by the Canadian example. Opened in 1835, Kingston Penitentiary was 'one of the first Canadian institutions to incarcerate women for long periods of time' (Arbour, 1996, p.239). From inception, provision of appropriate arrangements for women presented challenges for the regime. As Roger Neufeld notes (1998, p.101), when the first three women arrived at Kingston in 1835, 'authorities had no idea where to put them... [and they] were whisked to the prison hospital, which became female quarters until 1839, when other makeshift arrangements were made'. Along with mentally ill prisoners, women were viewed by the regime as 'nuisances by their presence in the penitentiary'. They 'seemed forever in the way of the prison's expansion' and were 'moved from the hospital to another wing [the North Wing], and in 1852 were again housed in the prison hospital awaiting the completion of the new dining hall' (p.102). In 1849 the Brown Royal Commission of Inquiry reported on 'severe abuses, the neglect of women prisoners, and a general lack of accountability on behalf of prison administrators'. The Brown Commission made recommendations including the 'construction of a separate living unit for women, who were forced to live in deplorable conditions' (cited in Arbour, 1996, p.240). Despite acknowledgement of the need for a separate women's unit, this was not provided until early in the 20th century.

A key development in the history of female incarceration during the second half of the 19th century in England was the women's reformatory movement inspired by Mary Carpenter. In 1846 Carpenter opened a 'ragged school' for destitute children in Bristol, England, followed by a reformatory for boys and girls in 1852 (Hendrick, 2006). The new profession of psychiatry influenced the ethos of the reformatories. In England, Zedner (1998, p.318) considers the reformatory objective was overtly 'eugenicist' with institutions created 'specifically to incarcerate those women who seemed to present a risk to the future health of the race'. Habitual women offenders who 'defied all reformatory efforts', presented a problem for the authorities and raised doubts about the potential of the reformatory project. The centralization of the English prison system in 1877 'sounded a death knell to innovation and individual treatment' and the reformatory project was 'largely abandoned'.

In the United States, the Indiana Reformatory Institution for Women and Girls was established in 1873 as the first discrete institution for offending women. In 1899 it was divided into an Industrial School for Girls and a Women's Prison. At the height of the reformatory movement, there were over 20 reformatories across the United States, based on cottage-style accommodation. In American reformatories, children were permitted to remain with their mothers until the age of two. Reformatory life was less harsh than the penitentiary, and some supervisors were committed to supporting women in their care. Accommodation was domestic in style with access to fresh air and education. Yet the reformatory was often more oppressive as women who failed to demonstrate their progress towards becoming reformed characters could be held for longer periods than the tariff they had received. Mentally ill women could be incarcerated indefinitely (Zedner, 1998). Race and class were significant in determining placement in reformatories while they were reserved primarily for White northern women, Black women continued to be sentenced to penal servitude (Craig, 2009). Rafter notes:

> The misdemeanants who at first filled the reformatories were mainly whites, women considered worthy of the expense and effort of rehabilitation. Most custodial units for women, on the other hand, held disproportionate numbers of black women.
>
> (Rafter, 1985, p.180)

In France, the École de Reform opened in 1891 on the site of the former Salpêtrière, for the confinement of up to 60 poor and 'morally abandoned' girls (Bosworth, 2000). In the École, young women were exposed to the 'new' science of psychiatry and placed in domestic occupations on release. Surveillance was emphasized with a relatively high 'staff-inmate' ratio (Bosworth, 2000, p.275) and 'incorrigible' girls were identified and excluded from the mainstream. The regime was based on a strict timetable involving sewing, embroidery, cleaning and education, each promoting clear gender conformity. However distinct from Salpêtrière, according to Bosworth (p.275), the École persisted in 'punishing morally suspect behaviour'.

In Freedman's (1984, p.109) assessment, 'by the close of the nineteenth century, women's prison reform had reached a point of stagnation' as reformers struggled to defend previous advances rather than progressing new ideas. In the United States during the First World War, public sympathy for women in prison was scarce (Zedner, 1998). Cuts in public funding generated worse conditions, increasing tensions in reformatories. Doubts were raised publicly concerning reformatories' apparent failure to achieve rehabilitation. By the 1930s, prostitution was 'no longer a source of national alarm', the momentum of the 'first-wave' feminist reform movement had abated and space was needed in central prisons for escalating male imprisonment (Rafter, 1985, p.182). The reformatory movement ended in the mid-1930s when custodial and reformatory institutions for women were merged, thus further marginalizing women and neglecting gender-specific needs. As Rafter states:

> No longer were women in prison the object of intense rehabilitative efforts by women outside the walls; no longer did legislatures fund elaborate programs for female inmates. Women held in reformatories came to be disregarded, just as women in custodial institutions had always been, by a correctional system designed around the demands of the larger male population.
>
> (Rafter, 1985, p.182)

The reformatories, however, produced a 'residue' and female prisoners 'continued to be treated as children' (p.183). In Britain a 'similar pattern of disillusionment and decline' occurred and by the 1920s all reformatories for female alcoholics were closed (Zedner, 1998, p.321).

A key development in the late 19th and early 20th centuries was the increased emphasis on 'medical' treatment of those labelled 'deviants' or offenders. In England, in 1861 a separate wing for 'criminal lunatics' opened in London's Bethlem Hospital, followed in 1863 by the Broadmoor asylum for 'criminal lunatics'. This did not signal the end of imprisoning the mentally ill as 'special provision' was developed simultaneously within the prison system for 'those who were not to be transferred to hospital' (Senior and Shaw, 2007, p.377).

In 1895 the Gladstone Committee recommended that 'all prison medical officers should have experience in the subject of lunacy' (cited in Senior and Shaw, 2007, p.378). In 1907 Aylesbury Convict Prison for Women was the first to segregate 'feeble-minded' prisoners (Zedner, 1998, p.320). Feminists argued that, given the impacts of poverty and mental ill-health, many women should not be imprisoned (Zedner, 1998). They lobbied for the appointment of female medical doctors and female inspectors in all women's establishments (Zedner, 2006). The role of prison medical staff expanded, 'most notably in the provision of psychiatric reports to courts' (Senior and Shaw, 2007, p.378).

Freedman describes similar developments in the United States where social scientists, influenced by eugenics, initiated and institutionalized extensive programmes based on the mental testing of prisoners. This led directly to the proposition that 'defective or disturbed' prisoners might 'benefit from special treatment' (Freedman, 1984, p.119). As Rotman explains (1998, p.159), 'progressives fully endorsed a medical or therapeutic model of rehabilitating inmates, on the assumption that criminal offenders suffered from some form of physical, mental or social pathology'. The impact of what became the 'psychiatrization' of prisons was dramatic. By 1926 in the United States, 'sixty-seven prisons employed psychiatrists, and forty-five had psychologists' while special institutions were opened for 'defective delinquents' (Rotman, 1998, pp.159–160).

Developments in 20th century women's penal regimes

Reviewing the treatment of incarcerated women during the 19th century, Pat Carlen identifies the following defining characteristics:

> evidence of paternalistic and patriarchal attitudes on the part of the prison staff; closer surveillance and regulation of prisoners than in the men's prisons; the isolation of women from each other for much of the time, and their employment in low-paid 'women's work' or domesticity when they are in association; special accommodation for prisoners' children being incorporated into the living arrangements; self-mutilation and suicides by prisoners; a greater number of punishments for offences against prison discipline awarded to female prisoners than to males; a narrower range of facilities than for male prisoners and recurring concerns about sexual abuse of female prisoners by male officers.
>
> (Carlen, 1998, pp.14–15)

Throughout the 20th century and across a range of jurisdictions, separate penal regimes for women were adopted. In Australia a separate women's prison was developed at Long Bay in 1909. Regarded as a 'model prison, founded on high-minded therapeutic lines', it was 'praised as one of the few purpose-designed women's prisons in the world' (McCormack, 2008). In 1913 in Canada a separate women's section was opened within Kingston Penitentiary's grounds. Two decades later women were moved to the newly developed Kingston Prison for women. The first purpose-built women's prison was developed in New Zealand in1944 at Arohata. Most of the new women's prisons in these jurisdictions were staffed by female officers, the chaplain being the only male permitted inside the institution.

Johnston (2009, p.29S) observes that as prisons expanded 'more highly differentiated institutions in terms of security level, age, gender, and mental status' evolved, and by the mid-1920s most states had separate penal institutions for women. While the 19th century was a period of intensive reform, Zedner (1998, p.320) states that on both sides of the Atlantic 'the early twentieth century was a period of disillusionment' as optimism regarding the potential for reforming 'deviant women' had waned.

The founding, development and consolidation of London's main prison for women, Holloway, encapsulates the contemporary history of women's imprisonment. Opened in 1852 in north London, initially it was a mixed 'house of correction' for men, women and juveniles, proclaiming its mission as a 'terror to evil doers' (cited in Camp, 1974, p.20). In 1900 a Prison Commissioners' report recommended that imprisonment in Holloway should be restricted to women. In 1902 it was designated women-only and those imprisoned for 'prostitution' or 'drunkenness' constituted two-thirds of its population. In 1907 Dr Mary Gordon was appointed as the first Inspector of Women's Prisons and introduced changes to women's regimes at Holloway and Aylesbury, including provision of drill, exercise and various, 'appropriate' work opportunities (Camp, 1974).

Reflecting on her 19 years as a warder in the early 20th century, Agnes Resbury describes Holloway: 'by far the nicest Prison, kept beautifully clean and wholesome, really quite comfortable, the women also looking clean. They are generally pretty lively, as far as they are allowed to be, but they must have discipline' (cited in Dodge and Forward, 2006, p.786). For Resbury, the majority of women were 'to be pitied after one hears the sad tales from their own lips of their outside lives' (p.787). Her fond depictions of Holloway, however, contrast markedly with suffragette Sylvia Pankhurst's account: 'the baths were indescribably dirty, the paint discoloured and worn off in patches, showing the black iron beneath, the woodwork encasing them sodden and shiny' (Pankhurst, cited in Dodge and Forward, 2006, p.803).

Between 1905 and 1914, the imprisonment of suffragettes raised the public profile of women's imprisonment. For the first time upper, middle and working class women were incarcerated together. Media reports of suffragettes' treatment, including handcuffing and force-feeding hunger strikers, provoked public outrage. In her memoirs, Resbury recalls attempts to forcibly strip approximately 40 suffragettes in 1906. On admission, the women refused to undress stating 'they were not going to obey the rules made by mere men'. Female warders attempted to strip women who resisted and, 'soon we were all on the floor, a tangled mass just struggling, and didn't know who we were tugging at, ourselves or a suffragette. They were allowed to go to their cells as they were for the time being' (p.799). Zedner considers the imprisonment of suffragettes was 'perhaps the greatest influence on the treatment of women prisoners' (2006, p.38).

In 1927 Mary Size was appointed as Holloway's first woman deputy governor. Soon after, Lillian Barker was appointed as the first woman Assistant Prison Commissioner. These were significant developments in the history of women's imprisonment in Britain (Camp, 1974). Size was committed to improving conditions and prisoners redecorated the prison, gardens were developed and the condemned cell demolished (in 1955, however, Ruth Ellis was the last woman to be executed in Holloway). Women were allowed to decorate cells with personal belongings and regular tuition in 'domestic' subjects was introduced. There was a small remuneration paid to women for their work, and they could purchase cosmetics with their earnings. 'Lights out' at 10 p.m. gave women the opportunity to read in their cells throughout the evenings.

Size's reforms included improvements in prisoner health care, particularly prenatal care. She faced initial opposition from prison officers for whom positive involvement with prisoners was anathema. Hampered also in progressing reforms by Holloway's austere buildings, Size and Barker proposed the construction of a new women's prison, the latter proclaiming that 'instead of parking women in prison I should like to imprison them in a park' (cited in Camp, 1974, p.100). In 1939 the outbreak of war resulted in the abandonment of their reform project. Prisoners nearing the end of their sentence were released, and those remaining were transferred to Aylesbury. Three years later women returned to Holloway, and Mary Size retired the following year. From

1948 pregnant prisoners were permitted to give birth in a community hospital as an alternative to Holloway. Babies could remain with their mothers in prison for nine months. If transferred to an open prison, the child could remain with its mother until the age of two. In 1949 Dr Charity Taylor was appointed as Holloway's first female governor (Camp, 1974).

Carlen (1998, p.15) notes that throughout the 20th century the prevalent view was that most women prisoners suffered mental ill-health requiring medical or therapeutic treatment. It was 'this belief in the fundamental pathology of female prisoners' (p.16) that informed the decision in 1968 to redevelop Holloway as a secure hospital for women prisoners. New Holloway had no hospital wing, thus confirming the regime's generic 'therapeutic nature'. It was proposed that a doctor be appointed as its first governor, 'reflecting the mixing of medical and disciplinary functions' (Maden, 1996, p.8). Tony Maden concludes that the Holloway experiment was 'a failure' and 'rather than a model for other prisons, the new Holloway became notorious for its repressive regime'. Violence, destruction and self-harm were common and 'a minority of seriously mentally ill women were held in unacceptable and squalid conditions' (Moorehead, cited in Maden, 1996, p.8). The Home Office concluded that 'most women in prison were "depressingly normal", in that their offending was not a result of psychiatric disorder and was not amenable to medical treatment'. Consequently, Holloway was 'reorganized to separate disciplinary and medical systems' (p.9).

Carlen states that in the 1960s, a period when women prisoners were identified primarily as potential mental patients, a new generation of campaigners emerged. They proposed that 'equal rights and responsibilities' should be 'tempered by a recognition of the special medical, emotional, psychological and social needs of female prisoners' distinct from those of male prisoners (Carlen, 1998, p.17). They considered holding petty persistent offenders within Holloway's secure hospital environment inappropriate. During the decades that followed, 'the notion of the "therapeutic prison" for women was abandoned by prison administrators', yet prison staff continued to treat women as 'mad', thereby justifying the maintenance of infantilizing regimes (p.17).

The global rise of women's imprisonment

In 1970 a UK Home Office Report predicted 'it may well be that as the end of the century draws nearer penological progress will result in ever fewer or no women at all being given prison sentences' (cited in Carlen,

1983, p.23). This aspiration proved unattainable as the prevailing punitive climate contributed to a steady rise in women's imprisonment
rather than a commitment to the development of constructive alternatives. In fact, while women have continued to comprise a small
percentage of the overall prison population, the increase in women prisoners has been disproportionate. In 1981 the average daily women's
population in England and Wales was 1,407 (Home Office, 1982 in
Carlen, 1998: 26). By November 2012, however, the women's prison
population exceeded 4,100 (Ministry of Justice, 2012a). There has also
been a disproportionate increase in 'foreign national' prisoners, their
numbers doubling within a decade (Ministry of Justice 2012b).

Although England and Wales have 'the highest overall imprisonment rate in Western Europe, coupled with serious overcrowding'
(Medlicott, 2007, p.245), the rise in women's imprisonment has been
global (Sudbury, 2005). It is estimated that more than 500,000 women
are imprisoned throughout the world at any one time (Ashdown and
James, 2010, p.123) including approximately 100,000 women in Europe
(UNODC & WHO 2009, p.1). Reviewing evidence from a range of jurisdictions, McIvor and Burman (2011, p.6) conclude that increased levels
of women's imprisonment have been a 'defining feature of western
jurisdictions in recent years' noting a 'particularly dramatic' rise in
the United States (p.9). Australia, New Zealand and many European
jurisdictions have also generated a significant expansion of women's
imprisonment (McIvor and Burman, 2011).

Instructively, the global increase does not reflect an increased frequency in or seriousness of women's offending behaviour. As Medlicott
(2007, p.247) states, women's offending is distinctive, it 'poses far less
of a threat to order and safety in society, and demonstrates a much
lower level of violence'. Women commit less serious and less violent
offences than men and are less likely to be repeat or persistent offenders. During the 1980s, a body of research demonstrated that women
were often sentenced 'not primarily according to the seriousness of
their crimes but more according to the courts' assessment of them
as wives, mothers and daughters' (Carlen, 1983, p.18). Further, there
has been a marked increase in women being sentenced for drug- and
alcohol-related offences (Medlicott, 2007, pp.246–247).

Loraine Gelsthorpe and Allison Morris (2002) note that the crimes for
which women receive prison sentences tend to be non-serious property
offences, suggesting that the relatively small increase in such offending is linked primarily to Class B drug offences. Most disconcerting is
Medlicott's (2007, p.249) finding that 'most of the rise in the female

prison population can be explained by the significant increase of severity in sentencing'. Gill McIvor and Michele Burman (2011, p.16) suggest that women's difficulties in meeting the 'technical' requirements of community supervision and the increased use of custodial remand are contributing factors to the increase in women's imprisonment. Consequently, Gelsthorpe and Morris (2002) propose a radical shift in sentencing policy and penal practice to reverse the punitive custodial trend.

Stephanie Covington and Barbara Bloom attribute the increase in women's imprisonment in the United States to

> the war on drugs; the shift in legal and academic realms toward a view of lawbreaking as individual pathology, ignoring the structural and social causes of crime; government policies that prescribe simplistic, punitive enforcement responses to complex social problems; federal and state mandatory sentencing laws; and the public's fear of crime even though crime in the United States has been declining for nearly a decade.
>
> (Covington and Bloom, 2003, pp.1–2)

Julia Sudbury's (2005) edited international collection on research into women's imprisonment connects the globalization of capital to the 'unprecedented incarceration and victimization of immigrants, women and people of color, and the poor' (p.15). This 'explosion' in women's imprisonment has resulted in 'spiralling incarceration rates, rampant overcrowding, and systematic human rights violations' in women's prisons, 'from Lagos to Los Angeles' (p.xiv). The transnational sex and drugs trades, together with legislation and policies criminalizing migration, have fuelled the industrial–penal complex. Sudbury tasks the anti-globalization movement with monitoring the spaces that 'warehouse those who are surplus or resistant to the new world order', emphasizing the need to bring together 'antiglobalization and antiprison praxis' (pp.xii–xiii).

Women's gendered prison experiences

A thematic inspection of women's imprisonment by the Prisons Inspectorate in England and Wales (HMCIP, 1997) found that issues facing women include difficulties in maintaining access to their children; homelessness; unemployment; educational deficits; background of local authority care; prior experience of physical and sexual abuse; legal and illegal substance use; self-harm and suicide attempts; and mental ill-health. During a 24-hour period, the inspectors recorded the complex range of incidents within one women's prison: a woman setting fire to herself; a fight; a woman's transfer to the high-security male environment of HMP Belmarsh; a woman's transfer to hospital to enable the breastfeeding of her premature baby; the separation of two mothers from their babies; a woman swallowing a needle; and a terminally ill woman declining a hospital appointment because she refused to be handcuffed.

Research by the Office for National Statistics (Singleton et al., 1998) found that 40 per cent of women prisoners had received mental health support prior to imprisonment, and 22 per cent of remand and 15 per cent of sentenced prisoners had been admitted previously to a mental hospital (p.8). Approximately two-thirds of women imprisoned in England are mothers, and of these over two-thirds are serving a first custodial sentence. Women prisoners are more likely than male prisoners to have experienced educational deficits. Most women in prison are 'tragically damaged and have suffered the very many kinds of social exclusion, abuse and marginalization, to which the defining stigma of prison is then added' (Medlicott, 2007, p.253). A thematic inspection of prisoners' mental health needs concluded that distress caused by earlier traumatic experiences was, for women, more likely to result in self-harm and suicide attempts – violence inflicted on the self – whereas for men their violence was directed towards others (HMCIP, 2007). In the United States, Bloom and Covington (2008, p.8) note high levels of mental ill-health and experiences of abuse and trauma among women prisoners, concluding that '[r]esearch on women's pathways into crime indicates that gender matters'.

As stated previously, because women prisoners constitute a small minority of the overall prison population, the identification, understanding and realization of their needs consistently, across jurisdictions, have been marginalized if not ignored (Carlen, 1983). This institutionalized neglect ranges 'from the architecture of prisons, to security procedures, to facilities for healthcare, family contact, work and training' (Bastick and Townsend 2008, p.1). The 'pains of imprisonment' (Sykes, 1958) for women are mediated by gender, class, culture and 'race' (McCulloch and George, 2009). Disciplinary procedures, strip-searching, physical restraint, use of punishment and isolation cells and access to education, health and other services are among the key practices experienced differentially (see Scraton and Moore, 2005, 2007). Jude McCulloch and Amanda George (2009, pp.121–122) focus on strip-searching as a form 'of sexual coercion, which reinforces women's sense of powerlessness and undermines self-esteem and self-worth'.

Carlen's pioneering research in Cornton Vale, Scotland's only discrete women's prison found that women were incarcerated as much for 'stepping outwith domestic discipline' (Carlen, 1983, p.16) as for 'criminal' acts. The relatively small prison population contributed significantly to their 'invisibility' within the penal estate (p.4). Their imprisonment was 'denied' on several levels: 'it is denied that the women's prison is a real prison, it is denied that the women are real prisoners and it is denied that the prisoners are real women' (p.211). Consequently, women were 'defined out of existence as being beyond care, cure and recognition' (p.17).

In her research, Carlen revealed a regime characterized by separation from families, dull unproductive routine, long periods of lock-up, few activities, limited training or vocational opportunities and high levels of surveillance. Daily monotony, alongside disciplinary processes and staff attitudes infantalizing adult women, resulted in their debilitation while provoking a constant atmosphere of tension. Simple acts of kindness, such as sharing sweets or tobacco with a newly admitted prisoner, were subject to disciplinary punishment. A small population of women sentenced for a wide variety of offending behaviours, from fine default to murder, were held in a single prison in which disciplinary and security regimes were founded on the 'most difficult prisoner' or the highest level security risk (p.21).

While women were incarcerated physically, they were also 'mentally and emotionally straitjacketed' by the application of a rigid, disciplinary system (p.102). Women diagnosed as 'personality disordered' faced a harsh regime. Mental health professionals viewed this condition as untreatable. They used their privileged, professional position to make '*judicial* judgements', including refusing to admit or transfer ill women to hospital (p.203). Incarceration offered no support and no relief for these women, often worsening their ill-health. Shunned by their families and communities on release, they quickly returned to jail. As Carlen notes, 'after several years in the revolving door syndrome they are beyond recognition' (p.210).

Audrey Peckham's personal account of Pucklechurch remand centre and Styal Prison illustrates women's gendered experiences. Following a hysterectomy, Peckham was spared the degradation she witnessed inflicted on others:

> Tampons were handed out sparingly, if at all. I can imagine what it must have been like to be locked up all night with a heavy period and no access to a clean towel; to have to use the pot and have nowhere

to wash your hands. And if, by any chance, you had managed to get an extra [sanitary] towel in the cell and could change, you then had to live in the cell with the soiled towel and its smell until you were next unlocked.

(Peckham, 1985, p.30)

Prison doctors were reluctant to provide medication prescribed to women by doctors in the community and those addicted to illegal drugs were withdrawn without therapeutic support in conditions that 'amounted to solitary confinement' (p.32). While being 'in need of therapy', Peckham soon realized that it was 'not part of any prison system'. The response was to put her in 'strips' to ensure she did not take her own life:

I was left with only a mattress and my plastic mug. I was told to take all my clothes off, and given a strip gown to put on. This was a tunic-like garment made out of specially strengthened material, so that it could not be torn up and used to strangle myself. Two strip blankets were given to me, which were of similar material, but quilted like an eiderdown. For two days and two nights that is all I had in my cell... I was left alone with my misery. (p.53)

Remand was tedious, with long periods of lock-up and few opportunities for association or activity. As the sole relief from monotony, mealtimes became a 'preoccuption' (p.79). Once sentenced, Peckham was transferred to Styal where staff were 'petty minded' in making prisoners' lives 'as difficult as possible' (p.172). The regime was strict and women faced arbitrary and inconsistent punishment, often without warning. There were 'no secure boundaries' in a prevalent atmosphere of 'fluid madness'. She states, 'I was suddenly returned to my small childhood, being shouted at by furious adults for some transgression which I did not even know was a transgression' (p.174).

Alexandra Mandaraka-Sheppard's primary research (1986, p.192) explores the causes of conflict and aggression in women's prisons in England, identifying the strategies adopted by women in their negotiation of 'institutional pressures'. She notes a higher level of physical violence in closed prisons as a consequence of the responses and reactions of individual women rather than collective action (pp.194–195). Having a history of violence in the community, however, was not a predictor of violent behaviour in prison. Prisoners who violated prison rules were, typically, young and single. Echoing Carlen on the management of women prisoners, Mandaraka-Sheppard records an 'obsession with security precautions, the pettiness of rules, the injustice in the enforcement of the rules and adjudications' (p.195).

Mary Eaton's research (1993, pp.18–19) identifies the damage caused by prison regimes to women's confidence and its inhibition on successful resettlement on release. Wybron and Dicker's (2009) research with Australian women prisoners finds that life on release is often confusing and lonely, emphasizing their disconnection from the community. Prison regimes based on strict routines and surveillance result in women's exclusion from minor decision-making, raising the spectre of institutionalization. Describing her release, one woman stated, 'I totally lost myself, I would sit on the couch with my knees up to my chest every day, I didn't know what to do, and I was so scared' (p.20).

Shoshana Pollack (2008) research documents the serious issues facing women on release from prison, including resuming addictions; obtaining employment; difficulties in dealing with banks and social services; and relationship-related stress. Challenging the concepts of 're-integration' and 'community', she notes that women often find themselves 'barred from the larger community' while 'no longer connecting to their former community' (p.27). She recommends the development of appropriate services including peer support, pre-release information, day-release programmes, half-way houses, addiction treatment and 'feminist-informed' trauma services. Critically, she proposes that community organizations should be autonomous from the justice system in establishing programme content and facilitating delivery.

Bree Carlton and Maria Segrave (2011) study of the deaths and near deaths of women post-release from prison in Victoria, Australia, identifies the significance of trauma on their lives. For many women, imprisonment is itself inherently traumatic. While for some it provides a 'temporary reprieve' from the hardships of life they endure in their lives outside, invariably it results in further 'marginalization and isolation' (pp.559–560). On their release from prison women experienced, 'loneliness, boredom, coping with disappointment and death and their self-identification as failed mothers'. Some who succeeded in finding a home or regaining custody of their children took their own lives, demonstrating the inescapable impact of their trauma.

Gender-specific reforms

As noted above, in most jurisdictions the last two decades have been marked by spiralling rates of women's incarceration, prison overcrowding and a significant increase in self-harm and suicide in prison. Paradoxically, during this period within most jurisdictions attempts have been made to develop alternatives to custody and to reform prison regimes. Compelling and consistent research findings, evidencing the dangers of holding women in male-oriented regimes, have contributed to the emergence in principle of gender-specific programmes and policies. Bloom and Covington (2008) argue that gender-specific programmes should provide 'comprehensive services that take into account the context and content of women's lives', recognizing that 'a woman cannot be treated in isolation from her social support network' while promoting 'continuity-of-care' in response to addictions, trauma and mental ill-health. Monica Barry and Gill McIvor (2008, p.6) suggest that 'gender specific intervention for women needs to be more informal, less structured and supportive of needs other than offending behaviour', offering 'emotional support' for women's complex problems at times of crisis. Effective community interventions should be developed to address the structural context of women's needs, focusing on 'empowerment' and 'mutual engagement', 'reducing their powerlessness' and 'promoting agency' (Sheehan, McIvor and Trotter 2011, p.xix).

Demonstrating the deeply institutionalized power of prisons, however, significant barriers to reform remain. For example, events in Canada in the 1980s brought reforms that have left an instructive legacy. A Task Force, involving civil servants and representatives from prison reform groups, was established in response to a crisis in Canada's only federal prison for women in Kingston. It was a consequence of a deteriorating, unsafe regime. The Task Force reported in 1990, recommending the prison's closure and its replacement by four smaller regional prisons. These would reflect women-centred principles and include a 'Healing Lodge' for Aboriginal women who were significantly over-represented within the criminal justice system. The Task Force anticipated that women prisoners would be housed in 'cottage style' buildings, with 'natural light', access to land and 'dynamic security' (Hayman, 2007). The Healing Lodge would embody Aboriginal principles of justice, incorporating a 'healing circle'. By 1997 four regional prisons had opened, including the Edmonton Institution for Women and the Okimaw Ohci Healing Lodge.

Yet, in 1994 events at Kingston threatened the apparently progressive outcomes of the Task Force's recommendations. Eight women in the segregation unit were forced to the floor, shackled in restraints and leg irons and stripped naked by an all-male search team. The riot-equipped team was deployed in a six-hour raid. Before the restraints were removed, prisoners were required to 'consent' to a 'body cavity search' by a medical doctor and a woman who refused to give consent was held in restraints overnight. In 1996 the Arbour Commission of Inquiry established that the treatment inflicted on the women had been 'cruel, inhuman and degrading'. It contested the authorities' proposition that women in restraints and leg irons had the capacity to volunteer 'consent' to intimate searches. The Commission's report led to the immediate resignation of the prison director and in 2000 Kingston Prison closed.

As Margaret Malloch (2013, p.81) states, 'reservations about the potential for creating a space of "healing" within a penal environment were expressed from the outset', yet at the same time there was a 'very real need to improve circumstances for women in prison generally, and a desperate need to do something for Aboriginal women prisoners'. Canadian penal regimes for women were in need of significant reform and while progress had been made, the core issues persisted. As the Arbour Commission was in session and within months of opening in 1995, the new prison in Edmonton was in crisis, following suicide attempts, self-harm and a murder (Hayman, 2007). Stephanie Hayman notes that when women first entered the prison, it was unsuitable for occupation. From the outset it held a high number of maximum-security prisoners, offered few programmes and its staff had not received appropriate training. Consequently, maximum security prisoners were transferred to discrete units within male prisons. Further, the Task Force had failed to plan effectively for 'difficult to manage women'. High levels of segregation were used and guards were unable to engage effectively or sensitively with women locked in isolation. Aboriginal women were disproportionately classed as 'maximum security', thus prohibiting admission to the Healing Lodge.

Hayman (2007) concludes that due to middle-class values and perceptions, the Task Force's recommendations reflected assumptions of 'idealized' womanhood. While ostensibly proposing to generate 'pathways into the community', its strategy remained 'grounded in the prison' (p.200):

> What this Canadian story…highlights is the way in which feminist interventions in the criminal justice arena have contributed to more oppressive regimes for women prisoners, even if the women involved have not necessarily been responsible for this outcome.

Similarly, Malloch (2013, p.86) identifies some positive aspects of the Healing Lodges, noting that Okimaw Ohci has the 'potential to make a difference to the lives of individuals able to access this resource' and women 'often appreciate the space that can be created through the opportunity to access support and "time" to collect the fragments of a life'. However, the 'effect of classification and assessment practices and the disproportionate number of Aboriginal women in Canadian prisons' resulted in few Aboriginal women gaining access to the Healing Lodge (p.83). Despite some positive initiatives within the prisons, Malloch concludes, 'there appears to be some evidence that circumstances *outside* the prison have worsened for women', leading to a rise in the proportion of Aboriginal women in the prison system (p.83).

The UK process of penal reform also has proved to be disappointing. In 2001 the UK Government published a *Strategy for Women Offenders*. This was followed in 2004 by the *Women's Offending Reduction Programme*, a multi-agency strategy aimed at creating an integrated or 'joined-up' approach to policy and practice. The establishment in 2002 of the Asha Centre in England and a year later the 218 Centre in Scotland are initiatives adopting alternative responses to women's offending, providing support including drugs and alcohol programmes, welfare services, education and training, and parenting. Evaluations of these initiatives have been mainly positive (see Loucks et al., 2006), yet there has been no significant reduction in women's imprisonment.

As a consequence of political and public concerns about suicides in women's prisons, Baroness Corston was appointed to conduct a review of vulnerable women in the criminal justice system in England and Wales. She expressed dismay at finding 'so many women frequently sentenced for short periods of time for very minor offences, causing chaos and disruption to their lives and families, without any realistic chance of addressing the causes of their criminality' (Corston, 2007, p.i).

While noting improvements in prison health care, and a corresponding reduction in the level of self-inflicted deaths, Corston concluded that 'radical change' was required in the treatment of women prisoners within the criminal justice system and she recommended a 'woman-centred' approach. She proposed that the Government should develop immediately a 'clear strategy to replace existing women's prisons with suitable, geographically dispersed, small, multi-functional custodial centres within 10 years'. The strategy should include improvements in conditions in existing prisons; reduction of strip searching to the 'absolute minimum compatible with security'; and a programme initiative for foreign national offenders, including measures to reduce the use of imprisonment (p.5).

Corston also proposed that women's custodial centres should be 'removed from the Prison Service', to be managed and staffed by 'specialists in working with women' under the direction of a 'Commission for Women who offend or are at risk of offending' (p.86). Each centre should accommodate between 20 and 30 women, prioritizing those receiving sentences of two years and above. Custodial sentences should be restricted to serious and violent offenders who present a demonstrable threat to the public. She considered there should be reduced levels of custodial remand and the development of supported bail placements. Primary carers of young children 'should be remanded in custody only after consideration of a probation report on the probable impact on the children'. Community solutions for non-violent women should 'be the norm' (p.9).

The UK Government's response to Corston, published in December 2007, accepted her broad analysis and most of her recommendations. Yet, six years on, Corston's key recommendations remain unimplemented. The Government's response regarding the development of small, local women's prison units has been evasive, agreeing only to conduct an evaluation on their potential (Ministry of Justice, 2007, p.11). The recommendation to abandon strip-searching was only 'partially accepted' (p.12). The Government did not fully accept the recommendation that women unlikely to receive a custodial sentence should not be remanded to custody (p.20), rejecting the proposition for increased 'flexibility' in sentencing when community orders are breached (p.23).

Conclusion

Several defining issues emerge from this necessarily brief excursion into the history of women's imprisonment in societies transitioning towards democracy. Since the development of the modern prison system, women's imprisonment has been marginalized within a penal system aimed at male prisoners under the direction of male managers and staffed by male guards. Women's prisons became institutionalized as adjuncts within male penal estates as had women's units been marginalized previously within male jails. It is also a history of subjugation to gendered punishments and sexual abuse.

Women held in predominantly male jails endured degradation, neglect and violence on a continuum leading to sexual assault and rape. As prisons and other sites of incarceration transformed from places of direct punishment on the body to places, at least in proclamation, of reform and rehabilitation, a primary objective was to accommodate men and women in separate locations. While the commitment to separation recognized the prevalence of sexual abuse and rape endured by women, perpetrated by male prisoners, it did not address their particular vulnerability to the discretionary power of male guards. As noted above, late 19th-century women reformists in particular sought resolution to the exploitation of women prisoners in campaigning for discrete accommodation for women under the management of women guards. Yet, in many jurisdictions, neither objective has been achieved.

As the literature demonstrates, separate units within male jails have persisted, and the establishment of separate women's prisons has presented new and significant challenges. However well intentioned, the reformist agenda – inspired initially by philanthropists and developed by feminism's 'first wave' – prioritized a form of 'emphasized femininity', transforming the 'rough' working-class woman, as she was depicted, to a state of 'respectability'. This objective underpinned all aspects of women's imprisonment: presentation of the 'self'; neatness and tidiness within cellular confinement; 'appropriate' skills development and prison work; discipline, respectfulness and obedience; acceptance and adoption of stereotypical, gendered roles and aspirations. In meeting this objective, women's regimes were established to instil discipline, maintain surveillance and undermine ties with families and communities.

Historically, the social construction of gender, derived in expectations that incorporate what is considered 'acceptable' behaviour, has had a significant impact on women's incarceration. As Corston's review shows, these ideas continue to influence policy and practice. In developing punishments that are more 'appropriate' for women, the unintended consequence is that they are more severe than those administered to male prisoners. More recently, responsibilization and risk have consolidated as significant themes in the imprisonment of women. Despite enduring histories of abuse and violence, women prisoners are often held responsible for their situation, thus neglecting social inequality, injustice and racism as contexts to their criminalization. They are viewed as 'dangerous' because they self-harm.

Mental ill-health has been a persistent and dominant feature in the history of women's incarceration – as a primary reason for women's entry into the criminal justice system and also in the condemnation and punishment of women viewed as failing to conform to the expectations of social norms. The consolidation of psychiatric intervention in prisons has established, both formally and informally, the classification and treatment of women as 'mad' or 'bad'. Either pathological label can result in admission to the isolation cell. In this context, the relationship between punishment and care becomes compromised, not least in the use of isolation cells and surveillance cameras when women self-harm. The introduction of appropriate health care within prisons has been undermined by security, control and punishment imperatives mitigating against the creation of therapeutic regimes. Women-centred units that have been established tend to accommodate 'conforming' women, with 'difficult' women threatened by transfer to harsher regimes.

The brief historical review presented above identifies periodic attempts to reform women's imprisonment, often inspired by concern about the abuse suffered by women prisoners. Malloch and McIvor (2013, p.3) note that there has been a 'growing international recognition that prison is an inappropriate response to women in conflict with the law'. Yet, despite the spread of community initiatives to address women's offending, the women's prison population has continued to rise. Community-based initiatives have tended to 'operate alongside reforms to the prison estate', rather than replacing prison as the dominant form of punishment (Malloch and McIvor, 2013). Jodie Lawsten (2013, p.111) also concludes from the American experience that 'community corrections are thought to be an alternative to prison' whereas 'in fact these are an expansion of punishment and confinement to communities' which do 'nothing to address the human rights of marginalized women'. Critics of recent reforms argue that the prison system historically has been adaptive in incorporating reform and protecting its institutions. In her critique of penal reform in Canada, Kelly Hannah-Moffat (2001, p.4) argues that gender-specific initiatives represent 'yet another flawed attempt to reconceptualise the meaning and experience of punishment to make it more "appropriate" and suitable for women'. Given that prison systems consistently have failed to address women's needs, she doubts their capacity to play a 'central role in the empowerment and healing of women' (p.199).

This chapter notes the limitations of attempts to reform women's incarceration, identifying the problems associated with well-intentioned initiatives. It is a recent history that reveals a framework in which women who failed to conform to gendered disciplinary regimes were categorized as aberrant rather than abhorrent, for the pathologization and medicalization of the 'deviant' had a particular, gender-specific resonance for women prisoners (see Sim, 1990). Often invasive, psychiatric interventions predicated and legitimated on assumptions of women's particular proximity to madness were matched by an expectation that as women they should submit to male authority – both personal and professional.

Thus, the strong, resilient and resistant woman prisoner, like her sister in the community, was identified as recalcitrant. Inevitably, a central judgemental element of emphasized femininity hinged on women prisoners' cooperation with infantilizing regimes and their daily, often petty, routines and interactions. In prison, the imposition of discipline and control of women's bodies, their identities and their associations developed as a more stark manifestation of the subjugation of women beyond the walls. Against this background, the following chapter considers women's incarceration in the context of structural and institutional limitations placed on their agency as women and as prisoners.

2

Agency, Violence and Regulation in the Incarceration of Women

Introduction

They were brought from their work and other activities and lined up, silent, in rows along a wide corridor. Uniformed prison officers stood at the front and back of the lines and patrolled the corridors. The boys stood expressionless, arms to their sides. Orders were shouted by officers many of whom had the peaks of their caps pulled down over their eyes, military style. Each line in turn was instructed to move and the boys immediately went into a parade ground jog along the corridor at right angles into the canteen corridor and in through the door of the canteen. They continued the jog around the outside of the canteen peeling off to their tables where they jogged, in time, on the spot until all were in the room. On an order, shouted above the tramp of feet they stopped. Then came a further order and they sat down. The canteen was silent save for the noise of cutlery on crockery.

> (Research field-note, Glenochil Detention Centre and Young
> Offenders' Institution, Scotland, June 1985)

This girl was no bigger than me. Fifteen of them came up. The ninjas came up, shields, the lot. Her mattress must have been against the flap. When they opened the door ... they bounced on her. We heard her screaming blue murder, I was sitting curled up. Put her two arms up her back, four of them sitting on her back. Put handcuffs on. Shouting, 'Keep still! It won't hurt'. They ripped her tongue bar straight out of her mouth. Put her in the Block and then she got bail. We never saw her. We said we wouldn't be surprised if her arms were broken. The squealing was terrible ... unbearable. They made her walk down to the Block. The atmosphere was awful after. We were

28

all shouting, 'Let her go! Get off her!' It was, 'Shut up or you'll all go down the Block – the whole effing lot of you!'

(Interview, Hydebank Wood YOI and Women's
Prison, Northern Ireland, January 2005)

These are two accounts, each from a different prison and from contrasting regimes. The first, a male detention centre, is an observation recorded in contemporaneous research field-notes; the second, a women's unit inside a male jail, is taken from an in-depth interview with a young woman prisoner. Distinct yet connected by the lack of negotiation and absence of self-determination in the face of institutional authority. The boys, many still children, were subjected to harsh, physically aggressive 'discipline'. They stepped out of line at their peril. Observing a guard throw a boy's mattress across the cell, because he found a feather on a pillow, raised the obvious question – what punishment would he have inflicted had the researcher not been present? The second account, from the research on which this book is based, describes the violence meted out by a control and restraint team to a young woman screaming abuse at male guards who refused her cigarettes. The barren isolation of the Punishment Block strip cells was used to break resistance and demand obedience. Tearing out her tongue bar and forcing her arms to breaking point constituted assaults on her body. The strip cell was an assault on her mind.

Chapter 1 provides historical context to the incarceration of women but also reveals the potential of prison regimes and discretionary powers afforded to prison guards and their managers to inflict pain and damage on the most vulnerable regardless of gender, age or ability. It concludes by noting that prisoners' resistance to the often petty and inherently punitive is met, as it always has been, with uncompromising discipline, restraint and isolation. The prison as a total, rarely transparent, institution imposes both subtle and raw power on those who fail to comply with its regimes and on those whose behaviour is considered troublesome or deviates from the expectations imposed. While the 'agency' experienced by individuals in their families and communities is circumscribed by the structural relations of class, 'race', gender, sexuality, age and ability, in prison behaviour, will and expression is non-negotiable. It is a form of determination supported by the administration of internal regulations and by the interventions of associated professionals, particularly prison doctors and psychiatrists. Together, law and medicine have been complicit in the reproduction of prisons as sites of rejection and marginalization.

Nelson Mandela considers there is no ambiguity about the 'purpose of prison', whether directed towards political prisoners or ordinary prisoners:

> The challenge for *every* prisoner...is how to survive prison intact, how to emerge from a prison undiminished, how to conserve and even replenish one's beliefs. The first task in accomplishing that is learning exactly what one must do to survive... Prison is designed to break one's spirit and destroy one's resolve. To do this the authorities attempt to exploit every weakness, demolish every initiative, negate all signs of individuality – all with the idea of stamping out that spark that makes each of us human and each of us who we are.
>
> (Mandela, 1994, pp.340–341, emphasis added)

Expanding on the previous discussion, this chapter considers the significance of notions of 'agency' within the context of imprisonment. It questions claims made within the prison-related literature regarding prisoners' potential to claim agency within the structural and institutional relations of power that prevail in regimes of incarceration. Of particular significance to this study is the imposition of gendered forms of discipline and control within prisons and their implicit and explicit denial of women's lives, experiences and potential.

Contextualizing 'agency'

People as 'makers of their own histories' has been, and continues to be, a long-standing philosophical debate about the relationships between the precise historical moment, geographical location and sociocultural and economic context into which individuals are born and their capacity to exercise 'free' will in actions that challenge constraints imposed on their lives. The conditions and circumstances that constitute the *determining contexts* of family, community and social order are established in culture, language, custom and identity rooted in not only recent, but also long-term, history. At birth, each child inherits and is placed within a social formation, inducted into relationships, community and institutions that together, in all their diversity, form the foundation and development of societies in constant flux and perpetual transition. While socialization is a process of determination that operates in the 'personal' sphere, combining encouragement, persuasion and regulation in achieving conformity with conventions and laws, the potential for conflict, resistance and rebellion remains ever-present – even in navigation of the most oppressive circumstances.

Clearly, individuals can and do exercise a will to challenge, to break with their past, to reject cultural or religious traditions that constitute inheritance and to take a stand against the manifestations of inter-personal, institutional and structural *power* that constitute their daily routines. They have the potential for rational thought, to be active participants within and against a social order that seeks to condition, contain and impose conformity. They also have the capacity, individually and together, to organize and collectivize opposition to power, to question its authority and to deconstruct its legitimacy. It is this often intensely personal and local spirit of opposition that, once shared and organized, manifests itself as a social movement informed by a politics of resistance. In mobilizing against the grain, however, the resilience of the oppressed, the subjugated and the marginalized is often matched by dogged, uncompromising and brutal resilience by the powerful. Those in power maintain a self-serving commitment to the *status quo*, ensuring social and political reproduction and managing conflict. The use of physical force and inhuman and degrading treatment is not confined to totalitarian regimes. It extends to 'advanced' democratic states.

Structural relations of production and distribution lie at the heart of all societies. In their advanced capitalist form, they underpin global relations between and within nation-states. From slavery and colonization to indentured labour and migration, capitalism was secured by its global reach. It took land, displaced people, destroyed civilizations and utilized genocide. One legacy is the over-representation in jail of Black and Hispanic people in the United States, of First Nations people in Canada and of Aboriginal Australians. It is also no coincidence that incarceration – in prisons, mental institutions and detention centres – is primarily class based. Poverty, mental ill-health, chronic physical health, homelessness, educational under-achievement, illiteracy and low life expectancy are ever-present factors of exclusion and criminalization within escalating prison populations. They emanate not from inherent pathologies of 'flawed' individuals, 'dysfunctional' groups or 'aberrant' cultures, but from the tensions, conflicts and exclusions created by structural inequalities. Such tensions, conflicts and exclusions are played out daily in communities blighted by persistent, structural poverty. State intervention through its institutions, whether caring or regulatory, does little to eradicate immiseration. Rather than developing the capacity to challenge economic marginalization and social exclusion effectively, individuals' roles and potential are circumscribed, operating within the social and political management of consequences and conflict.

What are the implications of this process of structural determination and its institutional manifestations for the individual in terms of her or his everyday life and relationships within home and community? Critical social analysis emphasizes the location of the experiential world of everyday life within the structural relations of power, authority and legitimacy. It accepts that, to an extent, individuals are agents in their own destinies, making choices, navigating pathways, thinking independently – acting, interacting and reacting. As 'agents' they oppose, resist and occasionally deny the imposition of controls and regulations, organizing, campaigning and collectivizing their actions. Yet, structural relations and the interventions of state and private institutions set boundaries to social interaction and personal opportunity. The overarching structural relations of advanced capitalism, patriarchy, neo-colonialism and age are inherently conflicted and subjugating. The ownership and control of the means of production and distribution; the politics and economics of reproduction and normative heterosexuality; the colonial legacies of racism, sectarianism and xenophobia; and the exclusion of children and young people from active participation, in both private and public spheres, reveal determining contexts that have consequences for all people in society. Power and authority are not limited to material (economic) or physical (force) interventions but are supported by deep-rooted ideologies constituting a social force of compliance and conformity.

The populist appeal of authoritarianism, using a vocabulary of negative reputation – folk devils, demons, monsters – is a tangible manifestation of social forces not only defining and categorizing people as outsiders but also carrying implications for social policy and law reform. Processes of marginalization, exclusion and criminalization are central to explanations and analysis of relationships between definitions of crime and antisocial behaviour, discretionary law enforcement, the administration of law through the courts and linked 'restorative' practices, and the presumed utility of punishment – especially the deprivation of personal liberty. The significance of critical research and analysis is that it considers offending and antisocial behaviour, like other life experiences and personal opportunities, within powerful determining contexts: poverty and class; 'race' and ethnicity; sectarianism; and gender and sexuality. While accepting that 'each individual's experiences are distinctively mediated, these are powerful ideological as well as material determinants' (Scraton and Haydon, 2002, p.326).

Consequently, in all social situations the possibility to act unfettered, to self-determine, to display volition and to experience 'free choice' is relative. Yet, particularly at a micro-level, there is always capacity, however limited, to hold and retain some influence over personal destiny within social, institutional and structural constraints. Limits to act freely, however, are not only material. They include the internalization of ideology and hegemony evident in established community and societal conventions. Laws, protocols and conventions place significant parameters to reflexivity of thought and to active resistance. The relativity that exists between determining contexts, structural or institutional or both, and the negotiation, conflict and mediation of social life challenges the false binary of 'structure' and 'agency'. Thinking and acting outside or beyond expectations, building and using alternative discourses as 'resistance' or 'starting point[s] for an opposing strategy' (Foucault, 1981, p.101), are central to social change opening possibilities for different social arrangements and realities.

What is also self-evident is that in *making* transitions and transformations in circumstances beyond their choosing individuals and movements are confronted by strong and persistent limitations, formal and informal, on their capacity to influence personal and collective, immediate and longer term, destinies. In conditions of conflict, agency takes diverse and contrasting forms: voluntary conformity; enforced compliance; strategic compliance; silent opposition; public protest; individual and collective acts of resistance; and counter-resistance. Within broader structural contexts, formal institutions engage, often simultaneously, in defensive and authoritarian discourses and direct interventions seeking to incorporate or eliminate opposition. How much ground is given by parties to such negotiation depends on relative power and the potential damage to their political legitimacy. The dialectic, however, plays out at a micro-level. It is in the ebb and flow of everyday life where it is felt and experienced the keenest – in those communities enduring the consequences of material deprivation, under-investment, alcohol and drug dependency, social and political exclusion and criminalization. Containment within the boundaries of these communities has an umbilical connection to incarceration within the walls of the penal and state hospital archipelago. What of 'agency' here?

'Agency' and prison

She ate with her fingers. They'd taunt her at the door by blowing smoke through the door. They would taunt her and laugh at her. She tried to hang herself and three of us saw her getting out of the ambulance. They walked her across the tarmac in February with a suicide blanket on. They had all the riot gear on. She was crying. They were bringing her back from hospital and she was put back in the Punishment Block. We just kept our heads down, just did our time.

This account, from a woman prisoner held in the Mourne House unit of Maghaberry Prison, who carried out occasional cleaning duties in the Punishment Block, introduces Ellie, an older woman prisoner:

When we arrived at the gate to the Punishment Block there was a woman out of her cell mopping what appeared to be an already clean corridor. Ellie is one of two women held on punishment. There had been three until yesterday. The officer opened the gate and we went with Ellie into her cell.

(Research field-notes)

Able and willing to hold a conversation, Ellie was in poor mental and physical health. She had urinary and bowel problems and used a colostomy bag. She suffered a severe skin condition, apparently untreated, epilepsy and diabetes. She had been sent to the Block because, allegedly, she had thrown the contents of the colostomy bag at guards. They had refused her cigarettes, she claimed, and 'blow cigarette smoke through the door'. Her 'intermediate' punishment cell was equipped with a wash basin, open toilet and bed, each bolted down. Until recently she had been on a 'basic' regime, locked in isolation for long periods without a mattress, pillow or chair. Only two weeks earlier, staff had been informed that Ellie suffered epilepsy. A week later they were told she was diabetic. Until that point her diet had not been controlled and much of the food she had been given exacerbated her condition.

Consistent with the prison's policy of denying medication prescribed in the community, Ellie no longer received creams for her visibly painful skin condition. Each day she was 'drip fed' 10 cigarettes because the governor considered that uncontrolled access to cigarettes encouraged chain-smoking and was 'bad for her health'. Distressed and confused, she was refused tea for several days and had been restricted to water. This arbitrary and unauthorized punishment was inflicted by guards because, they claimed, she refused to conform. Ellie's circumstances were demeaning and degrading. Locked in her cell 23 hours each day, she was unlocked only to mop the corridor. Her need to receive treatment for her physical conditions, and care for her fragile state of mind, was self-evident even to a lay observer: 'I shouldn't be in a punishment cell. I'm sick over mammy, my daughter and my grandson'. When, eventually, Ellie was released she left the prison without an after-care plan. Her first night of 'freedom' was rough sleeping in a bus shelter.

It is difficult to map or comprehend the full extent of institutional failure in the duty of care owed to Ellie. An ill woman with multiple physical needs, she was also deeply disturbed. After one incident she was transferred to the male prison hospital. Returning to the women's unit she was escorted by guards in riot gear and compelled to walk barefoot across a snow-laden yard to a 23-hour Punishment Block lockdown. Whatever the recommendations made by medical staff in composing her healthcare plan, several guards took apparent pleasure in baiting her until she lost control and became aggressive. Her angry outbursts resulted in further arbitrary punishment. The relationship between the abuse of discretionary powers by guards and the institutional failure to provide adequate and appropriate health care is a stark example of claims for agency laid bare. It confirms the 'fundamental contradiction between authoritarian and punitive functions of prisons and the non-judgemental basis of a therapeutic environment' (Faith, 1993, p.238). Consequently, prisoners 'resist [medical and discipline] staff efforts to gain their confidence because there can be no reciprocity of trust'.

Ellie fought back defiantly, using the contents of a colostomy bag. Her resistance to the cruelty she endured brought further deprivation of association and personal contact, persistent degradation and humiliation. She argued, screamed and swore at guards. They walked away, locked the outer gate and left her to her suffering. Although seemingly extreme, Ellie's experiences are not unusual. They raise profound questions about how 'agency', often conflated with notions of 'resistance', is conceptualized in understanding relationship dynamics in prisons. In discussing the 'investigation of identity', Mary Bosworth considers it 'introduces the related concepts of agency and resistance... requir[ing] an appreciation of inmates [sic] as independent actors whose actions help to determine the meanings and effects of punishment'. She continues:

> To be an 'agent', or to have 'agency' denotes the ability to negotiate power [and] requires a certain self-image as active and participatory... Power, in prison, is constantly negotiated on the level of identity. The prisoners are clearly at a disadvantage in this negotiation, because they are restricted not only in their movements and opportunities, but also in most of the characteristics deemed necessary for active, adult agency, namely choice, autonomy and

responsibility. Rather, the prisoners are able, to some extent, to 'get what they want done' and so assert themselves as agents.

(1999, p.3)

This suggests that 'agency', in the meaningful sense of 'choice, autonomy and responsibility', is tightly restricted and denied within prisons by the power dynamics vested in their formal and informal operation. While in certain circumstances of negotiation – even resistance – women prisoners are able to 'assert themselves', Ellie's assertiveness and rebelliousness significantly reduced her capacity to act freely. There is no way of knowing accurately the consequences of these episodes regarding her identity and self-esteem. Interviewing her in her cell, however, it was clear that a profoundly distressed and disturbed woman had been further damaged by callous disregard for her welfare.

Bosworth (1999, p.130) uses 'agent' to 'signify two distinct attributes of women in prison...their specific subject position or identity and their ability to act'. Her thesis, in part, is that rather than being undermined by constant negative judgements made about their femininity, women prisoners turn this against their critics as a form of resistance. In a similar vein, Pat Carlen and Anne Worrall (2004, p.88) discuss the 'especial utility and significance' attributed by feminist researchers to the notion of resistance. They suggest that in 'redress[ing] the balance' in order to correct 'portrayals of women as victims' that perpetuate 'traditional and sexist misrepresentations of women as the weak sex', their research demonstrates 'that even under the most violent and oppressive conditions women can resist their violent oppressors...and both contest and evade the rules that grind them down'. Noting the 'constant fascination with the interaction between prisoner and prison' they identify three significant 'processes': adaptation; institutionalization; resistance. Adaptation, also represented as 'prisonization', occurs 'when by the formation of prison subcultures prisoners manage to adjust the rules to serve their own ends'. Certainly, there is a well-documented history of carefully constructed and thought-through strategies invented by political prisoners to organize alternative frames of action in opposing the administration of the prison. Institutionalization is a consequence of 'prisoners becom[ing] rule-governed in at least some aspects of their behaviour – though seldom all'. Resistance occurs 'when prisoners directly evade or disobey rules; or engage in psychological strategies for the maintenance of identity and self-esteem'.

Catrin Smith's (2009) study of women prisoners' experiences of menstruation illustrates graphically the harsh restrictions placed on individual autonomy, extending to the intimacy of the body. She describes how women rely on permission from prison guards to access basic necessities such as sanitary protection or to use toilets/washrooms. Frequently, their requests are delayed or refused, ostensibly to accommodate the administration of the regime – staff discretion or availability. Not only is women's privacy violated, but 'personal control is taken away as the prisoner and her body become the objects of external forces' (Smith, 2009, p.11). Referring to Bosworth's previously noted observation that women possess agency despite oppressive circumstances, Smith's research confirms that some women attempted to subvert power relations through attempts to embarrass male guards who displayed discomfort at the mere mention of menstruation. Yet, Smith's unequivocal conclusion is that ultimately women were stripped of control. In enduring menstrual cramps, for example, women prisoners were constrained by what was permitted or resourced by the regime, thus having no authority to 'act as they would normally'. Even the 'simplest of actions' were restricted by 'regulation and enforced dependency' (p.17).

As these examples drawn from feminist prison research demonstrate, prisoners adopt a range of strategies, ploys and disruptions – informal and formal, individual and collective – to negotiate and challenge the authority to which they are subjected. Such negotiations are often anticipated and institutionalized, reflecting the complexity of power differentials between prisoners, between guards and prisoners and between guards and their managers. They also extend to other professionals employed within, or as consultants to, the prison. Without denying the strength and relevance of such oppositional strategies and the complexities of prison relationships, the limits to negotiation and the relations of power are evident from the moment of entry into prison.

Arriving at Wormwood Scrubs, a prison at the time notorious for staff brutality and institutionalized racism, Trevor Hercules recalls:

> I remember the van feeling cold as I hunched myself up against the window, one hand in my pocket while the other was in the middle of the seat cuffed to some white guy . . . I even thought about escape, but that was not on. The door was secured by several locks with one screw sitting at the front of the van carrying the keys while several more sat at the back and the sides of the van. Besides, where was I going to go, me a black man with a white man attached to him, like some kind of monkey . . . We had now arrived at the Scrubs. The driver bibbed his horn and the gates of hell swung open.
>
> (1989, pp.24, 30)

Hercules' graphic experience reflects how prisoners are 'torn' from the 'fabric of their previous life-world' to be 'infantilized and disempowered' (Leder, 2004, pp.64–65). Incarceration brings a 'massive disordering of temporality' with the 'experienced present...slowed almost to a halt by the lack of things to do, the boredom, the paucity of meaningful projects...as [prisoners] are "warehoused" for their duration' (p.54). As 'altered time...threatens to overcome the incarcerated', however, individual prisoners adopt 'a variety of strategies' to 'rework temporality' (p.54). These include cerebral 'escape' as the 'flight from an oppressive reality' and 'reclamation' in which the prisoner 'is back to "doing time" instead of having time to do' (p.55). To achieve this form of personalized escape and reclamation, however, demands a level of literacy and access to stimulating materials and educational opportunities often beyond the reach of prisoners.

Reflecting on his experience of prison, Ron Phillips (in Fitzgerald, 1974, p.84) discusses the passage of time, control of personal destiny and loss of identity. He notes how the 'value of an hour changes, and all the apparatus built up over the years for dealing with the passage of time suddenly becomes obsolete...measured as the outside world measures it, time becomes intolerable'. Prison time has no correspondence to outside time: 'it is possible to look at a clock and gain no information from it'. While the prisoner adjusts to prison time, the 'power of decision' also 'disappears'. Whatever 'happens to the prisoner, including the most personal functions, happens because, or when someone else decides that it should'. Any 'illusion of control over personal destiny' evaporates as the 'prisoner is all at once assailed by a realization of...impotence'. The 'most terrible' impact of prison, however, is the loss of 'value of a human being, as judged by his [or her] own value' as it 'changes out of all recognition'.

Beyond the prison gates the purposeful strategies adopted by regimes to isolate the prisoner and erode the value of self are captured eloquently in Erving Goffman's classic 1950s essay 'On the characteristics of total institutions'. He notes how the prisoner 'is immediately stripped of the support provided by these [stable social] arrangements' of her/his 'home world':

> In the accurate language of some of our oldest total institutions, he [sic] begins a series of abasements, degradations, humiliations, and profanations of self...systematically, if often unintentionally, mortified...The barrier that total institutions place between the inmate and the wider world marks the first curtailment of self.
>
> (Goffman, 1968, p.24)

Removed from routine familiarity of home and community the prisoner is 'dispossessed' of her/his role with 'losses' sometimes 'irrevoca-
ble' (p.25). Arrival in prison 'typically brings other kinds of loss and
mortification...taking a life history, photographing, weighing, finger-
printing, assigning numbers, searching, listing personal possessions for
storage, undressing, bathing, disinfecting, haircutting, issuing institutional clothing, instructing as to rules' (pp.25–6). Thus the prisoner is
'shaped and coded into an object that can be fed into the administrative machinery of the establishment, to be worked on smoothly by
routine operations'. It is a process of objectification that 'ignores most
of' the prisoner's 'previous bases of self-identification' (p.26). Compliance with the regime is demanded via an 'obedience test and even a
will-breaking test' and 'an inmate who shows defiance receives immediate, visible punishment'. Vulnerability is affirmed, physical safety is
threatened and personal initiative is derided.

The prisoner is reminded of her/his 'special low status even in this low
group' (p.27). Nakedness, loss of possessions, allocation of a number,
ill-fitting prison clothes together undermine physical integrity. Further
'indignities' extend to the imposition of 'humiliating verbal responses'
within the 'forced deference pattern of total institutions'. Prisoners have
to 'beg, importune, or humbly ask for little things such as a light for a
cigarette, a drink of water, or permission to use the telephone' (p.31).
Goffman identifies how 'territories of the self are violated' through, for
example, disclosure of a prisoner's 'social statuses and past behaviour'.
This focuses on 'particularly discreditable facts' that 'are collected and
recorded in a dossier available to staff' (p.32).

Other invasions of self include lack of privacy in sleeping, in using
the toilet and in slopping out. For many prisoners nakedness, con-
taminated food, forced interaction, sexual assault and strip searching
are stark departures from their home life. Beyond the directly physical
denigration of the self is the parallel 'disruption of the usual relationship between the individual actor and his [her] acts' (p.41). Impelled
to defer, comply and conform, the prisoner 'cannot easily escape from
the press of judgemental officials and from the enveloping tissue of
constraint' (p.45).

Writing at the mid-point of the 20th century, Goffman was not famil-
iar with the language of agency and structure. Yet, the dynamic between
personal experience, social interaction and institutional context and its
impact on the 'self' was central to his thesis: 'total institutions disrupt
or defile precisely those actions that in civil society have the role of
attesting to the actor and those in his [her] presence that he [she] has
some command over his [her] world – that he [she] is a person with

"adult" self-determination, autonomy, and freedom of action' (p.47). Thus adulthood is reduced as the prisoner is infantilized, losing all means of controlling even the most routine events. The currency of 'privileges' including access to taken-for-granted items in the outside world becomes the transactional process governing interpersonal relations inside jail. This includes bartering as well as sharing. On the flip side of privileges, however, are punishments; and the withdrawal of 'privileges' constitutes a foundational transaction of punishment.

Deeply imbedded within this transactional process is Goffman's notion of 'secondary adjustments'. These are 'practices that do not directly challenge staff but allow inmates to obtain forbidden satisfactions or to obtain permitted ones by forbidden means' (p.56). Prevalent, informal material and knowledge economies enable deals to be cut, guards to be compromised and interpersonal power to be realized. They also provide the prisoner 'with important evidence that he [she] is still his [her] own man [woman], with some control over his [her] environment . . . a kind of lodgement for the self, a *churinga* in which the soul is felt to reside' (p.56).

The presence and knowledge of secondary adjustments develop into a prisoner code of conduct alongside a system of 'informal social control' within which goods, services and information are bartered and exchanged. Camaraderie is restricted not least by the individualism at the heart of the formal, transactional 'privilege' system and the process of self-mortification. Withdrawal from social interaction, direct personal confrontation, adherence to rules and over-identification with the regime, each constitutes expressions of 'adaptation'.

In Goffman's exploration of mortification, adaptation and reorganization of the 'self', and his contextualization of 'the cultural milieu' that represent prison life at any given time and place, he does not claim that the 'sense of injustice, bitterness and alienation' endured by prisoners casts them as helpless and hapless. Yet, he argues, the prisoner's 'social position within the walls' is 'radically different from what it was on the outside' and on release her/his 'social position . . . will never again be quite what it was prior to entrance' (p.70). As Leder (2004, p.61) notes, the prisoner's 'body is everywhere constrained' and 'renders the self vulnerable to outside powers':

> The institution reinforces the experience of the 'I cannot': I cannot move freely, leave the prison, secure privacy, or pursue my preferences. The prisoner's bodily location, dress, and actions are largely dictated by the state . . . the forces of containment . . . blatant,

fashioned by bars and barbed wire...The imprisoned body...is associated with violence and deficit, objectified by a fearful gaze, appropriated by hostile others.

'Agency' and resistance

Over half a century after Goffman's defining essay, Victoria Law berates 'prison scholars and activists' who have 'omitted from the discourse' the 'ways in which incarcerated women have individually and collectively challenged' conditions and regimes under which they are held (Law, 2009, p.3). Because research and campaigns prioritize male prisoners, she argues, 'distinctly feminine' issues have been neglected and dismissed. These include 'the scarcity of sanitary hygiene products, the lack of medical care specifically for women, especially prenatal care, and threats of sexual abuse by guards' (p.4). Consequently, 'incarcerated women's activism and resistance' has been ignored 'prevent[ing] outside recognition of female agency' (p.5).

Law, however, also notes how prisons 'further erode low self-esteem' and how women prisoners 'who do challenge the system face extreme levels of administrative harassment' (p.6):

> Solitary confinement – euphemistically called 'Special Housing Unit' or 'SHU', 'control units', 'administrative segregation', depending on the prison – is increasingly used to isolate and punish prisoners who challenge their conditions of confinement...Even in their cells, the women have no privacy – toilets are in full view of the cell door windows, guards can look through those windows at any time and male guards often watch the women in the showers. If the women complain, the guards turn off the water...Often this threat of staff retaliation [solitary confinement] dissuades others from acting.
>
> (pp.7–8)

What is apparent in Law's work is the fine line that exists for women prisoners, of which they are well aware, between resistance and compliance. That is not to suggest that in being compelled to comply with rules and orders women sacrifice their agency but they do moderate direct acts of defiance. The forces deployed against resisting women are significant.

Karlene Faith's research on women's imprisonment in Canada notes how women classified as 'disorderly or uncooperative' can so easily 'gain direct knowledge of the foul segregation units in which prisoners are strip-searched' (Faith, 1993, p.241). These are 'super-maximum security segregation units, the prison within a prison' where women are

> kept in virtual cages under bright lights and camera surveillance; have food pushed through a slot in the bottom of the bars; are denied privacy for toilet activity; are harassed, ridiculed and humiliated by uncaring guards; are denied visits with their children and other family members; and are otherwise subjected to the indignities of extraordinary powerlessness within already-disempowering circumstances. (p.241)

Following extensive interviews with women incarcerated at the Valley State Prison for Women in Chowchilla, California, Cassandra Shaylor (1998, p.386) condemns the 'emerging use of the control unit, the prison within a prison, as the ultimate expression of the regulation of the female body'. The use of solitary confinement, she argues, underlines an 'increasing brutality in prisons, particularly in prisons for women'. In her study of women's imprisonment in Queensland, Australia, Tamara Walsh (2004, p.16) notes that the 'special needs' of mentally ill women are addressed by 'segregation in the event that they are engaging in self-harming behaviour'. Former prisoners reported their experiences inside as 'brutal, humiliating, traumatising', and several 'alleged that they had been raped by correctional officers' (p.19). The impact of segregation and the potential for physical and sexual assault inhibited women's disclosures. As 'merely crying' could bring reallocation to segregation the women 'learn[ed] quickly to disengage from their emotions'. Any indication of weakness 'will be reported to corrections officers by psychologists' (pp.22–23).

Law, however, is concerned that in representing women prisoners as 'passive' their capacity to resist authority and militate for change is undermined and underestimated. Yet, she acknowledges that women who resist in prison 'face an additional burden' as 'they have already defied societal norms by transgressing both laws and acceptable notions of feminine behaviour and morality' (Law, 2009, p.9). In challenging the authority of the guards, and/or the rules of the regime, women 'continue to defy proscribed gender roles, often leading to further disdain and dismissal' (p.10). Prison research and activism, Law argues, regularly acknowledges male prisoners' resistance and acts of rebellion while neglecting women's ownership and realization of agency through acts of protest and resistance. This includes a range of strategies, interpersonal and collective, through which women support each other, share resources and organize challenges – within the prison and beyond – to the power of the guards and the institution. She proposes that lawsuits, grievance procedures, peer education, contact with children and public education are each expressions of women's resistance to oppressive regimes derived in their agency. These successes, however, also risk inviting tighter and harsher regulation of personal space and bodily integrity; and her case studies show that acts of defiance or resistance rarely go unpunished.

Punishment for those considered 'recalcitrant' is variously and thinly disguised as 'time out', 'special observation' or 'crisis support'. Walsh (2004, p.15) found that 'crisis support units' were used as a 'behaviour management tool to house difficult as well as disturbed prisoners' yet women were held in a unit that included '17 year old prisoners, prisoners who have received a disciplinary breach and women with "discipline problems", in addition to prisoners with mental illness'. Observation cells were 'barren rubber rooms where prisoners are subjected to 24 hour a day lighting, stripped down and dressed in a suicide gown, and often physically restrained' (p.25). A woman prisoner commented that disorientation of permanent lighting 'plays games with you, and it sends you mad, and wanting to smash their TV and stuff like that' (p.15). Another objected to being watched on camera, 'having a shower, or having a piss' (p.15). Walsh notes that 'women ex-prisoners reported that they witnessed women miscarrying in the toilet blocks, and seriously ill women being told to take two Panadol' (p.26).

As discussed in Chapter 1, these recent experiences are neither new nor are they confined to the jurisdictions in which they occur. In her 1974 autobiography, Angela Davis recounts her prison experience in the United States. She notes that while 'jails and prisons are designed to break human beings, to convert the population into specimens in a zoo – obedient to our keepers but dangerous to each other' the response from 'imprisoned men and women' is to 'invent and continually invoke various and sundry defenses' (Davis, 1990, p.52).

Consequently, two layers of existence can be encountered within almost every jail or prison. The first layer consists of the routines and behavior prescribed by the governing penal hierarchy. The second layer is the prisoner culture itself: the rules and standards of behavior that come from and are defined by the captives in order to shield themselves from the open and covert terror designed to break their spirits. In an elemental way, this culture is one of resistance, but a *resistance of desperation*. It is, therefore, incapable of striking a significant blow against the system. All its elements are based on an assumption that the prison system will survive.

(pp.52–53, emphasis added)

Thus Davis witnessed directly the institutionalized neglect of women's physical and psychological health needs in the operation of the jail's daily routine. While her resistance was predicated on the politics of her imprisonment, supported by an international campaign for her release, it is instructive that she identified the routine resistance of ordinary prisoners as one of desperation.

The prescription of routine and the imposition of behavioural constraints are central to the regimes imposed on women prisoners. In the daily interaction between guards and prisoners they are reminded constantly of their failings as women. Blanche Hampton (1995 p.143) quotes a woman prisoner's experiences in a New South Wales prison where prison guards 'wanted the women to be completely oppressed, like you work in the laundry or the kitchen or you can be a sweeper, doing women's duties'. Women's crimes are not only committed 'against society' but 'against womanhood'. She continues: 'That's reinforced continually, you abandoned your children. So all this added guilt comes on top of your own problems'. Another woman commented:

There is little understanding shown towards any inmate who uses initiative or fights for just causes. They seem threatened and disorientated when the system or an officer is challenged... Some male officers exercise their personal desires on a sexual level. One prison officer offered sex for rewards to any [woman] who wished to participate. Cells were unlocked at night to cement these rewards, which created a lot of aggravation and violence, knowing what was going on after the lock-in. (p.143)

The impact of these intense interactions in the daily negotiation of women prisoners' lives is profound. Inevitably, in a system that already offers 'privileges' in exchange for compliant behaviour, the delivery of additional 'rewards' by guards in exchange for sex created tension and violence between women prisoners. Hampton's interviews reveal the male guards' selective exploitation of women prisoners. Another woman prisoner drew distinctions between 'screws who would actually take the prisoner's side on occasion', those who 'feel it was a job with an occasional bad day', and those 'who... seemed to derive real delight from ruining your day' (p.142). Such discretion was not without consequences: 'You get so used to having your privacy intruded upon and your dignity destroyed that you develop a *kind of tolerance* which stops you questioning insensitive, degrading and abusive behaviour' (p.142, emphasis added). There was constant, deliberate and purposeful intrusion into women's lives – daily, hourly, momentarily. They were humiliated or exploited according to appearance and vulnerability and any woman who complained about 'sexual advances' or threats from the guards was 'thrown in the bin' (punishment block). A 'kind of tolerance' was developed as a survival mechanism – and most were silenced.

In considering acts of collective, political resistance as effective challenges to the system it is also instructive to consider the significance of gender. Ahmed Kathrada – found guilty of sabotage in June 1964 alongside Nelson Mandela, Walter Sisulu and five others and sentenced to life imprisonment – reflects on a quarter of a century's political imprisonment. Writing from his cell in 1988 he states:

> The most common form of measuring one's time in prison is by calculating the number of years; in our case in terms of cold statistics this amounts to 25 years, 5 months and some days. Looked at from *such a restricted* angle, one simply gets a picture of fragmented units of time – monotonous, drab, unchanging, unexciting and tedious. It does not cover the *essentially vibrant* community that inhabits the world within a world – its spectrum of experiences, its collective and individual emotions, thrills and responses, its fears, its joys and sorrows, its hopes, its confidence, its loves and hates, the *unbreakable spirit*, the fellowship, the hardships, the morale... find[ing] expression in a myriad [of] specific forms in every hour of every day of every year.
>
> (Kathrada and Vassen, 1999, p.244)

The collective strength, optimism and celebration of political commitment by male comrades united in their struggle against apartheid defied the prison and its 'forbidding high walls... grim, cold atmosphere, prosaic, harsh, vulgar, violent... desperate, unsmiling faces; anger, bitter and frustrated beings' (p.247). Whatever the extent of debilitation wreaked by the 'nightmarish existence' of apartheid's prisons, it was met by the camaraderie of men that inspired a community of resistance. These resistances, however, reflect the political dynamics of collective resistance, organized and orchestrated. They are in marked contrast to the isolation of individual prisoners discussed previously. Significantly, even in the context of political struggle, women prisoners' experiences of incarceration were different, isolating, violating and a direct consequence of gender.

In her evidence to the Truth Commission in South Africa, Thenjiwe Mthintso reveals the fear unique to misogyny:

> When they [Security Branch] interrogated, they usually started by reducing your role as an activist. They weighed you according to their own concepts of womanhood ... they said you are in custody because you are not the right kind of woman – you are irresponsible, you are a whore, you are fat and ugly, or single and thirty and you are looking for a man. And when whatever you stood for was reduced to prostitution, unpaid prostitution, the licence for sexual abuse was created. Then things happened that could not happen to a man. Your sexuality was used to strip away your dignity, to undermine your sense of self.
>
> (Krog, 1998, p.179)

Anjie Krog notes how basic necessities such as 'deodorant and sanitary towels' had to be requested. Women were forced to 'strip in front of a whole range of policemen making remarks about your body', to 'do star-jumps naked, breasts flying, Fallopian tubes were flooded with water until they burst, rats were pushed into vaginas' (p.179). Thenjiwe Mthintso's evidence was explicit:

> Women have been made to stand the whole day with blood flowing down and drying on their legs. Did they gain strength from looking at their blood? From asking you to drink your own blood? ... a woman's refusal to bow down would unleash the wrath of the torturers. Because in their own discourse a woman, a black *meid*, a *kaffermeid* at that, had no right to have the strength to withstand them. (p.179)

In writing and delivering her evidence to the Commission she 'realized how unready I am to talk about my experience in South African jails and ANC [African National Congress] camps abroad' and 'despite the general terms in which I have chosen to speak, I feel exposed and distraught'. Under the constant threat of rape and locked in isolation except for the company of rats, another woman, Greta Appelgren recalled how it 'taught me something':

No human being can live alone. I felt I was going deeper and deeper into the ground. It felt like all the cells were like coffins full of dead people. I had to accept that I was damaged. That part of my soul was eaten away by maggots and I will never be whole again. (p.181)

The point of selecting and focusing on these harrowing accounts from many others available is not to create or endorse a gender hierarchy of pain suffered by those politically imprisoned. Male activists were degraded, beaten, tortured and murdered by the police, the security services and prison guards. Yet, what distinguishes these accounts – Ahmed Kathrada's 'unbreakable spirit'; Thenjiwe Mthintso's undermined self; Greta Appelgren's destroyed soul – is their distinctive, powerful gender testimonies in a time of war.

The isolation of women political prisoners and the degradation of their bodies as sites of persistent punishment are clearly evident in the accounts of Irish Republican women prisoners, Ella O'Dwyer and Martina Anderson, while held on remand in London's Brixton Prison:

We had four body searches that day which also, of late, include the warden putting hands inside the trousers. On Tuesday we had four of these body searches... On Wednesday we had a strip search each and three body searches... Thursday was even more eventful as we had two strip-searches each, before and after court, and three body searches... Martina had a strip search on Friday even though she was visibly sick... and had been vomiting all morning... Yesterday, Saturday, I had one strip search and we both had body searches, Martina having four and I had five. Today we have had six body searches... Our association to me is almost non-existent and spent washing and ironing. We spend almost all day alone in our cells.

(Ella O'Dwyer in Mama et al., 1986, p.162)

The relationship between agency and resistance, particularly when the latter is collectively and politically organized (McKeown, 2001; Corcoran, 2006), has been of considerable significance in Northern Ireland. Mary Corcoran's work, specifically on the 'paradoxes of women's political imprisonment', progresses the continuing debate regarding the lived reality of prisoners' agency and its actual potential for successfully unifying and mobilizing women's collective resistance against (she quotes Pat Carlen) 'the complex power relationships and penal practices within which *women's imprisonment* is constituted'.

Once the political prisoners were released, however, the harsh regimes lived on and were imposed on 'ordinary' prisoners. As our research shows, women political prisoners feared for the women left in prison: 'When we were there we protected them, not just ourselves, but when we were gone there was nobody to take the screws and the governors on' (Interview, former Republican Prisoner).

Gender, violence and unsafety

Davis (2003, p.61) argues that while prisons are isolated, closed institutions their 'deeply gendered character of punishment both reflects and further entrenches the gendered structure of the larger society'. As Carlen notes, women's imprisonment 'incorporates and amplifies all the anti-social modes of control that oppress women outside the prison' (1998, p.10). In her earlier ground-breaking research, she introduces women prisoners through deeply moving accounts of their family lives and social context. As working-class women their lives embodied a 'contradiction' – they carried 'heavy responsibilities as breadwinners and homemakers' while suffering simultaneously 'brutal and familial repression at the hands of bosses and husbands' (Carlen, 1983, p.27).

Far from being safe havens, the Church ('Kirk') and the home reflected misogynist histories. When 'women talked about their lives outside the prison' they concentrated

> on family life which they thought other people had and which they themselves hoped to have one day; on the family life which they had rejected; on the family life which, somehow, had eluded them; on the family life that had left them physically bruised and emotionally battered; on the family life which, in a minority of cases, had engendered in them (too late?) a burgeoning awareness of the rights and wrongs of women.
>
> (Carlen, 1983, p.36)

While her research revealed many instances of violence endured by women in their relationships with men, Carlen notes that the 'non-penal and informal disciplining of women' was not restricted to 'extreme physical violence' but by being 'controlled and increasingly isolated in a multitude of non-violent ways, ways which initially they had found difficult to define, blaming themselves for their sense of unease, isolation and powerlessness' (p.36). Not wanting 'to give the impression' that the women she interviewed 'were merely downtrodden, weak or broken' (p.55), Carlen also records how women were often isolated and lonely within their homes 'as the major symbol of their bondage' (p.54). In her later work she explores the 'different social role of women within the family' establishing the 'expectations about women's proper place in the family which can materially affect women's experiences of imprisonment even when they might not have, in fact, been living out the conventional roles of mothers, wives and daughters before they went into prison' (Carlen, 1998, p.134).

In an engaging analysis of 'women, crime and punishment', Adrian Howe (1994, p.163) discusses the wider context, rooted in material conditions, of regulation and coercion in women's lives. 'Imprisonment' in this context extends to all aspects of many women's experiences, a 'coercion of privacy', of isolation and of limitation – physical and psychological. She argues that conceptualizing the 'private prison' is significant 'for understanding the restraints placed on women's lives all along the "freedom" – "imprisonment" continuum' thus 'an historical analysis of the social control of women should shift away from the formal custodial institutions to informal sites of social control' (p.163). She also warns of the 'absurdity of infinite relativism... not forget[ting] that incarcerated women are more coerced than those outside the prison walls and that some women, notably black and other minority women, suffer from the coercion and oppression of institutionalised racism within Western criminal justice systems' (p.164).

In extending the scope of 'imprisonment' to consider women's experiences in intimate relations, families and communities – especially connected to material dependency and social isolation – Howe raises, 'a distinctive aspect of women's experience – namely, "our" injuries' (p.171). These are

> the hidden injuries of all gender-ordered societies, the injuries associated with lower gender status, the once privatised injuries which we have begun to name over the last twenty years, such as domestic violence (now criminal assault in the home), incest (now father-daughter rape) and sexual harassment which is now, at least in the workplace, sex discrimination... while these injuries have become public issues they are still trivialised in the wider culture... Insisting that our private injuries become public issues is not enough: to ensure that our distinctive mode of alienation as women is not lost in translation into a legal claim, we need to demonstrate that the injuries

we feel at a private, intimate level are socially created, indeed, social injuries, before we demand they become public issues.

In advancing a 'social injury strategy' Howe's 'starting-point' is 'women's pain' (p.170), recognizing 'it need not rest on a universal, essentialising notion of "woman"... is not dependent on gender identity... [is] not intended as a strategy for all women prisoners' (p.176). There are several important issues here. When people enter prison they bring with them the specific context relating to the events for which they have been prosecuted (whether guilty or innocent) while also carrying the resilience and/or burdens of personal history. It is self-evident that their material conditions, their social experiences and their self-esteem are crucial in adjusting to an environment that diminishes initiative, punishes resistance and undermines potential. This was Goffman's point. In recounting her work with the Prisoners Action Group in New South Wales, Howe notes the principle of 'aggregate social harm' as applied to the experiences of Aboriginal men in police custody. 'Social injury strategy' is not reducible to gender identity but has direct relevance to 'any member of a marginalised group who recognises a harm or discrimination as an injury to themselves or members of that group' (p.176).

Gender specificity, however, is not simply an analytical frame of reference. It is a key element of the incarceration of women and men, of girls and boys. Carlen's definitive study of Cornton Vale found that on receiving a prison sentence, women entered 'no-woman's land'. The courts 'appropriate knowledge of their domestic lives and incorporate it into a public and apposite history of maternal failure and dereliction of duty'. This leaves women prisoners 'outwith family, sociability, femininity and adulthood' – 'beyond help... beyond cure' (Carlen, 1983, p.155). In this context of rejection by medical and social care agencies women experience prison that is gender specific, employing 'two modes' of control that dominate women's lives in the community: 'family life and isolation from each other... also incorporated into the prison regime to produce a very fine disciplinary web which denies the women both personality and full adult status' (p.16).

As Carlen (1998, p.133) notes in her later analysis of interviews with staff in women's prisons, they were clear that

throughout the women's prison sector there is a strong awareness that women's imprisonment is different from men's for three main reasons: biological – women's physical needs are different to men's;

social – women's role in the family is different to men's; and cultural – women's experiences of imprisonment are different to men's and have different meanings attached to them by both the women themselves and all those for whom, subsequently, they become 'prisoners' or 'ex-prisoners'.

According to Carlen's research, and as discussed in Chapter 1, by the late 1990s UK women's prisons 'had not even begun to take seriously women's difference' there was 'no holistic approach to the basic issue of the operationalizing of regime and security concepts in a woman-friendly fashion; and an almost complete avoidance of the issue of women, gender, identity and *sexuality*' (pp.133–4, emphasis in original). She asserts the 'lip-service paid to gender issues' has to be transformed into a 'holistic approach to the theorizing of penality and gender difference; together with a gender-testing of all new regime innovations' (p.138).

Further, Carlen (p.99) emphasizes how, 'in addition to the ideological baggage about appropriate and legitimate femininities and women's proper place', women 'carry with them into prison all the material consciousness of their family responsibilities'. They are 'especially vulnerable to the pains of separation from their children' and live with 'constant fears about risks to gendered sensibilities whose violation can, in turn, threaten the physical, emotional and sexual composure constitutive of female self-esteem'. In part, those threats emanate from 'the prison's usurpation of their domestic roles; the constant hijacking of any control they might temporarily establish over their living quarters; the infantilization still inherent in some disciplinary regimes in the women's institutions; and the psychic coercion which is a routine feature of the relationship between the gaoled and her gaolers' (p.91).

As discussed above, women prisoners express 'even more distress and anger about those aspects of penal power which are exercised most directly on their bodies':

Food, health and hygiene, and institutional sexual abuse (in the form of violations of bodily privacy and enforced submissions to inspections of body parts normally protected from the public gaze) have perennially been the most frequently mentioned causes of concern. The volume and the complaints about these intimate intrusions have not been diminished by innovations such as integral sanitation, mandatory drug testing or cross-gender postings . . . .

That is the nub of the matter – the vulnerability of women prisoners' naked bodies or exposed sexual parts to the possible lusts, derision or merely coldly casual inspections of their gaolers – whether those gaolers be male or female, heterosexual or lesbian.

(pp.91, 143)

As adjuncts to the mainstream male prison system, conditions and regimes for women regularly fall below minimum standards of decency, humanity and international rights standards. The inherent, generic processes of dehumanization within prisons mirror gendered violence endured by women in essentially patriarchal social and societal relations. In analysing gender-oppressive regimes and the range and extent of subjugation within operational practices, Liz Kelly's (1988) conceptualization of a 'continuum of sexual violence', whether related to intimacy in the private sphere or danger in the public sphere, is apposite. As Elizabeth Stanko (1985, p.9) notes, within 'male-dominated society' women's 'experiences of sexual and physical violation take on an illusion of normality, ordinariness'. Taken together, 'ordinariness' and 'continuum' cover a range of threatening and abusive behaviours including acts of emotional, physical and sexual violence. Analysis of the intimidation, fear and experience of violence should not be confined to interpersonal relations but should include collective and institutional manifestations. The continuum lifts the focus from the 'different forms of violence and abuse as discrete issues' to recognizing 'commonalities between them in women's experience and theoretically as forms of violence underpinning patriarchal power and control' (Radford, Harne and Friedberg, 2000, p.2).

For Stanko (1988, p.12), vulnerability is connected directly to powerlessness, particularly the 'ever-present potential of sexual violation'. She notes the 'reality of physical and/or sexual vulnerability is part of women's experience of being in the world' (pp.12–13). Elsewhere, she argues that women's lives 'rest upon a continuum of unsafety ... a common awareness of their vulnerability' regardless of 'direct experience, class, race, sexual orientation, or physical abilities' (p.85). Women 'constantly negotiate their safety with men – those with whom they live, work and socialise, as well as those they have never met'. Stanko concludes, their 'life experiences – as children, adolescents and adults – are set in a context of ever present sexual danger' (p.86).

Writing on women's experience of prison as 'a kind of freedom' from intimate violence, Lisa Vetten and Kailash Bhana (2005, p.265) note the profound 'similarities between imprisonment and abusive relationships'. Each is 'characterized by authoritarianism, a marked power imbalance, enforced restriction of movement and activities, lack of freedom of association, violence, and enforcement of arbitrary and trivial demands'. Not only does this replication create problems for women regarding recovery, but it requires the same strategies of survival used in resisting intimate abuse: 'compliance with others' demands, denial of one's own wishes and thoughts, defensive violence, suppression of feelings'. Drawing on the life histories of women prisoners – a Jamaican, an African-Canadian and a Colombian – Julia Sudbury (2004, p.23) concludes, the 'state's punishment of women is often the culmination of years of gender violence and exploitation, reminding us that the criminalization of surplus labor works in specifically gendered ways, often taking as its starting point the abuse of women of color and children by men in our communities'.

The prison, then, becomes an institutional manifestation of gendered powerlessness and vulnerability. As George (1995, p.17) states: 'The institutional prison contains women who have suffered the worst excesses of a highly stratified, sexist, racist and class-based society'. As discussed earlier, for girl and women prisoners the threat of violence and violation within their communities remains significant in their experiences of prison. Also consistent are processes through which women are judged as 'good', 'respectable' or 'moral'. There is a considerable literature on the dynamics underpinning the ascribed negative reputation of 'aberrant', 'deviant' and 'criminal' women. Non-conformity and refusal to comply with gendered and sexual norms within patriarchies, however socially and culturally diverse, invariably results in discipline, banishment, punishment and even death. The imprisonment of women and girls cannot be removed from such frames of reference and determination.

3
Researching Prison, Women's Voices

Introduction

Considering that the prison or detention centre is predicated on the loss of a person's liberty and removing from the prisoner every vestige of personal and social identity, it is remarkable that they are places of fascination. For researchers in part this is a consequence of seeking to understand and explain the inner workings of total institutions. Whether their location is urban or remote, the prison is highly visible, forbidding and intrusive. In contrast to its outward appearance, its most mundane and its most spectacular events are invisible even to the most astute observer. It is self-evident that walls, fences, gates and bars are structural barriers to prisoners' freedom and movement. When the prison is locked down for the night its prisoners, like Russian Dolls, are celled within multiple layers of confinement; layers that hold prisoners in, while keeping others out. Prison security is not one dimensional. It imposes absolute control of access to prisoners and absolute control of access to information.

Metaphorically, and in some cases literally, the prison is an island operating beyond the referent points and parameters of regular social life. It determines, for itself, time and motion. Prisoners are locked or unlocked according to institutional routine and convenience. A prisoner occupying a single cell will spend the majority of her sentence alone. The only variation on out-of-cell time will be during periods of extended lockdowns, justified by 'staff absences', unattributed 'incidents', work shortages or adjudicated punishments. If the guards on duty decide that lockdown will be early it will be early. If they decide unlock will be delayed it will be delayed. The use of time as currency, whether it is unlock or access to the phone or shower, is an

54

essential element of transactional relationships between guards and prisoners.

Whatever its paper accountability to prison service headquarters and government justice departments, the prison is its own jurisdiction. While serious charges against prisoners involve police investigation and prosecution through the courts, the disciplinary code – its rules and regulations – create a form of law unto itself. Cursing, swearing, insubordination, challenging authority, refusal to work, failure to obey guards' instructions and, most significantly, malicious allegations against guards are each examples of 'offensive' and 'offending' behaviour leading to governors' internal adjudication. At the internal hearing the prisoner has no legal representation and probably no supporting witnesses or corroborating evidence against guards who invariably, if necessary, will produce verification from their colleagues. The consequences can be severe; for example, relocation to the punishment block and 23 hours a day lockdown with access prohibited to a radio, newspaper and other prisoners.

Prisoners regularly comment that to take complaints outside the prison is futile as they are rarely upheld. Many also fear reprisals. Of course, prisoners do use the complaints process, a few with some regularity and persistence. Prison adjudications, however, demonstrate clearly how prisoners' compliance is maintained and reproduced without the acknowledgement and protection of natural justice. The operational discretion afforded to prison staff at all levels is extensive, penetrating into every aspect of prisoners' daily lives and experiences. This can be as petty as changing the television channel in the recreation room to suit guards' preferences or handing over a newspaper with the crossword already completed. It extends to more serious matters such as physical and mental health care, decisions on assessing and referring a 'prisoner-at-risk' or observing the expectations of care plans that have been established for the health and well-being of a 'prisoner-at-risk'.

It is in this context that prison guards, without specialized knowledge of mental health or challenging behaviour, take decisions that have a major impact on a prisoner's state of mind. At best their actions are well intentioned but ill-informed, at worst they are dismissive and vindictive. Prisoners understand this and, as discussed in the previous chapter, they evolve strategies that range from quiet negotiation to outright hostility. Such strategies are often confused by prison researchers and theorists as expressions of their agency. Yet, the 'power' of staff rests in the discretion they bring to bear on any given situation, however trivial and insignificant it might appear to the outsider.

Researching the view from below

> A society that separates people through the institution of the prison
> creates populations of incomplete and wounded lives, whether we are
> inside the prison or outside the prison. This is the dance of the slave
> and the slaveholder, inmate and captor, prisoner and non-prisoner.
> No-one escapes the damage caused by the fact that the prison exists.
> The damage is pervasive – on levels economic, social, psychological,
> and, ultimately, spiritual.
>
> (Quinney, 2006, p.270)

Richard Quinney (2006, p.270) argues that while there are 'real and con-
sequential differences' between the 'lives of those in prison and the lives
of those outside the prison' the harm and 'injuries caused by the prison
are shared by all'. In reality, there is no outside and all in society are
'doing time together'. Recognizing the dialectic between those inside
and those outside establishes a distinctive premise for critical research
into places of incarceration. There is personal responsibility as well as
self-interest in viewing the pains of confinement as pain administered
in 'our' name, pain that is financed through the public purse. It also
carries other costs – social, political and emotional.

In the most accurate conceptualization of alienation, those who experience the diminution of their humanity through intellectual and material exploitation share their condition with those who create and operate
the means through which alienation occurs. So it is with prisons. The
prison–industrial complex has become all-pervasive. Its corporations are
permanently and globally open for business, their entrepreneurs genuinely seeking exploitation. Prison architecture and regime mechanics
are promoted at trade fairs as the industry's self-anointed 'experts' speak
to potential customers at quasi-academic conferences. Whether the 'war
on crime', the 'war on drugs' or the 'war on terror', the crude mar-
keting of prisons and detention centres is plumbed in to what Mike
Davis (2001, p.45) refers to as the 'fear economy' in which state security
and protection of the public are presented as 'fully-fledged urban utility[ies] like water and power'. Prisons are taken for granted as essential
services.

Quinney's (2006, p.270) message is as simple as it is profound: 'anything done to others is done to ourselves…what is done inside the
prison is done to everyone outside the prison'. Regardless of whether
people show concern, are ambivalent or consider prisons 'too soft',

within civil society there is a collective moral as well as political responsibility for the fate of prisoners. What cannot be dismissed lightly is that 'we are witnesses [active or passive] to their suffering' (p.271). In Quinney's analysis, complacency or indifference towards the inhumanity of the prison cannot be rationalized until awareness is awakened by personal experience. In discussing shared perceptions of a death in custody within communities that are 'poor working class and marginalised', Helen Shaw and Deborah Coles (2007, p.9) note that people identify and 'empathize' with the victim and with the bereaved. It is empathy derived in familiarity – with prisons and with institutionalized 'poor conditions... inadequate treatment and medical neglect', particularly in women's incarceration (Sandler and Coles, 2008, p.4).

An instructive comparison is Susan Sontag's (2003) reflection on the brutality and brutalization of war in which she considers the dynamics through which ordinary people living routine and settled lives unexpectedly become recipients of atrocity inflicted on them or on their community. Those outside the community, even within the same society, remain external to the suffering and 'don't understand' (p.125):

> We don't get it. We truly can't imagine how dreadful, how terrifying war is, and how *normal* it becomes. Can't understand. Can't imagine.
> (pp.125–126)

Those who survive the direct experiences of war 'stubbornly feel' the lack of real understanding, whatever reassurances are given to the contrary. So it is with prison. In the course of the research on which this book is based, a woman prisoner made this very point:

> We have a counsellor who we rarely see. She's always saying, 'I know exactly what you are going through. I know what it's like'. But she doesn't. She'd have to be here 24 hours, seven days a week. She'd have to be locked in her cell. She'd have to see three shifts change. She'd have to feel what it's like to have no say in your own life – to feel humiliation deep down. Then she could say she understands.

What is the relevance of this to prison research? To grapple with Quinney's lucid commentary the researcher has to move beyond the assigned interview room, the permissible questions, the guided tour, the escorts and the set itinerary. Critical research is about asserting the 'right to know', it is investigative and it is revelatory. It bridges the inside–outside physical divide by informing the outside of what happens on the inside; it achieves the 'view from below' by the 'view from within'. It goes further, responding to Susan Sontag's call to stretch the imagination. Reporting, recording and interpreting mind-numbing routines as well as the harsh punishments and occasional cruelties are parts of the process of engagement with the prison as total institution. Critical research bears witness to the humiliation and lack of self-determination normalized in the lives of the incarcerated.

Joe Sim (2003, p.239) opens a discussion of researching medical power in prisons with a 'stark and compelling' account of a deeply distressed prisoner being aggressively dealt with by a prison doctor. After the consultation a healthcare officer dismissed the prisoner as a 'troublemaker' and the doctor referred to 'malingerers'. The doctor considered that '95 per cent of prisoners were "the scum of the earth"'. The account is disturbing and is illustrative of the

> operationalization of Foucault's 'micro physics of power' in that it captures a specific but not unusual penal moment in which a group of powerful men – a prison doctor and two health care officers – exercised their medical power over the body and mind of a powerless, individual man – a distressed prisoner. (p.240)

As Sim comments, the administration of prison medicine is a 'hidden, micro-world'. Central to his revelatory account is the researcher's commitment and responsibility to be present at that moment of interpersonal interaction when the politics and ideology of micro-relationships within prison are most evident, laying bare the rhetoric of care and rehabilitation.

Sim reflects on the importance of Lisa Maher's notion of 'being there' when the 'politics of domination and the power relations that inhere in ethnographic encounters' surface (Sim, 2002, p.241). This is difficult terrain, 'often a gruelling experience which was saturated by a sense of outrage, not only at the abject and corrosive physical conditions in which the prisoners were detained and examined, but also at the often callous, off-hand and brutally capricious medical treatment they received' (p.241). The research enabled prisoners, whose lives were subjected to the double jeopardy of being incarcerated and being ill in prison, to challenge the 'particular definition of epidemiological "truth" with respect to their lives' in establishing 'their own records with respect to their experiences of prison medical power' (p.242).

Researching state institutions

In presenting 'reflections on doing research in prisons' internationally, Roy King (2000, p.286; revised as King and Liebling, 2008) makes the contentious claim that Britain 'probably now leads the English-speaking world... in terms of [academic] research in prisons'. He provides an extensive list of studies to illustrate the consolidation of a 'sizeable group of academics with a detailed, first-hand knowledge of what goes on inside prisons' (p.287). Accepting that punishment 'is a political issue' he notes a 'principal issue of concern... is that the Home Office is *both* gatekeeper as far as access is concerned *and* principal funder of research' (p.288, emphases in original). Whatever 'dealings' operate between officials and researchers, the 'real power' lies 'largely in the hands of officialdom'. Despite this concern, however, he comments that 'some criminologists... regard almost everything done with Home Office funding or approval as necessarily tainted'. He argues that the 'reality is much more complex and nuanced' with the relationship providing a 'reasonably steady flow of good quality research' resulting in a 'cumulative base of knowledge and understanding' (p.288). The 'process' is 'two-way' in that 'getting access and funds need not mean that one automatically loses any sense of independence, scholarly judgement, or personal integrity' (p.289).

King maintains that prison researchers are aware of the politics of access and have the capacity, once inside, to pursue their independent agendas unfettered by officials. In realizing this potential he concludes that the influence of the Home Office and the prison service can be circumscribed. This is the 'complexity' or 'nuance', he states, that is missed by sceptical criminologists. Yet, critical approaches to prison research are also complex and nuanced. It is not simply that they reject all Home Office approved research as 'necessarily tainted'. Rather, they question the management and manipulation of the research process by official bodies at each developing level: proposal; access; location; itinerary; movement; association; information; and publication. At each level restrictions are both demanded and imposed by the prison service and the specific prison. Aspirant researchers also impose self-regulation to secure access, retain cooperation and maintain relationships for future work. This has become a significant issue in universities as research funding has become a vital element of their assessment as research-based institutions.

In seeking funding, particularly from state institutions, researchers are well aware of the political agenda underpinning the commission. The research proposal secures the contract in a tendering process. Its content is not necessarily determined by academic merit and is affected by perceptions of what will and will not impress the contractors. This includes the theoretical and conceptual framework adopted by the researchers, including the previous research referenced in the proposal and whether its inclusion could influence the award of a research contract. For example, in an article exploring and advising on 'routes into prison' for aspirant researchers, Carol Martin (2000, p.218, emphasis added) states, 'it is vital to remember the most *obvious fact* of all – individuals *are not allowed* inside a prison simply because they want to get inside, for whatever reason'. Consequently, 'it is important to decide what type of research project is to be carried out and, crucially, whether it is likely to meet with *official approval*' (p.218, emphasis added).

Martin also comments on in-house funding of unsolicited projects: 'the scope of the research must fall within the overall research agenda of the Prison Service' (p.219). The 'value' of research is the '*outcome value* to the Prison Service' without which 'the research is likely to be sanctioned' (pp.219–220, emphasis in original). She concludes, 'a key factor is being able to identify the ones [questions] which are most likely to represent the best value available to the prospective client, that is, the Prison Service as a whole or an individual establishment' (p.220). This is the prison–industrial complex, now an integral element of what Nils Christie (1994) identified as a burgeoning 'social control industry'. It has consolidated as a process that sets the research agenda, establishes priorities to be investigated, allows access and confers legitimacy. It bears no relation to independent research and severely undermines academic freedom.

Once the contract has been awarded and extensive terms and conditions applied, what follows is the negotiation of access, the precise location in which research interviews will be conducted and limitations on observing the regime in process. This negotiation determines agreed daily itineraries, the spontaneous movement of researchers within the prison and opportunities for informal association with prisoners and staff. The prison's operation, access to documentary information on regime implementation and prisoners' case files are tightly controlled with access restricted and discretionary. Martin is unambiguous in her assessment of discretionary access:

> [E]xperienced prison researchers who have a track record of working with the Prison Service are likely to be accorded a high degree of co-operation…a study commissioned by the Home Office or

Prison Service and employing Home Office researchers would probably gain the highest level of co-operation, enabling carrying of keys, and facilitating access to all parts of the prison and prisoner records. (p.221)

While prison researchers often use the inappropriate metaphor, 'going native', in warning against over-identification with prisoners, they are reticent in commenting on their over-identification with management and staff or the ready acceptance, usually for 'safety' or 'security' reasons, of restrictions placed on freedom of movement within the prison.

Finally, publication of research findings, their dissemination at conferences and disclosures to the media or interested parties, are tightly restricted by permission clauses. Breach of conditions or findings highly critical of official policy and practice carry the ultimate censure of disqualification from further research contracts. Roy King and Alison Liebling (2008, p.441), neither of whom 'can speak to the problems associated with getting materials published, because neither of us has experienced serious problems', warn that in 'to-day's climate it would be folly to take a publish-and-be-damned attitude if *one wanted to gain future research contracts*' (emphasis added). The issue is not about adopting a cavalier approach to publishing, but it raises the significance of publicly controversial findings in the knowledge that this may compromise future research opportunities.

In anticipating exclusion, self-regulation becomes a significant factor in all state-contracted research. This applies particularly to circumstances that have potential to reveal what Stan Cohen (2001, p.296) names 'troubling information', previously denied, neutralized or reconstructed by powerful state institutions. Following the publication of the first Human Rights Commission research project on which in part this research is based, the researchers were refused access to the Young Offenders' Centre to carry out research on behalf of the Northern Ireland Commissioner for Children and Young People. Further, they were banned from conducting follow-up research with women in prison. Eventually this decision was rescinded.

The negotiation of independent research in prisons raises significant ethical questions as the 'prison industry' has become intertwined with academic knowledge as industry. Christie notes the all-pervasive attack on academic freedom via the 'invasion' of 'management ideology' and vocational 'correspondence' within universities. Central to this is the long-standing construction of 'useful knowledge' demanded by 'managers within the state and business' and its imposition on research and teaching. This utilitarian process has compromised 'university standards of critical thinking' while reducing 'the moral power of the question-makers'.

As C. Wright Mills (1959) noted in his seminal text *The Sociological Imagination*, many sociology and other social sciences departments within universities owed their expansion and consolidation to their 'correspondence' with the requirements and demands of private and public institutions and their political management of structural inequalities through welfare as well as business programmes. They served and serviced the post-war military–industrial complex, and as the crime control industry has expanded administrative criminology serves and services the prison–industrial complex.

In mainstream criminology textbooks critical analysis regularly has been misrepresented and caricatured, yet its significance and impact remains undiminished. It has developed and consolidated an impressive range of theoretical publications, established a critical mass in empirical research and inspired several generations of researchers and teachers through offering excellent, challenging programmes. This body of work foregrounds analysis of state alongside the corporate interests of a global political economy. It remains closely associated with the daily realities of people's lives within societies where class divisions, neo-colonialism, patriarchal oppression and ageism remain entrenched.

In her searching analysis of penal policy and punishment Barbara Hudson argues that 'legal theory and criminology' cannot deliver convincing explanations of crime, social problems or the differential and discriminatory administration of criminal justice. She proposes a 'critical theory of the contemporary state' exploring the 'structural context in which criminal justice is enacted' demonstrating how the 'rhetoric of law and order, crime and punishment has prevailed over treatment' (Hudson, 1993, pp.6–7). The 'defining tradition' of 'critical social science' underpinning Hudson's analysis is intellectual engagement 'on behalf of those on the downside of power relations'. As Lee Harvey (1990, p.6) notes, critical social research prioritizes and exposes 'how social systems really work, how ideology or history conceals the processes which oppress and control people...direct[ing] attention to the processes and institutes which legitimate knowledge'.

The converse, however, is the affiliation of 'mainstream', administrative criminology as it nurtures 'the most dangerous relationship to power: the categories and classifications, the labels and diagnoses and the images of the criminal being both stigmatizing and pejorative'

(Hudson, 2000, p.177). The potential of critical analysis for challenging and affecting change in the established politics and practices of criminal justice is well illustrated by Thomas Mathiesen's (1990) important critique of prisons and punishment. Concerned with the 'material underpinnings' of the ideological functions of imprisonment he notes that society's bifurcation 'between the productive and the unproductive ... places prisoners in a [structurally] powerless position' (Mathiesen, 1990, p.138). While the crimes and conventions of the powerful are neglected, those of the powerless become increasingly stigmatized. Thus prisons 'appear meaningful and legitimate'. He concludes: 'By relying on the prison, by building prisons, by building more prisons, by passing longer prison sentences' politicians and civil servants 'obtain a method of showing they act on crime ... that they are doing something about it, that something is presumably being done about law and order' (p.139). Mathiesen's vision of prison expansionism was prophetic.

> Sponsors of research include government departments [local and central], especially the Home Office, institutions of criminal justice, such as the police and legal profession, and pressure groups ... Each of these stakeholders has interests to promote and interests to protect ... each has differential levels of power with which to promote and protect such interests. The exercise of such power is ingrained in the research process from the formulation of problems through to the publication of results.
>
> (Jupp, Davies and Francis, 2000, p.170)

Reflecting on a discussion with a senior civil servant at the Health and Safety Executive (HSE) while researching safety in the offshore oil industry, David Whyte (2000, p.420) was told that 'government funding would be forthcoming only for research ... constructed around the HSE's agenda'. Access and funding would be granted only in association with substantial restrictions on the 'freedom to publish and disseminate findings'. As Whyte concludes, once researchers accept a 'grant-holding relationship with either government or corporate funders' their 'research activities will, to some extent, be structured by those who hold the purse strings' (p.421).

Victor Jupp (1989, p.158) notes that when funders commission research focusing on their policies and practices, or those of institutions for which they are responsible, 'they will be concerned with the way in which they are portrayed, with the way in which their management and control of institutions is portrayed and with the way in which conclusions might be used by others'. Funders and influential gate-keepers 'who have the power to protect their interests' present the most 'serious threats' to the publication and dissemination of research findings.

As Jupp (1989, p.175) argues, and is evident in what follows in this book, 'the balance of power between different parties (subjects, researchers, gatekeepers, sponsors) and the way in which it is exercised, determines what gets studied, by whom and with what outcome'. A revealing article by Alison Leibling, a prolific prison researcher regularly commissioned by the Home Office, discusses a long-term research project on incentives and earned privileges in prison (alongside other state-commissioned research) (Liebling, 1999). Following brief mentions of 'emotion', 'feelings' and 'turbulence' experienced by prison researchers, and the 'risks' associated with interviewing male lifers in a volatile situation, she states:

> Our interviews were becoming harrowing, as prisoners vented their frustration for us, or told us that they would commit suicide by the year's end – life as a life sentence prisoner was becoming unbearable. Our interviews were traumatic encounters – long enough to empathize with some of their feelings, structured enough to limit our ability to respond with more than sympathy or occasional suggestions. We saw (for the first time, to this extent) what was meant by the term 'difficult prisoner': angry, hostile, resentful, suspicious, articulate men questioning the staff, challenging us and beginning to take their own action against what they saw as unreasonable change. (p.150)

Over two years the ten person research team with whom she worked conducted '1000 structured and 250 semi-structured interviews' across five prisons. Liebling describes the researchers' experiences of the aftermath of the project: 'It was tempting to drink and smoke more than usual, listen to extra-loud music, drive too fast and resort to other stress-related behaviours, to let off steam. We did' (p.150). In the aftermath of the research, issues were raised concerning methodology, proximity, objectivity, personal experiences and their impact on knowledge formation. Researchers' crises included the 'continuous nature, pressure and speed' demanded by the research alongside its political context and feelings of personal dissociation when communicating experiences of the closed world to those not involved. The 'associations' of the prison 'summoned' by researchers, 'indicate as much about us as well as about the prison: confinement, authority, power, control, injustice, violence, relationship, hope, pain and sadness' (p.152). Prison reveals the 'extremes of human nature – its capacity for good and evil ... in perhaps their starkest form'. Such extremes encompass 'compassion and wisdom' as well as 'abuse and life-threatening violence' in institutions that are 'raw, and sometimes desperate, special places' (p.152).

This rare but important glimpse into the netherworld of prison in which the researcher faces her dilemmas, her associations, her relationships and her worth in terms of knowing and knowledge is soon overtaken by the job-in-hand. Liebling describes the 'pressures' associated with state-commissioned research. She describes the 'pilot work', the 'structured, quantifiable interviews', the 'randomly selected sample' and the 'evaluation' of the 'outcome', 'implementation' and 'process' of a policy initiative. Yet, there is no exploration of the tensions inherent in assessing the relationship between research and evaluation, of directing interviews with prisoners that measure the effectiveness of policy rather than exploring prisoners' profound experiences of incarceration in a broader context. The 'research pace', therefore, was directed by those who commissioned a policy evaluation rather than by the prisoners' experiences. In agreeing to be interviewed, what did the prisoners consider they had signed up for?

While acknowledging the honesty, openness, distress and emotion of some of the qualitative interviews and their 'brave and terrible stories' (p.158), what emerges from Liebling's account is a project in which the researchers are presented as 'players' who each 'spent different amounts of time in the field' (p.160). They contributed to 'debriefing' meetings which developed the 'interplay between experience in the field, analysis of the data and reflection' lending important support 'for those in the field' (p.160). Further, a 'dialogue' was 'engaged' with 'representatives of the field' as 'different players in the world we studied' (p.160).

Liebling selects one prisoner's story to illustrate the impact of a punitive political climate on long-term prisoners. The reader is placed in the prison, in a prisoner's life, rather than a 'field'. It is a moving account concluding with the following reflection:

> It was a sad conversation, that left its mark for days afterwards. What do we do with such experiences? ... We were in danger of 'going native' by this stage, identifying so powerfully with the feelings of

prisoners and of some staff groups, that we were becoming less able to bear the interviews. It was time to leave the field. The task was how to reconcile our powerful emotions with 'our data'. Or was it? (p.162)

In her lengthy conclusion about the 'nature' of prison research, Liebling does not address the significance and implications of working to a state-commissioned agenda. However demanding, distressing and emotional, the 'research' was an evaluation of a policy initiative derived in a political context. The framework of 'incentives' and 'privileges' in prisons is in immediate tension with internationally agreed standards on the rights of and protections afforded to prisoners. In conducting the research the prison becomes a 'field', people become 'players' and more profound excursions into prisoners' lives run the 'danger' of 'going native'. It is here that the dilemma of independent prison research is located and can be so easily compromised.

A research project of this scope, the size of the research team, its duration, access and finance is dependent entirely on the commission and the commission establishes the parameters. It is obvious that interviewing inside a prison, with the range of emotions trapped inside a total institution, is always difficult and often harrowing. Most, but not all, prisoners have deeply considered stories to offer, not bounded by prescribed questions or time limits. It is not unusual for prisoners to request a further interview, having reflected on their initial discussion. Returning to the discussion is not merely about further reflection and memory-work, it is also about trust. In opening up to researchers prisoners are immediately vulnerable. They have no guarantees about how their words will be used, who by or where they will be published. In prison there is minimal trust, limited confidentiality and numerous instances of commitments made and broken by those in authority. Researchers are perceived, and often are, extensions of that authority and cannot ignore Howard Becker's (1967) defining question, 'Whose side are you on?'.

Conveyor-belt research driven by interview targets and policy evaluations cannot respond sensitively or responsibly to the depth, complexity and significance of prisoners' revelatory stories. This is best summarized in a previously unpublished comment from a prisoner serving a life-sentence:

I'm fed up with researchers coming in here and expecting us to answer questions about the latest changes. It's pretty simple. This place is a shit-hole, the conditions are crap, you're locked up most of the time and most of the screws can't be trusted. I did it once. Spilled out everything to this researcher about my life, home, kids, the lot. I went back to my pad and hardly slept for two days. It fucked me up and you know what? I never heard from her again. That was the last time. When they ask now [for an interview] I just say 'No way'.

(Field-notes, Glenochil, 1995)

The empirical research

The final quote above clearly summarizes the potential for exploitation inherent in prison research. We maintain there is an ethical responsibility in social research equivalent to the Hippocratic Oath in medicine – to guard against harm and injustice while maintaining confidentiality (see Scraton, 2004). The primary research discussed in Chapters 5–8 was conducted in two phases: the first during 2004 and the second during 2006. The initial field research took place in Mourne House, the women's unit within the male high-security prison at Maghaberry. Follow-up research was conducted after the women's unit had been transferred from Maghaberry to a unit within the medium-security male Young Offenders' Centre at Hydebank Wood. These units within male jails were the sole accommodation for women prisoners in Northern Ireland as remains the situation at Hydebank Wood.

The impetus for initiating the project was a 2003 visit by Human Rights Commissioners to the Mourne House Women's Unit at Maghaberry Prison. This visit followed the death by hanging of a woman prisoner in the punishment block and the publication of a highly critical Prisons Inspectorate report on Mourne House. Concerned by what they experienced during their visit, the Commissioners established independent research prioritizing the human rights of women prisoners in Northern Ireland. Their concerns were evident in the research remit:

[T]he extent to which the treatment of women and girls in custody in Maghaberry Prison is compliant with international human rights law and standards, and in particular with Articles 2 [right to life] and 3 [right to be free from torture, inhuman and degrading treatment] of the European Convention on Human Rights.

The Commission's powers included independent, investigative research into custody but at that time it could not compel access to documentation or to places of detention (the latter became a problem during fieldwork).

In planning the Mourne House research it was apparent that the Prison Service intended to transfer women and girl prisoners from Mourne House to Ash House, a unit within Hydebank Wood male Young Offenders' Centre. The then Director General, Peter Russell, suggested postponement of the research beyond the transfer. As conditions at Mourne House had been the focus of the Commission's initial concern, the research proceeded. A second phase was planned following the transfer to Hydebank Wood.

Mourne House

Following meetings with the Director General and the Maghaberry Prison Governor, research access was granted in consultation with the Governor for Mourne House. Daily access was overseen by the Principal Officer who managed the unit. Access arrangements were agreed in advance but flexibility was negotiated in the schedule. Throughout the research access was uncontested, the accommodation provided was comfortable and arrangements went according to plan. The researchers agreed to usual security checks on arrival and were issued with palm-activated passes, their movements within the prison unencumbered and unescorted. Access was granted to all parts of the unit including the punishment block (special observation unit). Most guards were courteous, regularly referred to the researchers as 'human rights' and respected the requests to ensure confidential interviews with prisoners. The documentary records maintained on prisoners and held on the landings were made available. Record-keeping, however, was poor.

It was not possible to conduct interviews during lock-up and this proved restrictive. Following a death early in the research, access was denied to the cell in which the woman prisoner had died as the case was under police investigation. Access was granted, however, to an adjacent cell to demonstrate the physical conditions under which the young woman had been held. Two interviews with a 17-year-old child were held in the punishment block, but a third interview on the landing to which she had been relocated was denied by the Governor. In fact, the interview eventually took place in the closed visits area. Most women prisoners agreed for the interviews to be tape-recorded.

On the first visit, the researchers requested access to all policy documentation related to women's imprisonment within the unit. It was several weeks before this documentation was supplied. In total, it amounted to a four-page introduction to the Mourne House unit giving brief descriptions of accommodation, landing routine, tuck-shop, visits, parcels and wages; a two-page guide for prisoners explaining 'progressive regimes'; a two-page guide, 'Booking a visit at Maghaberry Prison'; a two-page description of the daily routine for the committal and assessment landing; the Committee for the Administration of Justice's brief guide to prisoners' rights; a card introducing the Board of Visitors; and the Maghaberry Prison *Health and Safety Policy*. In fact, the latter was the only policy statement provided to the researchers by the prison authorities. The researchers were informed that the Prison Service did not have policy documentation on the custody of women or girls.

Relevant Prison Service documentation, accessed from other sources, were *Life Sentence Prisoners in Northern Ireland: An Explanatory Memorandum* (July 2000); *Review of Prison Healthcare Services* (April 2002); the draft *Policy on Self Harm and Suicide Prevention Management* (March 2003); the Maghaberry Prison Board of Visitors *Annual Report 2002–2003*; and the explanatory guide *Compact for Separated Prisoners* (February 2004).

Focus groups were held with representatives of the Mourne House Branch of the Prison Officers' Association (MHPOA) – on two occasions, with members of the Maghaberry Board of Visitors and education staff. Semi-structured interviews were held with women prisoners who wished to participate in the research, and anonymity was guaranteed. In evaluating the research evidence, and establishing its reliability, wherever possible triangulation was used alongside cross-referencing. A relatively small number of prison officers asked or agreed to be interviewed. Individual interviews were also held with staff from health care, the probation service and the clergy. Formal meetings and informal discussions were held with prison governors. Throughout the research contemporaneous field-notes and a diary were used to record the operation of the daily routine of the prison.

Responding to the proposed transfer of women to Hydebank Wood, the Human Rights Commission published an interim report opposing the transfer: *The Transfer of Women from the Mourne House Unit, Maghaberry Prison to Hydebank Wood Young Offenders Centre*. The full research report was published in October 2004: *The Hurt Inside: The Imprisonment of Women and Girls in Northern Ireland*. A revised and updated edition followed in June 2005.

Hydebank Wood

On 28 June 2004, all women prisoners were transferred to Ash House, Hydebank Wood. In July, the Chief Commissioner of the Human Rights Commission requested access to visit women prisoners to ensure that the conditions in the prison were rights compliant. Access to the prison grounds and accommodation landings was denied. The Director General agreed that Commission staff could visit women who requested a visit, in the legal visits area. The researchers were permitted to visit an 18-year-old young woman who was self-harming and had been detained in the Special Supervision Unit (SSU). Despite restrictions on access the researchers interviewed ten women in the legal visits area, and interviewed family members and friends of prisoners, as well as women released from Hydebank Wood who made contact following the extensive publicity generated regarding the work. The second phase of the research, however, was in jeopardy.

In December 2004, a new Director General was appointed to the Prison Service. In November 2005 access was negotiated for the second phase. The methodology was consistent with the Mourne House research. Following initial discussions with Prison Service management and the Governor of Hydebank Wood the on-site fieldwork took place over several weeks in late 2005 and early 2006. As the women were moved from their initial accommodation in Ash House to refurbished accommodation in Beech House, a further period of on-site fieldwork was negotiated. An unexpected development occurred when a number of 'foreign-national' detainees were admitted. This extended the scope of the research.

Managers, prison officers, health-centre staff, teachers, clergy, professionals working on-site from outside agencies, the Independent Monitoring Board and the Prison Officers' Association (POA) were interviewed. The level of women prisoners' participation was highly enhanced by publication and media coverage of the first Report. Prison guards, except for a small minority, refused to participate in interviews. The researchers experienced a courteous but distant reception from most, but not all, guards on the landings.

The primary research with women used semi-structured interviews based on a schedule covering all aspects of their imprisonment. As in Mourne House, some prisoners were interviewed on several occasions, the interviews taped and transcribed in full. Focus groups were convened during association and some women, particularly those serving short sentences, preferred to be interviewed as a group. Routine access to landings and recreation rooms allowed the researchers considerable time to observe the regimes in action.

The researchers also observed meetings in progress, including 'prisoner-at-risk' sessions. Documentary evidence was provided when requested, particularly policy documentation or operational guidelines. Quantitative data was supplied on request but was often incomplete. Further interviews were conducted with outside professionals and former prisoners. Meetings were held with senior managers at Hydebank Wood culminating in a final meeting with the Director General and colleagues at which the researchers raised issues that had emerged from the work.

Subsequent research

Following publication of the second report, *The Prison Within*, in 2007 the research became the focus of significant media interest and public debate. The researchers' direct involvement in cases and in two inquests provided a range of access to documentation via the Human Rights Commission as an interested party. Although the researchers had no right of access to Hydebank Wood, and the Human Rights Commission decided against further research, interviews with women prisoners continued to be conducted in the visits area. Between 2008 and 2010 reports of the Independent Monitoring Board and the Prisons Inspectorates were analysed, and the researchers participated in the post-devolution review of prisons established by the Minister of Justice. This range of documentary research and active participation informs the final chapter of the book, enabling analysis and evaluation of the impact of the research and the slow rate of progress towards affecting necessary change.

4
Women's Imprisonment, Conflict and Transition

Introduction

Imprisonment in Northern Ireland operates within the context of a society and criminal justice process emerging from three decades of violent conflict and a longer history of sectarian politics. Penal regimes have developed and consolidated within this context. High rates of political imprisonment and the dynamics of prison struggles have had a profound impact within local communities. Throughout the recent Conflict, over 3,700 men, women and children were killed, the majority by republican or loyalist paramilitary organizations (McKittrick et al., 2004, p.1528). Tens of thousands were injured and countless others made homeless, traumatized or bereaved. Approximately ten per cent of killings were by state forces (McKittrick et al., 2004, p.1534). Allegations persist regarding the extent of state collusion with loyalist paramilitaries. It is estimated that half of Northern Ireland's population (1.8 million in 2011) has been affected by the death or injury of a close relative or friend (Fitzduff and O'Hagan, 2009).

Paramilitary ceasefires and the subsequent multiparty 1998 Good Friday/Belfast Agreement resulted in the devolution of powers to an elected Assembly and to significant reform. Delayed for over a decade, justice and policing were finally devolved early in 2010 and a justice ministry formed. Following the Agreement, the early release of politically affiliated prisoners was viewed by many commentators as a prerequisite for a lasting peace settlement. Despite a shared commitment, at least publicly, to securing a political resolution, the transition from conflict has been inconsistent. Two decades on from the ceasefires, a level of paramilitary violence continues and policing remains contested, particularly within working-class communities.

Throughout the Conflict, Northern Ireland had a unique prison system' with high levels of long-term, indeterminate and life sentence prisoners, more than 50 per cent of convicted prisoners were imprisoned for politically motivated offences (McEvoy, 1998, p.40). It was a system steeped in the Conflict, producing 'charged sites' within which 'larger battles' were fought (McEvoy et al., 2007, p.293). Significantly, a leading Republican activist predicted that the 'war will be won in the prisons' (cited in Coogan, 1980, p.14). At all levels – management, operation and regimes – the prisons were shaped by sectarianism and the overwhelming majority of prison guards were male, recruited almost exclusively from Protestant/Unionist/Loyalist communities. Throughout the Conflict, therefore, prison managers and guards were considered 'legitimate' targets by Republican paramilitaries. Twenty-nine prison guards were killed and many more had their homes fire-bombed or were forced to flee following paramilitary threats (Ryder, 2000). In November 2012, David Black became the 30th member of the Prison Service to be killed, shot dead by a Republican paramilitary group opposed to the political settlement.

The history of the state's use of and reliance on imprisonment to repress protest and rebellion provides the essential context to understanding contemporary penal policy and practice in Northern Ireland. This includes politically affiliated prisoners' resistance to penal regimes and the impact of imprisonment within communities, extending to the formal political process and the central role played by former prisoners in political transition. This historical context provides the foundation on which analysis of the current situation for all prisoners in Northern Ireland, whether or not politically affiliated, has been developed. This chapter provides that context, then discussing the experiences of politically affiliated women in prison in Northern Ireland alongside the experiences of women imprisoned for politically motivated offences in other conflicted and transitional jurisdictions.

The impact of the Conflict on the prison system

Kieran McEvoy (2001) notes that the British State's use of imprisonment during the Conflict progressed through three stages: reactive containment (1969–1975); criminalization (1976–1981); managerialism (early 1980s onwards). He considers 'reactive containment' as a 'relatively crude' and 'military led' approach by the State to repress politically motivated violence (McEvoy, 2001, p.204). In the early 1970s, reactive containment involved mass arrest and detention without trial under emergency legislation, practices which sparked community unrest and rioting. Internees, detained under special powers legislation, and not charged with crimes, were subjected to 'interrogation techniques' including sleep deprivation, 'white noise', hooding and being forced to stand for long periods spread-eagled against walls.

In November 1971 the Compton Inquiry concluded that although some detainees had suffered physical ill-treatment and 'hardship', this did not extend to 'physical brutality' (para. 14). In January 1976, the European Commission ruled that detainees had been subjected to 'inhuman treatment' and torture, breaching Article 3 of the European Convention on Human Rights (ECHR) (European Commission, 1976). A subsequent European Court judgment in January 1978 (Ireland v UK), however, ruled that the techniques constituted inhuman and degrading treatment but did not amount to torture (European Court, 1978; for analysis of Ireland v UK, see Donahue, 1980).

Internment was used primarily against members of Catholic/Nationalist communities. Between 1971 and 1975, 1,874 Catholics/Nationalists and 107 Protestant/Loyalists were interned (CAIN webservice). They were held in a range of places of detention including a prison ship and internment camps at Long Kesh and Magilligan. Internees were recognized by the authorities as having political status. Separated within the camps by their political affiliations, they were not obliged to carry out prison work and could wear their own clothes. Those convicted through the courts for conflict-related offences, however, were refused special status and treated as 'ordinary' prisoners. Demanding the extension of special status to include those convicted of politically related offences, Republican and Loyalist prisoners in Belfast prison went on a hunger strike and in June 1972 'special category status' was extended. The court process was also shaped by the Conflict and in 1973 'Diplock' courts were introduced for a range of scheduled, mainly terrorist-related offences, thus abandoning trial by jury.

In Long Kesh detainees and prisoners organized their own huts, each compound having an 'officer-in-command' responsible for all communication with the prison authorities. Some Republican 'cages' were designated 'gaeltacht' (Irish speaking) areas. A 'camp council' drawing representation from each paramilitary organization was established. A former Loyalist prisoner reflected that daily routine was controlled 'not by prison staff, but by the prisoners themselves' (Gusty Spence, cited in Crawford, 1999, p.33). Prison guards were 'permitted' into the compound only to conduct a morning head count or occasional searches. On days of cultural celebration or remembrance prisoners held military-style parades. In Colin Crawford's assessment (1999, p.26), the British State inadvertently had introduced a 'humane' form of imprisonment that 'did not institutionalise, dehumanise, criminalise or alienate prisoners, but afforded them a degree of dignity and liberty, unknown and without precedent in recent British history'. Republican former prisoner Laurence McKeown (in Sharoni, 1999, p.2) described the atmosphere created by Long Kesh prisoners as 'vibrant, energetic, supportive, progressive', a 'luxuriant oasis in the midst of a harrowing desert'. Despite this unique form of self-governance, by the mid-1970s within Long Kesh tensions and protests emerged, provoked particularly by new security measures following escape attempts, poor food and inadequate health and mental health care (Ryder, 2000).

In the mid-1970s, as the security situation worsened, Government strategy shifted to a policy of 'criminalization', an approach characterized by a 'law and order' response to politically motivated violence. The Gardiner Commission (1975) recommended the abandonment of political status, the phasing out of internment and the construction of a new cellular-based prison. On 1 March 1976 Merlyn Rees, UK Secretary of State for Northern Ireland, announced that special category status would no longer be granted to prisoners sentenced after that date. A month later the IRA responded by killing prison guard, Pacelli Dillon, the first of 19 guards killed during the five years of 'criminalization'. On 14 September 1976 Kieran Nugent, the first Republican prisoner sentenced under the new conditions, on entering Long Kesh (renamed HMP Maze) refused to wear a prison uniform:

> They [prison guards] pushed me into one of the cells and told me to put the uniform on. I said: 'No, I'm not putting that gear on'. So they said 'Right, take your own clothes off'. I refused, so then they jumped on me and forcibly removed my clothes, and held me down and punched me about. One of them then threw a blanket at me – so in fact he started the protest.
>
> (cited in Ryder, 2000, p.166)

Eventually over 300 Republican prisoners engaged in the blanket protest including women prisoners held in Armagh jail. Some Loyalists also went 'on the blanket' but were withdrawn from the protest by their organization (Crawford, 1999). Protesting prisoners were punished by 24-hour lock-up in isolation with 'no radios, televisions, books, newspapers, magazines, writing papers, pens; no exercise; nothing but a piece of foam for a mattress, a piss pot and a container of water' (McKeown,

2009, p.21). From March 1978 the action escalated into a 'no wash' and then a 'dirt protest', the origins of which remain contested. Confined to their cells and reliant on chamber pots for defecation, prisoners complained that guards returned pots to cells only half-emptied – guards and prisoners made counter-accusations of pots being thrown.

Following a visit to the Long Kesh/Maze, a Catholic Archbishop (later Cardinal) Tomás Ó Fiaich expressed shock at witnessing the 'inhuman conditions', reminiscent of 'the spectacle of hundreds of homeless people living in sewer-pipes in the slums of Calcutta' (cited in Coogan, 1980, p.157). In June 1980 the European Commission ruled that while it considered conditions self-inflicted, the UK Government had been inflexible. A former prison guard explained guards' hatred for the 'blanket men':

> The screws [guards] regarded the prisoners as scum bags, they called them 'fuck dogs'. They didn't see them as human beings, so they didn't care what they did...The system [criminalization] changed men. Decent officers I knew from the compound side came to the blocks, and went power mad.
>
> (cited in Crawford, 1999, p.166)

Another guard described the 'brutal' strip searches:

> There were rules about how men should be strip-searched. We were told not to worry about them, they were 'English rules'. The prisoners would be forced to strip and squat over a mirror before their visits. If they refused, they were either beaten into submission or the visit was cancelled.
>
> (Crawford, 1999, p.174)

In one guard's view frequent strip searching was worse than beatings as the 'beatings were human; this [strip searching] was official, institutional' (Crawford, 1999, p.175). Denis O'Hearn (2006, p.168) describes the mutual enmity between Republican prisoners and prison guards during this period: '[t]he warders were mostly loyalists who considered themselves at war with the IRA. The blanketmen were mostly IRA members who made no secret of the fact that they could pass on intelligence about hated prison officers'.

In October 1980 seven Republican male prisoners in Maze/Long Kesh and three women in Armagh went on hunger strike for political status. The action was halted in December, the prisoners believing that the reintroduction of special category status was imminent. Yet no progress was forthcoming and a further hunger strike began on 1 March 1981. Bobby Sands was the first prisoner to refuse food followed by others in a staged process, on this occasion without women's participation. The hunger strike was based on five demands: prisoners' right to wear their own clothes; withdrawal from prison work; freedom of association; education and recreation; and restoration of lost remission. As the hunger strike consolidated it drew significant support and widespread protests within Nationalist/Republican communities.

Five days into Bobby Sands' hunger strike, the Member of Parliament (MP) for Fermanagh-South Tyrone died and a by-election was called. Standing as an 'Anti H-Block' candidate, on 10 April Bobby Sands was elected to Parliament having received over 30,000 votes. Prime Minister, Margaret Thatcher responded with the words: 'Crime is crime is crime. It is not political, it is crime' (cited BBC News, 5 May 2006). New legislation, the Representation of the People Act 1981, was rushed through Parliament to ensure that prisoners could no longer stand for election. Following 66 days on hunger strike Bobby Sands died and approximately 100,000 people attended his funeral. As more prisoners died, others joined the hunger strike which inevitably became an international issue.

With no apparent resolution forthcoming, several families requested medical intervention once their sons lost consciousness. By 3 October 1981, 10 men had died, and the hunger strike was over. It had become clear that families of those remaining on hunger strike planned to intervene before they died. The prisoners had won their demand to wear their own clothes and could leave their cells for association and exercise. Former hunger striker John Pickering comments, 'what they did in trying to criminalize us was they opened up our imaginations beyond anything they could have dreamt of' (in Howard, 2006, p.91).

The prisoners' demand for exemption from prison work was refused and in October 1982, in a strategic move, Republican prisoners 'presented themselves for work'. From the authorities' perspective it appeared that 'at long last the policy of criminalisation was beginning to work' (McKeown, 2009, p.22). Their optimism, however, misread the situation as the prisoners' objective was to escape (McKeown, 2009). On 25 September 1983, Republican prisoners took control of H-Block 7 and 38 escaped. A prison guard was stabbed and later died following a heart attack. A further six guards were shot or stabbed.

The Hennessy Inquiry (1984) into the escape described how the Maze/Long Kesh had developed from a small internment camp into a 'huge maximum modern prison', 'unique in size', noting 'the continuity of its protests and disturbances'. The task of the Governor and his staff was challenging given the Government's persistent policy of defining those it labelled 'terrorists' as ordinary prisoners (para. 10.4). The resistance of a hard core of prison guards to any 'concessions' to prisoners had reinforced a prevalent 'laissez-faire' attitude within the prison (para. 10.5) underpinned by 'complacency' and 'lazy practices' (para. 10.10). Hennessy made 73 recommendations directed towards improvements in physical and environmental conditions and security. His inquiry recommended new leadership and removal of 'dead wood' among prison guards (para. 10.18).

Returning to McEvoy's three-stage classification (2001), the strategy of 'managerialism' adopted from the mid-1980s, involved the State's acceptance that political violence could not be overcome via use of imprisonment. Rather, political solutions were required, with prisons managing the out-workings of conflict. Thus, pragmatic engagement with prisoners on day-to-day issues was viewed as a positive management strategy rather than a capitulation to the demand for political status. Managerialism was projected as the means to achieve organizational efficiency and effectiveness, 'value for money' and planned business outcomes (p.252).

The opening of the new high-security prison HMP Maghaberry in 1986 was central to this strategy. The new prison's first occupants were women, transferred from the closed Victorian Armagh Jail. A year later, 'ordinary' male prisoners were accommodated in Maghaberry. It was expected that modern physical conditions and possibilities of early release would tempt paramilitary prisoners to transfer to the new regime from Long Kesh/Maze and accept integration into the 'ordinary' regime (McEvoy, 2001).

Further incidents, however, demonstrated that the Northern Ireland prison system remained locked into the Conflict. In 1992 the Colville Inquiry reported on the death of a Loyalist prisoner in Belfast Prison when a device exploded in the prison dining hall. Five years later, in December 1997, Loyalist Volunteer Force (LVF) prisoner, Billy Wright, was shot dead in Long Kesh/Maze Prison in an operation mounted by three Irish National Liberation Army (INLA) prisoners. The Cory Report into Wright's death (2004, para. 3.14) found that, 'two dangerous and warring hostile factions had been billeted in the same H Block. The victim and murderers were just a stone's throw away from each other in a prison where the prisoners exercised a great deal of control'. Cory reported that by the time of Billy Wright's death, prison guards' control over the 500 remaining prisoners had 'diminished almost to the vanishing point' (para. 3.30). Moreover the State had turned a 'blind eye' to guards' warnings (paras 3.222–3.223). Subsequently, the Billy Wright inquiry (2010) found serious failings and negligence by the Prison Service, but no evidence of collusion.

Political imprisonment constituted a central element of the Conflict, thus prison issues were integral to its political settlement. As Bill Rolston (2002, p.92) comments, 'Republican and loyalist negotiators could not sign up to an agreement which did not promise the early release of their prisoners'. In January 1998, Secretary of State for Northern Ireland, Mo Mowlam visited the Long Kesh/Maze for discussions with Loyalist and Republican prisoners and the 1998 Good Friday/Belfast Agreement included provision for their early release. Prisoners who were members of paramilitary organizations on ceasefire were offered the opportunity to apply for 'early release on licence'. Over 400 prisoners were granted early release during the following two years. On 28 July 2000 the last prisoners left Long Kesh/Maze. Following the closures of HMP Armagh in 1986, HMP Belfast in 1996 and HMP Maze in 2000, all remaining or newly-held politically motivated prisoners – male and female – were held in Maghaberry.

The intention to operate Maghaberry as an integrated and 'normal' regime immediately ran into trouble as prisoners belonging to paramilitary groups not on ceasefire increased in numbers. In summer 2003, protests were staged by Loyalist and Republican prisoners demanding separation from each other and from ordinary prisoners. A safety review was commissioned under John Steele (2003), former head of the Northern Ireland Prison Service. It concluded that separation was necessary for prisoner safety but that this should not be presented nor interpreted as 'segregation' as in the previous regimes. While conducting his review, Steele was confronted by rooftop protests demanding segregation on political grounds.

Following Steele's recommendations, two of the six male accommodation units at Maghaberry, Bush and Roe, were adapted to house male politically affiliated prisoners separately. A Parliamentary Select Committee inquiry (2004: summary) stated that no 'concessions' should be made to separated prisoners which 'might undermine or diminish the control exercised by prison officers'. Arrangements for the separated regimes for male prisoners were set out in a 'prisoner compact', establishing conditions on which 'separated status' was granted. The findings from the primary research on which this book is based, discussed in Chapters 5 through to 8, coupled with evidence from inspection and other monitoring reports, subsequently challenged the depiction of the 'managerialist' approach as a pragmatic resolution to the problems within the North's prison system.

The imprisonment of women for politically motivated offences

As Mary Corcoran (2006, p.xvii) observes, the 'gendered organization of punishment' has been neglected in most academic research and commentaries. It is clear from the few accounts that have been written, that the management of and resistance by politically motivated women – approximately five per cent of those detained throughout the Conflict – had a clearly gendered dimension.

Northern Ireland's oldest prison, Armagh gaol, was built between 1780 and 1819, comprising three prisons housing women, 'felons' and debtors. Historically, Armagh was used for the imprisonment of Republican women during periods of political unrest. In the 1930s the leading Republican suffragist, Hanna Sheehy-Skeffington, was imprisoned in Armagh for breaching exclusion orders. During the Second World War, 18 Republican women, the majority very young, were interned there for up to three years. Their testimonies provide a graphic illustration of cold cells, isolation and monotony. They were locked up for 20 hours a day; 'only one visit a month was permitted and boredom hung heavy for three years. Knitting, embroidery, drawing, singing, an old gramophone and Nancy Ward's violin were the only forms of diversion' (McGuffin, 1973, p.81). Madge McConville, interned in 1942, described the enduring hardship and poor conditions in Armagh. Yet she recalled the friendship, collective support and shared resistance to the regime:

> Then we had the mutiny in November and they brought the peelers in. They turned the hose on us. The place was wrecked. They took everything out of our cells. They took us out of our cells, emptied the cells, and put us in a cell with nothing in it, only the bed which was attached to the wall. They couldn't take that away. Oh but you could bang it; it was great.
>
> (cited in Brady et al., 2011, pp.23–24)

While identifying as political prisoners and resenting the criminal classification imposed by the State, Republican women were affected by witnessing the lives and experiences of 'ordinary' prisoners. Mary Keenan, a Republican prisoner, commented 'I began to be less intolerant...I saw them [ordinary prisoners] more and more as the victims of society' (McGuffin, 1973, p.81). During the IRA's 1956–1961 'Border

Campaign' only one woman was interned. Bridie O'Neill was held 'on her own' for seven months in Armagh (McGuffin, 1973, p.83).

In the 1960s the civil rights movement in the North expanded and consolidated as a broad-based campaign for equal rights for Catholics. Marches were met with violence and repression from the police, the Royal Ulster Constabulary (RUC). In 1970, having been convicted of rioting, Bernadette Devlin, civil rights leader and (MP) for Mid Ulster, was sentenced to prison for six months. On arrival in Armagh she was strip-searched: 'I think the officer who received me was more embarrassed than I was'. She was given prison regulation clothes: a

> vast dress...two pairs of heavy-knit stockings, one pair of shoes...slippers two sizes too large...one elasticated suspender belt...and a garment which, with due respect to those who feel strongly about such niceties can only be described as your original and genuine knickers – which wouldn't stay up they were so big.
>
> (cited in Target, 1975, p.316)

Put to work sewing shirts she later described how:

> If you followed the routine religiously in a quite numb kind of way, just let your mind go blank, then the time passed so that you knew where you were in the day. If you were thinking hard, using your mind, time just got out of control.
>
> (cited in Target, 1975, p.316)

Devlin recalled relatively positive relations with prison guards, most of whom were young. Slopping out was, 'a humiliation lessened for us because, being few in number, we carried out our own ablutions'. Food was 'unnecessarily unappetising' and prisoners washed themselves and their dirty dishes in the same plastic basin (Target, 1975, p.314).

In the early 1970s, internment without trial was targeted mainly at Catholic men, while women occupied the heart of community protests including a mass 'rent and rates' strike (Corcoran, 2006, p.5). Nineteen-year-old Elizabeth McKee was the first woman to be interned, followed by 30 other women between 1972 and 1975 (p.5). According to Corcoran, the State's concerns were 'not without foundation'. From the early 1970s Republican women became more actively involved as Irish Republican Army (IRA) volunteers, operating in 'auxiliary' roles such as weapons transport, as lookouts and, more directly, in bombings, kidnappings and assassinations (p.6). Women's imprisonment expanded during the Conflict. In 1969 there were nine 'ordinary' prisoners and no politically-affiliated prisoners in Armagh. By 1981 there were 29 sentenced Republican women held alongside 27 'ordinary' prisoners (Fairweather et al., 1984, p.212). There were significantly fewer women from Loyalist organizations.

Corcoran (2006, p.131) notes that while male Loyalist and Republican prisoners adopted 'combined strategies', there is 'little evidence of any corollary working relationship between women prisoners, except where they were commonly victimized by administrative actions'. Corcoran's analysis of custodial patterns (p.8) shows:

> Of the 3,945 women who passed through the prison system between 1972 and 1998, approximately one half were interned or remanded (awaiting trial), a quarter were sentenced to immediate custody and another quarter was made up of 'civil offenders' and fine defaulters.

The expansion of women's incarceration was a consequence of emergency legislation, breaches of which included the 'wearing of "paramilitary-type dress", resistance to personal or property searches, and various acts of obstructing the security forces' (p.10). Republican prisoner Rose McAllister described how the political women in Armagh differed from other prisoners, 'because we were neither victims nor passive' (cited in McCafferty, 1981, p.18). Political status also offered some limited protection against abuse, 'I think we were lucky in gaol because we had our political status. A lot of girls who came behind us were in prison without status and they were persecuted in every way' (Anne-Marie McWilliams, internee Armagh, 1973, cited in Brady et al., 2011, p.40). Empathy for the plight of ordinary prisoners is shown in an account by Margaret Gatt, imprisoned in Armagh in 1971. She recalls the imprisonment of teenage girls, as young as 14:

> These girls had been deemed disruptive in the institutions where they had been previously so they were now housed in Armagh. We were appalled by this and thought we should do something about it. However, when we spoke with them, they pleaded with us not to do anything as they thought Armagh Gaol was a much better place than where they had come from.

> (cited in Brady et al., 2011, p.27)

The increase in women's imprisonment led to overcrowding, compounded by the use of Armagh as a borstal for boys and for 'overspill' accommodation for male internees and remand prisoners (Corcoran, 2006, p.21). From 1974, Armagh's Republican women were designated 'A' Company of the Provisional IRA. Communication with prison management was conducted through the prisoners' 'commanding officer' who 'interceded in disputes with staff, negotiated with the governor on behalf of prisoners, and maintained an ethos of internal discipline and community by allocating work to the company, conducting roll calls, wing inspections and holding political meetings' (Corcoran, 2006, p.26). On hearing that the Maze/Long Kesh had been set on fire, women in Armagh (Republican and one Loyalist) held the Governor and three female prison officers hostage, demanding assurances that their male comrades would not be subjected to ill-treatment (Ryder, 2000).

Although the paramilitary structure was similar to male prisons, Corcoran (2006, p.27) notes differences in approach: 'the women's political formations tended to develop more tacitly, and in accordance with the quality of reciprocal relationships that could be established with senior staff'. In 1974 Rose McAllister was imprisoned again in Armagh. She found the prison 'alive and humming...you still had to do your time, but the prison staff hardly interfered with us at all'. It 'wasn't a holiday camp, but you didn't feel you were dying from the neck up' (cited in McCafferty, 1981, p.20). Ann O'Neill, interned in 1973 confirmed the impact of solidarity and friendship despite the barren regime:

> The genuine care and support I received from Republican women in A Wing was unbelievable and the sound of their laughter I will never forget. It was so good to hear and I can hear it still. From that day on I would enjoy many more days of laughter and good times as well as sad and difficult times.
>
> (cited in Brady et al., 2011, p.34)

The introduction of the 'criminalization' strategy had a profound impact on politically affiliated women in Armagh. Republican women had rejected the labels 'criminal' or 'terrorist', and women entering the regime from March 1976 joined the campaign to restore political status. Unlike male prisoners, women wore their own clothes, providing they did not resemble paramilitary uniforms. 'Non-cooperating' women refused prison work, lost 50 per cent of remission and other 'privileges' and endured extended periods of lock-up. Allegations emerged that women ill with diarrhoea were refused access to toilets and women's access to sanitary protection was restricted: 'if a girl had had her period on say the third of a month then she got her sanitary towels on the third of the following month, even though the period might have arrived earlier' (Coogan,1980, p.115).

In February 1980 a 'general search' was carried out, ostensibly to find clothing worn during a parade held inside by Republican women prisoners in honour of an IRA volunteer 'killed in action'. Approximately 60 male and female guards conducted the search (Coogan, 1980). A woman prisoner, Maureen Gibson described the violence involved:

> In my own cell the mattress was pulled off the bed, the bedclothes lay on the floor, the cupboard was upended, photos of my family were torn up and the small holy statue the priest had given me was smashed. After that they came down to the association room and took us out one at a time to be searched. I walked into the room and all the screws were lining the walls. Naturally I was terrified. All I could see were blue uniforms everywhere. I didn't even have a chance to look at their faces before I was spreadeagled against the wall and searched. Then it was back to my cell. Four of the women had been up for adjudication for supposedly breaking some prison rule. After the whole thing the screws went up to their cells to get them. They went in full riot gear with shields and batons, and carried them down the stairs. One of them was actually kneeling on Anne-Marie Quinn's stomach – a huge big man – pushing her on to the bed while they were taking out Eilish O'Connor. One of the female screws even said, 'Go easy with her, there's no need to be so rough'.
>
> (cited in Fairweather et al., 1984, pp.219–220)

Following adjudications conducted in the prison, the women were locked in their cells and refused access to adequate sanitation. When chamber pots were full, the women poured the contents through the 'spy holes' of their cells:

> Then they [the guards] boarded them up, but we managed to unblock them and stop the waste from accumulating in our cells. We were never used to filth and dirt. Our cells were always spotlessly clean.
>
> (Rose, cited in Fairweather et al., 1984, p.223)

A Northern Ireland Office press release stated, 'a number of women had been confined to their cells and deprived of toilet facilities except for their "slop-pots" ' (*Irish News*, 8 February 1980, cited in Corcoran, 2006, p.37). During the 'dirt' protest, women remained locked in their cells 23 hours a day, smearing faeces and menstrual blood on cell walls. Officers wore 'blue nylon jump suits and white wellington boots, like space age women' (Liz Lagrua, cited in McCafferty, 1981, p.11).

> The stench was unbearable. Everything was dirty, as we weren't allowed to get washed. Even when you took your period you had nothing clean to change into. When you asked for sanitary towels they just threw them into the cells, and because of the strain some women were taking their periods when they shouldn't have. I was taking mine every two weeks, but I never got enough sanitary towels. They were rationed, like everything else... Before they boarded up the windows we could see houses in the distance, the sky and other parts of the jail. Then suddenly we couldn't see anything at all except shit.
>
> (Rose, cited in Fairweather et al., 1984, pp.221–222)

> If the smell is overpowering you can use the sanitary towels as a mask around your mouth, but you try to be sparing of that because the number of sanitary towels per month is restricted. They know we wear them even when not menstruating to provide some protection against our knickers or jeans and avoid disease, but even so they restrict us to two packages a month. That's the kind of thing that freaks you out about them and about the doctor... Criminalisation and sanitary towels go together. Criminal means clean. Political means dirty, they try to tell us.
>
> (Liz Lagrua, cited in McCafferty, 1981, p.13)

Days were monotonous, the routine disturbed only by meals and one hour of exercise. Yet the women organized classes and socialized through cell walls:

> Every night at 9.00 p.m. we have the Rosary in Irish. One shouts it out the door and the rest respond. Afterwards we have our Irish class shouted out the doors. Our voices are good and strong now from persistent shouting. Then perhaps bingo from our own made cards. It's good crack [craic – fun]. Anne-Marie next door persists in cheating but is always found out. Then at eleven the ghost story is continued from the night before as most lie in their beds under the covers to

keep warm... At mid-night all noise ceases – an order lain down by
our own [IRA] staff.

(woman prisoner, cited in Coogan, 1984, pp.129–130)

A different entertainments officer [prisoner] was appointed from
among us once a month and she drew up the weekly activities... The
fourth night there'd be a debate and those were the nights we liked
best... We talked about abortion, which many of them thought was
murder, contraception and sexuality.

(Liz Lagrua, cited in McCafferty, 1981, p.14)

Women suffered illnesses as a consequence of, or exacerbated by, the
conditions (McCafferty, 1981, p.15). The case of 23-year-old Pauline
McLoughlin raised concerns regarding the role of healthcare professionals within the regime. Told by the prison doctor that 'under the present
conditions on "A" wing she was going to die', but also that her situation
was self-inflicted (Coogan, 1984, p.131), in October 1980 she suffered
a heart attack in prison. Following hospital treatment outside, she was
returned to Armagh to continue her sentence (Corcoran, 2006).

In Corcoran's (2006) view the media constructed women prisoners'
protests as particularly abominable because they contradicted social and
cultural constructions of female cleanliness. Yet, conversely, women's
actions were used to garner support for the cause:

Men are expected to go to jail, men are expected to fight, men are
expected to die, men are expected to get battered. But when a woman
does this, it's something different. *So everybody uses that.*

(Meg, cited in Corcoran, 2006, p.180)

Fairweather et al. (1984, p.222) observe that leaving women to 'sit
in their own menstrual blood amidst excreta and urine', the authorities' objective was to 'break the prisoners in an exclusively female
way'. For Theresa O'Keefe (2006, p.535) menstrual blood was used by
Republican women as both an 'instrument of war' and a 'weapon of
resistance'. Taboos in Irish society regarding menstruation gave the
protest particular resonance. The incarceration of politically affiliated
women prisoners, the conditions in which they were held and the
treatment they received gained their cause international prominence:
'Women all over the world were campaigning for us; it was a very big
issue and the British government didn't like it' (Eilis O'Connor, cited in
Brady et al., 2011, p.202).

Women in Armagh continued on the 'dirt' protest from February until 1 December 1980 when it ended to enable participation of three women in the hunger strike (Corcoran, 2006). Although the Government sent proposals for ending the strike to prisoners at Maze/Long Kesh and Armagh, Corcoran doubts whether Mairéad Farrell, the women's officer in command (OC) was actively involved in negotiations to end the strike. During planning for the second hunger strike, it was agreed that women would participate. O'Hearn (2006) suggests that Bobby Sands wanted to ensure that women Prisoners were treated equally, believing that they had been made to feel like 'second-class participants' during the first hunger strike. The Armagh women agreed on three volunteers, but the first, Mairéad Farrell, then wrote a letter explaining her withdrawal from participation:

> All I can say is that I have real fear of letting the Movement down and possibly breaking the H/S [hunger strike] at a crucial stage because of this doubt. I don't thing I'm good enough or strong enough to embark on H/S. This has left me completely shattered.
>
> (cited in O'Hearn, 2006, p.329)

Within days the other women also withdrew. Sands wrote a supportive letter, stating it was 'not only the right thing but a very admirable thing that you and Mary did and for that matter the same applies to anyone who does the same. You shouldn't feel bad about it or defeated in any manner' (cited in O'Hearn, 2006, p.329). Following her release, Mairéad Farrell and two other IRA members were shot dead by the Special Armed Services of the British Army in Gibraltar in 1988. While they were part of an IRA 'active service unit', all were unarmed at the time they were confronted and killed.

Former Republican prisoner, Laurence McKeown describes discussions regarding women's role in the protests:

> The idea of women prisoners playing an equal role shocked many though I don't think we looked upon it at the time as anything to do with equal roles. They were regarded as the weaker sex. They had to be protected from their own recklessness. It was not expressed in such terms of course. The debate was more centred on what would be thought of us men if it were seen that women had to go to the fore in such an extreme form of protest as a hunger strike. Some did however express the opinion that women being on the hunger strike would be beneficial as this would horrify the public, outrage them so much,

or garner sympathy that people would respond to our demands for support.

(interview with Sharoni, 1999)

Following the 1981 hunger strike, as discussed earlier, attempts were made by the State to integrate 'ordinary' and 'politically motivated' women in Armagh, a process which met with resistance (Corcoran, 2006). The 'managerial' phase of imprisonment was gendered throughout. From 1982, there was a significant increase in the use of cell searches and strip searching. Previously, women had been stripped on arrival in the prison and on some occasions when leaving the prison. From November 1982 routine strip searches were introduced for all women – young, old, pregnant or menstruating – before and after all visits, whenever they left or entered the prison, including court attendance, and during increasingly used 'random' searches. The authorities justified this extension of strip searching ostensibly because keys had been found in the possession of two remand prisoners returning from court:

Despite my medical condition [having recently given birth] I was strip searched. Once naked I attempted to cover my breasts with my arms as I was embarrassed with my breasts leaking with milk. I was ordered to remove my arms to facilitate the warders' inspection of my naked body.

(Jacqueline Moore, 1984, cited in Stop the Strip Searches, undated, p.10)

Women who refused to remove clothes were forcibly stripped by groups of officers. Strip searching in Armagh brought local, national and international protest from women's, civil and human rights organizations. It 'came to epitomise, for many, the resolve of the security services to have women submit to the process of criminalisation and surveillance by taking control of women's nakedness' (Pickering, 2002, p.181). Officers labelled women as 'whores', 'sluts', 'bad mothers' and the authorities adopted 'firm assumptions about how women should behave' (p.181). Corcoran (2006) describes strategies used by women to regain control:

I would try to embarrass them with my nakedness. And they hated it. They hated it because we made them feel more uncomfortable with what they did.

(Kathleen, cited in Corcoran, 2006, p.165)

Strip searching extended beyond Armagh, to London's Brixton Prison where two Irish Republican women, Martina Anderson and Ella O'Dwyer, were strip-searched 400 times each between July 1985 and September 1986 (Stop the Strip Searches Campaign, undated, p.14). They were stripped up to three times a day, although 'the place is littered with cameras and a metal detector or one of their many sniffer dogs would successfully replace strip-searching as a security measure' (Ella O'Dwyer, cited in Stop the Strip Searches, undated, p.15). For O'Dwyer, strip searches constituted a 'form of psychological rape' and '[i]nsult' was added to 'injury' by the 'fact that a female prime minister [Margaret Thatcher] orders female prison staff to enforce strip-searching' (Stop the Strip Searches, undated, p.15).

Following Armagh's closure in 1986 women prisoners were transferred to Mourne House, the purpose-built unit within the new high-security Maghaberry Prison complex. Male prisoners were transferred to the main prison in 1987. With a capacity of 59 distributed between four wings, Mourne House held politically motivated and 'ordinary' prisoners. The Prison Service suggested that Maghaberry was a modern, 'state of the art' prison, based on an integrated, 'normal' regime. Yet, a mass strip search of Republican women in March 1992 suggests otherwise. Begona Aretxaga (2001, p.1) describes the search as disrupting the 'crafted monotony of prison routines', purposefully 'inflicting a political and psychological wound on the body of IRA female prisoners'. The strip search began at 10.30 a.m. and ended at 9 p.m., broken only by staff lunch and dinner breaks (Aretxaga, 2001 p.10). Male and female prison guards wore riot clothing, visors and carried shields, making it difficult to tell their gender. They entered cells, some accompanied by dogs. Women physically resisted and Aretxaga's account, based on handwritten narratives and interviews, documented the anger and distress:

Around 10:00 a.m. I heard that they were going to strip all of us. I couldn't believe it because we had jail searches before but they never involved us being stripped. Then I saw the search team coming in with full riot gear and I heard one of the men screws singing 'happy days are here again'.

(Bernie, cited in Aretxaga, 2001, p.9)

I saw a stream of screws in full riot gear entering the front gate of the jail and advance towards our wing. They were all dressed in navy-blue, boiler suit type of outfits with helmets and carried shields and batons, I don't know if they were all females as it was difficult to see their faces. I felt bewildered and frightened.

(Anne Marie, cited in Aretxaga, 2001, p.9)

They came into my cell and threw me to the floor, they held me between four screws and two others removed my clothes forcefully. I was taking my period. They took the sanitary towel and threw it to a corner as if I was shit! They had the door open and the male screws were outside, I don't know how much they could see. They were coaching the female screws and could hear everything.

(Carol, cited in Aretxaga, 2001, p.13)

Republican prisoner, Karen Quinn (cited in Calamati, 2002) describes listening to women's 'screams of pain' as they resisted the guards' searches, waiting and crying in her cell until her own 'turn' came. Confronted by women guards in riot gear she refused to undress and was thrown to the floor where she was forcibly stripped:

My arms were twisted so far back that I thought they'd break. I yelled that I was having my period but that didn't stop them... They grabbed me by the hips and managed to get the trousers down below my waist and then they yanked them down over my ankles... I couldn't breathe for the pain... they managed to strip me naked. As I lay there on the ground they threw me a blanket and a sanitary napkin. The warder who held me down with her knee wasn't finished... as she was leaving, she landed me a violent kick in the ribs.

(Calamati, 2002, pp.87–88)

Karen was particularly sickened by the role played by female prison guards in the brutality:

the following morning one of the warders who attacked me was on duty. I felt sick to my stomach at the sight of her; just a few hours before she had made me stand naked before her while my menstrual blood trickled down my legs. She was the one who should have been ashamed and embarrassed at what she had done to me. How could this woman, who had forcibly stripped twenty-one women, act as if nothing at all had happened when she came face to face with one of her victims?

(Calamati, 2002, p.89)

Charged with disobeying an order she lost all sentence remission.

> I feel as if I had been raped... I was helpless to do anything to protect myself from the warders... they can attack me any time they feel like it... Our bruises are fading, but the memory of what we were forced to endure will not fade so quickly.
>
> (Karen, cited in Calamati, 2002, p.89)

As Corcoran (2006, p.112) argues, the 'process of liberalization and constructive engagement' associated with managerialism, dubious in its implementation generally, was clearly 'more tenuous' in relation to women prisoners. The primary research on which this book is based, demonstrates the continued impact on women prisoners of the legacy of the Conflict and the persistent failure of the Prison Service to generate significant reform. Since the Good Friday/Belfast Agreement (1998) and the programme of early release, few Republican women have entered the prison system. Those who have been imprisoned have experienced greater isolation than did their predecessors. The separation of Republican and Loyalist male prisoners from the 'ordinary' regime – and from each other – initially was not extended to include women who were accommodated alongside 'ordinary' prisoners. Subsequently, separation for political women prisoners was granted in principle but the circumstances of its implementation have resulted in extreme suffering for isolated female prisoners, discussed further in Chapters 5 and 9.

Political imprisonment of women in an international context

While it is evident from the preceding discussion that the incarceration of politically motivated women in Northern Ireland has been and remains unique, there are clear similarities to the imprisonment of politically motivated women elsewhere. Analyses of jurisdictions in conflict demonstrate the extraordinary security measures adopted as states routinely 'abandon human rights and rule of law' and proclaim a public interest justification to engaging in a 'war on terror' (Scraton and McCulloch, 2009, p.13). In Northern Ireland, the use of special powers through internment without trial, and trial through non-jury Diplock courts, heightened resistance and contributed to a loss of confidence and legitimacy in the criminal justice process.

Recurring themes in research on imprisonment of women during times of war and conflict include the marginalization of regimes for women political prisoners and lack of political and media engagement; attempts by states to criminalize politically motivated women; and gendered experiences of punishment and abuse. Globally, politically motivated women prisoners have resisted their oppression, often using their bodies in individual and collective struggles against their criminalization and the arbitrary abuse of power in oppressive regimes.

Women prisoners in Armagh were largely neglected by national and international media. Notable exceptions were coverage of strip-searching and the 'dirt' protest when women were portrayed as particularly deviant and, because of menstruation, more unclean than male prisoners. Addressing the marginalization of politically motivated women's experiences in political and media discourse, Elham Bayour (2005) notes that the contribution of women political prisoners in Palestine also has been overlooked locally and ignored by Western scholars. Similarly, Laura Sjoberg (2007) comments on the lack of media coverage of women prisoners in Iraq. Women were incarcerated in Abu Ghraib but there is no published record of numbers or length of time held and the systemic abuse of female prisoners has been 'downplayed' in media analysis and official accounts.

Women's experience of gendered abuse is common within penal regimes and is particularly prevalent in the subjugation of political prisoners. In a personal account exemplifying such abuse, Nasrin Parvaz (2003) recounts her experiences in Iran from 1982 until 1990, during which she was imprisoned and sentenced to death following her campaign for women's and civil rights. Blindfold, handcuffed and whipped on the soles of her feet by male guards, her imprisonment was a 'nightmare world' from which she emerged bearing physical and mental scars (p.75). She recalls bloody handprints on cell walls left by a pregnant woman who had been tortured and subsequently had miscarried. Despite the violence, women resisted the regime, passing messages and hiding letters in 'secret post-boxes' including a flowerbed in the recreation yard (p.78). Relationships between women prisoners, however, were complex. Parvaz's outright rejection of the chador led to tensions, regarding her refusal to participate in a campaign by women for the right to wear coloured, rather than only black, chadors.

Focusing on Palestinian women in Israeli prisons, the UN Women project (2011) notes that women detainees routinely experienced neglect of their health care including gynaecological needs, lack of access to exercise, fresh air and poor diet. Psychological and physical forms of interrogation were used that 'were bordering on or can be considered forms of torture'. Often their interrogators were male, imposing further stress and intimidation. Individual accounts of physical abuse are documented within the project:

> They beat me with clubs. I'd have my face to the wall and they would beat me on my head and back. This method was used for 60 days of interrogation... The music would be turned up very loud and we would be beaten to the beat of this music. They would hit us as we heard songs, very loud Israeli songs. The interrogator... would stand me with my back to the wall and push his foot forcefully into my chest until I choked and my tongue hung out.
>
> (Fairouz Arafa, prisoner from Gaza Strip, cited in UN Women, 2011)

Gendered verbal abuse was also used: 'the thing that hurt me most were the insults that were hurled at me' (27-year-old Ghoufran Zamel, prisoner from West Bank, cited in UN Women, 2011). Bayour (2005) also records the sexual abuse and humiliation experienced by Palestinian women punished for resisting the Israeli occupation. She cites the case of two older Palestinian women, forced by soldiers to remove their traditional clothes and wear 'tight, short, sleeveless dresses', thus 'symbolically erasing the women's adherence to their national cultural heritage' (p.205). Bayour describes female political prisoners threatened with rape, beaten on their breasts and genitals, fondled and verbally abused. Pregnant women were kicked in the stomach and handcuffed during labour. Using sexual threats and assaults, the regime intended to extract information while bringing shame on women and their families. Jameila, a young Palestinian woman describes her experience:

> During interrogations they brought in an African Palestinian male political prisoner and ordered him to rape me. They beat him near death because he refused. I asked him to do it to stop his torture. They put a bag on my head and ordered me to climb up on rows of tables assembled over each other to the electric chair, still naked. They electrocuted me for four hours. The electric shocks were administered until I turned blue. Then they threw me in extremely cold

water, and then more beatings. They forced me to stand up on one leg with my hands raised upward and they covered my head with a *burlap* bag full of faeces.

(cited in Bayour, 2005, p.207)

During her imprisonment Jameila menstruated for the first time and was 'very scared' that she had been raped by soldiers: 'A male soldier heard my screams and told me, "Yes, we have raped you". They left me for three days covered with blood, without napkins or underwear' (cited in Bayour, 2005, pp.206–207).

As evidenced above, political prisoners regularly experience particularly harsh forms of oppression as a direct consequence of their oppositional status, and punishments are gendered. Yet the acquisition of political status occasionally offers increased protection and it is clear from international research that politically motivated prisoners, as part of their struggle, are likely to mount sustained and collective resistance to prison regimes. Irish Republican former prisoner Laurence McKeown expresses the importance of collective, motivated action both within and outside the prison:

> Given our conditions of incarceration we appeared, at least at first sight, relatively powerless... Yet, the combination of our strong political conviction, the support of our communities on the outside, our unity of purpose and discipline, we had a power not manifested in normal prisoner communities.
>
> (cited in Sharoni, 1999, p.3)

McKeown recognizes the uniqueness of the collective power of political prisoners. This contrasts markedly with the isolation and despair of a woman interviewed by Amanda George:

> I removed my clothes one piece at a time as requested... I honestly felt the only way to prevent the search becoming more intrusive or sexual was to remain as quiet and docile as possible. I always wondered why I was so passive. All I could answer was that it was an experience similar to sexual assault. I felt the same helplessness, the same abuse by a male in authority, the same sense of degradation and lack of escape.
>
> (cited in George, 1992, p.1)

As a consequence of conscience collective action, women prisoners in Northern Ireland gained concessions. Brady et al.'s (2011) collection of stories from Republican women ex-prisoners notes the illicit victories, such as the smuggling of notes and alcohol, and taking photographs. Marian and Dolours Price record their victory in winning a transfer to Armagh from an English prison following a lengthy hunger-strike and forced feeding: 'Two volunteers returned home, still ecstatic at the thought! It was a victory, the girls saw it as a victory, damn it, it was a victory; scream all you like girls' (cited in Brady et al., 2011, p.135).

Reconsidering the parameters of political imprisonment

A consistent focus of prisoner resistance in Northern Ireland has been the rejection by Republican and Loyalist prisoners of their classification as 'criminal' and being placed on general association with ordinary prisoners. Yet, despite their commitment to separation and recognition of their political status, some Republican women have recognized the vulnerabilities of 'ordinary' women prisoners. The research on which this book is based evidences the 'pains of imprisonment' which are experienced by all prisoners – whether politically-affiliated or in the general prison population. It argues that it is possible to recognize the particular context regarding the imprisonment of those with political motivation, without stigmatizing or excluding those who have been imprisoned through different routes.

Angela Davis (1971, p.29) identifies a difference in motivation between those who break the law for 'individual self-interest' and those who break law 'in the interests of a class or a People'.

> The former [individual self-interest] might be called criminal (though in many instances he is a victim), but the latter, as a reformist or revolutionary, is interested in universal social change. Captured, he or she is a political prisoner.

This analysis extends the parameters of 'political' imprisonment. For Davis, the State seeks to reduce the political to the criminal 'to affirm the absolute invulnerability of the existing order' (p.32). The use of political imprisonment, however, has increased the extent to which prisons and places of detention have become sites of struggle. The campaigns generated by political prisoners and their supporters influence public perceptions of prison regimes, inhumane conditions and penal policy.

While recognizing the unique issues faced by politically affiliated prisoners, and the specific role they play in social change, Davis raises the profoundly political nature of all imprisonment. For her, racism and class inequality are central elements to understanding incarceration: 'the prison has actually operated as an instrument of class domination, a means of prohibiting the have-nots from encroaching upon the haves' (p.34).

While the distinction between 'political' and 'ordinary' prisoners is significant, the latter experience a criminal justice process that reflects and sustains institutionalized structural inequalities. They are imprisoned because they are poor or Black, often innocent yet unable to afford adequate legal advice. Further, 'ordinary' prisoners may be radicalized by their experiences of oppression in penal regimes:

> Prisoners – especially Blacks, Chicanos, and Puerto Ricans – are increasingly advancing the proposition that they are *political* prisoners in the sense that they are largely the victims of an oppressive politico-economic order, swiftly becoming conscious of the causes underlying their victimization.
>
> (Davis, 1971, p.36)

Also challenging orthodox constructions of female prisoners as 'offenders', Biko Agozino (2005, p.186) notes that 'what is considered "criminal" is situational and culturally specific'. Agozino argues that from the slave economy, through to contemporary contexts, the 'entire colonial system of criminal justice' is based on the 'criminalization of innocent black women'. Linking the growth of imprisonment in Nigeria to the impact of globalization, he states that 'the crushing poverty imposed on Nigerians as part of the "global lockdown" has led to popular protests by the masses of the people resulting in the widespread arrest of women either for participating in such protests or for being family members of suspected men' (p.190). By situating women's imprisonment within the context of neocolonial, gender and class relations, the political dimension of all imprisonment can be observed.

In his defining research in Australia, Chris Cunneen (2009, p.211) proposes that, in states with legacies of colonial rule, 'indigenous people are massively over-represented' in the prison system and young Aboriginal girls and young women regularly report assault, including sexual and racial harassment in custody. Cuneen argues that while Aboriginal prisoners disproportionately are remanded or sentenced for alleged criminality, this occurs within the context of discrimination and marginalization leading to arrest, detention and imprisonment. As a consequence of their marginalization and the systemic inequalities they endure, therefore, their imprisonment is political. While the criminalization of politically motivated actions is demonstrably an institutionalized strategy of the state, all forms of imprisonment that reflect the twin processes of material marginalization and criminalization are also inherently political.

Two significant issues arise from the preceding discussion. First, the state's institutional denial of the political motivations of Republican and Loyalist prisoners created persistent conflict within the prisons and extending to communities. It also had the consequence of deterioration in regime and conditions and the development of a mindset of non-engagement with prisoners – whether politically-affiliated or imprisoned through other routes. Second, the characterisation within prison discourse of 'ordinary decent criminals', including those unconvicted, contributed significantly to the isolation, stigmatization and neglect of prisoners without political affiliations across the penal estate.

5
Inside a Deteriorating Regime

Introduction

Based on primary research with women prisoners, conducted by the authors for the Northern Ireland Human Rights Commission (the Commission), this chapter documents the deterioration of the regime in the Mourne House [women's] unit of Maghaberry Prison from 2002 to 2004. As discussed in the previous chapter, Maghaberry was built as a high-security establishment. Following the closure of Long Kesh/Maze it held a complex mix of prisoners: male and female, children and adults, remand, sentenced, short- and long-term prisoners, politically-affiliated prisoners and immigration detainees. Women constituted a small minority and Mourne House was a satellite, self-contained unit outside the walls of the male prison but inside the walls of the Maghaberry estate – a prison within a prison. In July 2003 the Commission embarked on an investigation of the treatment of women in prison using its statutory powers under the Northern Ireland Act, 1998. The investigation's remit was to examine 'the extent to which the treatment of women and girls in custody in Maghaberry Prison is compliant with international human rights law and standards, and in particular with Articles 2 and 3 of the European Convention on Human Rights'.

The Commission's attention was drawn to the issue by a highly critical report on Mourne House conducted in 2002 by an inspection team from England (HMCIP, 2003). Commissioners were also troubled by the death in September 2002 of 19-year-old Annie Kelly in a Mourne House punishment cell. In April 2003, they visited Mourne House and were alarmed by their observations: lack of empathy, verging on hostility, shown to prisoners by guards; a high ratio of male staff, especially on night duty when regularly there were no women guards on duty;

lengthy lock-ups and isolation; overuse of the punishment block where women were locked often in bare cells for 23 hours each day; limited access for women to fitness and leisure activities; persistent difficulties in accessing mail and telephone calls.

Responding to correspondence from the Chief Commissioner, the Director General of the Prison Service robustly defended the Mourne House regime, stating that a number of the Inspectorate's recommendations had been implemented while others remained 'on hold pending the outcome of a feasibility study into the possibility of accommodating women prisoners at Hydebank Wood [male young offenders' centre] instead of Maghaberry' (letter to NIHRC, dated 27 June 2003). The Director General noted that should the feasibility study prove favourable, the timing of the transfer would be affected by operational matters, 'not least the growing total prison population, which may add pressure to accelerate the transfer'. Fears not allayed, the Commission decided to investigate and the first phase of the independent research on which this book is based was commissioned.

At an initial meeting with the researchers, the Director General suggested that as the move to Hydebank Wood was anticipated, the research should be postponed. The researchers maintained that an investigation *prior* to the move would establish a baseline against which future conditions could be evaluated, thereby significantly contributing to developing a long-term strategy. The research agenda was agreed and conducted intensely inside the prison over three months in 2004. Partly observational, it also involved interviews with women prisoners; prison officers at different grades; professionals working in the prison including teaching, probation, healthcare staff and clergy; the Mourne House branch of the Prison Officers Association (POA); and the Maghaberry Board of Visitors. Research questions covered all aspects of women's lives including daily routine, education provision, activities, health care, discipline, contact with families and relationships between prisoners and prison officers.

The researchers had passes to the Mourne House Unit on a daily basis and unrestricted access to interview staff and prisoners. Early in the research it was apparent that the project would be considerably more extensive than initially envisaged as the complexity of the issues became evident: the proposed transfer to Hydebank Wood; the death by hanging of a young woman, Roseanne Irvine, during the first days of fieldwork and two other serious suicide attempts; the involvement of the authors in judicial review proceedings and a bail hearing regarding the treatment of a 17-year-old girl on 23-hour lock-up in the punishment block; and a hunger strike involving a Republican woman prisoner.

The 2002 inspection

The Prisons Inspectorate's 2002 inspection of Mourne House (HMCIP, 2003) provided several significant benchmarks for the research. The Chief Inspector noted that Maghaberry was 'the most complex and diverse prison establishment in the UK' (p.3) and the Inspectorate's report warned of 'the potential dangers' inherent 'in situations where the needs of a small group of women . . . can become marginalised' (para. MH.17). It stated that, because of the distinct contexts of women's imprisonment, 'safeguards, such as *total* separation, *distinct* management and staffing teams and *separate* healthcare facilities' [emphases added] should be established. Yet, despite a highly critical report, inspectors considered that Mourne House had 'the potential, in our view, to operate as a high quality facility' for women. It had 'some high quality living accommodation and excellent physical facilities, not least the potential for its own healthcare provision' (paras MH.1–2). Evidence of 'good interpersonal relationships', and 'effective education and training', were noted.

The inspectors, however, were concerned that Mourne House operated and was managed simply as another unit within Maghaberry with 'no recognition of the different needs of those held there' (para. MH.03). Staffing levels were inappropriately high, not reviewed since the unit held significant numbers of politically-affiliated prisoners (para. MH.04). At the time of the inspection 87 guards were dedicated to Mourne House to manage an average of 25 female prisoners (para. MH.14). A consequence of this extraordinary level of security was women were 'routinely escorted over short distances from house units to the healthcare centre' (para. MH.24). The regime was based on lengthy periods of lock-up offering minimal activity. Although the standard of teaching in the educational department was praised, classes were frequently cancelled for operational reasons (para. MH.82). The kitchen in Mourne House had been 'mothballed', preventing women from preparing their own food (para. MH. 54). Their meals were sent across from the main prison kitchens.

The Inspectorate recorded an unhealthy balance of male staff to female prisoners and criticized the transportation of women to and from court in vehicles shared with male prisoners. On the journeys women prisoners experienced taunts and verbal abuse. There was complacency over record keeping, extending to the inadequate recoding of a young woman's long history of self-harm (paras MH.26–28). Fifty per cent of women interviewed by the inspectors stated 'they did not feel safe' on 'their first night' and 'had not been given any written or spoken information about what was going to happen to them' (paras MH.30–33). Almost all, 89 per cent, 'did not feel confident that they knew what was going to happen to them on their first night'. The Inspectorate found 'no structured programme of induction'. It recommended an interview with a member of staff before first-night lock-up, access to a free telephone call, a self-harm risk assessment, induction reception packs, a two-day induction programme with cross-discipline inputs and information on the regime, responsibilities and incentives.

Inspectors were highly critical of the treatment of suicidal and self-harming women who often found themselves in the male prison hospital or in punishment or isolation cells. The consequences were marked:

> The perception among female prisoners was that, should they declare their vulnerability to self-harm, then there was the possibility that they would be taken over to the observation cells in the healthcare centre in the main prison or to the punishment unit on Mourne. It was not appropriate to accommodate distressed female prisoners in what were little more than strip cells in an environment which essentially centred on the care of male prisoners, many of whom had mental health problems. This was more likely to increase feelings of vulnerability.
>
> (para. MH.36)

The inspectors raised the case of a 15-year-old self-harming girl dressed in strip clothing and located in the punishment block. They queried whether prison was the most appropriate place for the child, particularly as staff had no training appropriate to children's often complex and challenging behaviour (paras MH.37–38). They were also critical of resettlement provision for women which 'lacked strategic direction and planning' (para. MH.108).

Among the inspectors' key recommendations were: that Mourne House should be declared a discrete women's facility under Maghaberry management; the Prison Service should establish a gender aware policy and strategic plan for women prisoners as the operational framework for Mourne House; all staff and managers should receive training specifically preparing them for working with women prisoners; the unit should function as a low-security facility within a secure perimeter with significantly reduced staffing levels; the healthcare facility within the unit should be reopened and all healthcare delivered in the unit or in the community (paras MH.6–11).

The Mourne House research

At the time of the research, all women prisoners in Northern Ireland were held in Mourne House. In 2003 they constituted one per cent of the overall prison population, and five per cent of receptions into prison during the year were women (McMullan et al., 2004, p.1). The daily average female prison population was 22, typically comprising eight remand prisoners, one fine defaulter, 12 sentenced to custody and one 'non-criminal' – immigration detainees or people in prison for non-payment of debt (p.9). Three women were serving life sentences and most sentenced prisoners were serving five years or less. The majority were aged between 20 and 40 years. On average two girl children (under 18) were held in the Mourne House Young Offenders Unit – a landing within the women's unit. Among the sentenced female population the most significant category of offence was violence against the person, with small numbers sentenced for burglary, robbery and drug offences. During the research the groups of women in Mourne House included: life prisoners; remand prisoners; committals; an immigration detainee; Republican prisoners; 'young offenders' (remand and sentenced).

Arriving at reception, the woman prisoner provided information on next of kin and personal contacts. She removed her clothes, was searched and given a sheet to cover her body. A guard recorded distinguishing features and identifying marks. Clothes and property were searched, recorded and put into storage. She showered, washed her hair, dressed and was escorted to her cell in the accommodation block. Each cell had integral sanitation and a television rented for 50 pence per week. Prisoners were locked up Monday to Saturday before 8.30 p.m. and unlocked after 8 a.m. Lunch was at 11.30 a.m., followed by lock-up before 12.30 p.m. They were unlocked after 2 p.m. and had tea [dinner] at 3.45 p.m. They were locked again at 4.30 p.m. and unlocked after 5.30 p.m. until 8.30 p.m. Although there were kitchens within the unit, these had been closed and food was transported from kitchens in the male prison. On Sundays women were locked for the night at 4.30 p.m. Evening unlock, however, created considerable tension as it was 'subject to change, regarding staff availability' (Mourne House, HMP Maghaberry, undated document). Regularly, evening unlock was replaced by a 'rolling unlock', with each landing unlocked one at a time and only for a brief period. This placed significant restrictions on telephone calls and was particularly difficult for women wanting to speak with their children. Observing the regime in action, it was difficult to understand why women were locked down so regularly and arbitrarily.

On the normal regime, the maximum possible out of cell time was nine hours, the minimum six. In every full day for between 15 and 18 hours women were locked alone in their cells and on Sundays they were always locked for 18 hours. Given the regularity with which evening recreation was cancelled or subjected to brief out-of-cell time due to rolling unlocks, women spent 75 per cent of their sentence alone in their cells. That women prisoners, including those on remand, were in solitary confinement for at least three quarters of their time in jail exposed the fallacious claims made by the criminal justice system, the Prison Service and the Government that women's incarceration was based on rehabilitative, progressive principles. Certainly there was no acknowledgement at the point of each woman's entry into prison that a significant majority of her time would be served in solitary confinement.

Morning and afternoon unlocks were scheduled for work, education or physical activity in the gymnasium. Yet all workshops, except for gardening, had been closed. The education timetable appeared comprehensive, scheduling 17 classes over 10 periods including Craft, Hair and Beauty, Cookery, Maths, English, Art, Music and ICT. The class lists presented a positive impression of a varied and well attended curriculum with five to seven women listed for each session. Yet this proved to be false as discussed later. Women prisoners who cleaned the prison earned £10 per week spent on essentials, food and expensive phone cards. Each convicted prisoner was allowed one 60-minute visit each week which could not be suspended and carried over. Remand prisoners were allowed three 1-hour visits each week, which could be exchanged for a single 2-hour visit.

The regime was based on progression through three levels – Basic, Standard and Enhanced. 'Basic' was applied to prisoners 'who through their behaviour and attitude demonstrate their refusal to comply with prison rules generally and/or cooperate with staff'. 'Standard' applied to those 'whose behaviour is generally acceptable but who may have difficulty in adapting their attitude or who may not be actively participating in a sentence management plan'. The highest classification, 'Enhanced', applied to prisoners 'whose behaviour is continuously of a very high standard and who co-operate fully with the staff and other professionals in managing their time in custody' (*HMP Maghaberry Progressive Regimes Guidance for Prisoners*, undated). Prison guards had formidable discretion in operating the regime and classifying prisoners who had to achieve four consecutive weekly reports with 'favourable recommendations' to climb the progression ladder. Enhanced classification required 'continuous exceptional behaviour... judged on areas such as conduct, personal hygiene, participation in work and education and attitude to staff and other prisoners'. Two consecutive negative reports resulted in a reduction in regime level. The women endured the ever-present threat of 'being zeroed'.

As previous research and prisoners' personal accounts have demonstrated, the first hours and days of imprisonment are a time of significant vulnerability. In interviews, women described their anxieties on entering the prison:

> I was absolutely petrified coming into prison. I came after long interrogation. I don't know how I coped. I came into reception. It was regimental: 'Get a shower.' 'Fill in this form.' No question 'Are you alright?' It was all oppressive, no kind of reassurance. You were terrified.

> I know myself, when I came in, I was terrified. I'd never seen a jail, never mind been in one. And I was just thrown onto the wing. It was one of the other girls, actually, who told me the ropes and what to expect. It was the girls who were there for me, not the staff. It's still the same to this day.

> When we came in we were up in the committal wing for about 14 days. During that time we were on 23 hour lock up. When someone is coming in to prison for the first time it's hard, 23 hour lock up.

Another woman, who had been in Mourne House for some time, commented:

> There's an elderly woman in at the minute. When she came in, it was about 10 [night] and she was just thrown in a cell, with a pint of milk and a tub of butter and she was told not to press the buzzer unless she was dying. That's what they said. Now that's not the way to treat anybody coming into prison.

Although some women had been provided with an arrival leaflet, 'it didn't explain tuck or visits or anything like that'. The Mourne House Principal Officer provided the researchers with a schematic information leaflet outlining accommodation, routine and facilities, including weekly wages, but the women disputed that it had been issued on their arrival:

> It wasn't until the next morning that I was able to start asking questions. I asked if there was an induction booklet I could read but I didn't get that. If I could have read something to answer some of my own questions. Basic things: Can I ring my family? Can I ring my children? When can my family come up and see me?

Many women commented on prison guards' indifference to their needs, for example:

> The staff don't sit down and explain to the girls what they have to do. They don't explain that, if you're on remand you get three visits a week, and this is what you're expected to do or not to do. You find out all that information from other prisoners.

> If you're a prisoner, 'Go to your cell and don't bother anyone else'. That's the attitude I get from them.

Prison guards were not trusted, particularly regarding personal confidences, and women voiced their need for independent support:

> I felt desperate. I need to talk to somebody...My family was always there for me, but I need to talk to somebody that could better understand what I was going through. Even though I was talking to my mum, I couldn't say because I knew it would break her heart, you know. I needed somebody who didn't know me personally.

The unpredictability of the evening unlock was a persistent frustration, with no information on time out of cell provided until 4 p.m. each day. The pressure, especially on women with children, was considerable and well illustrated by two long-term prisoners:

> Lately we're getting rolling unlocks, out for half an hour. All of us have children on our wing. You can't speak with them. I've two children – you can't speak to one and not the other.

> My only priority in my day is contacting my children. There's nothing worse than a day goes by and you don't speak to them. There's nothing worse than going to bed that night knowing that you've not spoke to them. If it's very limited access to the phones the chances

are you won't even get on the phone and if you do it will only be for two minutes and that's no good especially if there's any problem at home and they want to talk to you about it. They and I have such a close bond and there's things they don't want to say to [other family members]. You know what children are like with their own mammy. I just want to get through the day, one day at a time. One day less 'til I get back with my children.

Maintaining telephone contact was expensive: 'The telephones are dear [costly]. I'm spending £30 a week on telephone calls and [if unlocked] I get about 20 minutes [each time]. I can't understand why it's so dear'.

With the workshops closed, education classes offered the only available activity other than working in the gardens. Despite the impressive range of classes claimed and the number of women registered, classes were rarely held. A long-term prisoner said: 'You get up in the morning, you're ready to go to class and they [prison guards] will say "Classes are cancelled", so then I have to go and change and put on my work clothes [for the gardens]'. Another long-termer had ceased preparing for class: 'Education can be cancelled at the last minute. When you get up you put on your old gardening clothes because you'll be in the gardens; not putting on something better to sit in front of a computer'. For long-termers classes were important, not only for the opportunity to study but also for the quality of contact with teachers:

> The education staff are dead on [very good]. They're used to me and they're used to my ways. If I was over and upset they'd know. They're there for you, not only for education but to talk to as well. You can talk to them and you know it's not going any further.

A prison guard escort was mandatory for women to walk the 150 metres from the residential accommodation to the education block, yet the route was under constant electronic surveillance at all times. Teachers were not permitted to escort prisoners. A woman prisoner commented that given a 'wee element of trust' women could 'walk unescorted to education'. Work in the gardens was rarely disrupted only because the work was managed by a prison guard who collected the women and escorted them to the greenhouses and gardens.

Visits were also a matter of concern, as voiced by a long-term prisoner:

> The system for visits is disastrous. Often you're lucky to get an hour, sometimes 45 minutes. It is dreadful on the children. Children are every bit as much doing the sentence as their mother is. If you try

to maintain standards you're regarded as a snob that needs to be cut down to size.

Some women on shorter sentences did not take family visits because they wanted to protect their children from the ordeal: 'It's too much being locked away from my kids. The kids' father hung himself. The kids think I'm in hospital having a baby'. Another woman was 'too afraid to talk to them [her children] because I know I'll cry'.

The impact of receiving a long-term prison sentence is immense. Apart from the emotion and upset of the trial, often accompanied by intense and unbalanced media coverage, the adjustment to facing many years in jail can be overwhelming. Central to that adjustment, the importance of assessment, sentence planning and management has been recognized within prison policy and practice across jurisdictions. It is now usual for long-termers and life-sentence prisoners to be accommodated in an assessment unit throughout the first months of their sentences during which time their progression is discussed, planned and mapped. The rationale being that, while effective programmes geared towards release can be put in place immediately for short- to medium-term prisoners, they are not appropriate for prisoners who expect to be held in custody for longer periods.

The sense of despair and futility, together with guilt and remorse, places long-termers at risk early in their sentence. Assessment programmes, such as those pioneered in the National Assessment Unit within the Scottish Prison Service, have been developed to establish the needs of individual prisoners while agreeing effective and appropriate sentence plans. Whatever the advances of such initiatives, however, the reality is that prisoners face long periods of 'dead time' when time itself becomes the problem and prisoners feel themselves to be 'languishing' in jail. Not underestimating the impact of a long sentence on male prisoners and their families, for most women with children and family responsibilities the loss of role as well as freedom brings desperation. Without induction or counselling, with no information or planning, the isolation leaves long-termers particularly vulnerable:

I was moved from the remand wing to the sentenced wing. I asked to speak to the long-termer governor but he never came. I don't know what the story is about a sentence plan.

I sat there for nine months staring at the ceiling and staring at the walls. I could have been using my time more productively but I was just not in the right frame of mind for it.

The monotony is crucifying. Before I came in here I had such a busy lifestyle. I went from one end of the scale when I didn't have time to see the news at night to suddenly having hours and hours on my hands. That's what hit me when I first came in. I couldn't get used to that. I kept looking at my watch, thinking, 'What am I going to do with my time?'

It is well established that, once settled, long-termers and lifers devote considerable effort to 'personalising' their surroundings, often decorating their cells, communal spaces and landings. This sense of 'ownership' of space benefits prison staff as well as prisoners. The problem for long-termers in Mourne House, of being few and not having discrete accommodation, was significant:

On the male side long-termers are separated. I did fight for a long-termer's wing about two years ago and was told we would get one. And I scrubbed D1 and brought it to the way I'd like it. I moved all my stuff down from my cell and was told to move all my stuff back. They were playing with my mind; playing mind games with me.

Apart from noise and disruption, the emotional impact was persistent:

As a long-termer, when there's people who come in and are on parole, it's difficult. I haven't even got a tariff yet. I don't think it's fair to put people on the wing who are going out. You can't expect girls not to talk about their parole because of course they're excited about getting out. Management should see what that does to a long-termer.

Another long-termer agreed:

On our landing there's a few short-termers. We get on ok but it's very disruptive when they come in and are on home leave . . . two weeks to go . . . one week to go. It's very unsettling. And short termers have no real respect for where they live. We have a high standard of hygiene and want to care for what we have. Let's face it, that's got to be our home for the next lot of years and we want to make it as homely as possible and we just really want peace and quiet and we don't want to hear music blaring out all hours of the night and people shouting out of windows to one another.

With workshops and kitchens closed, education classes regularly cancelled and evening unlocks severely limited, it was clear that lifers could expect to spend up to 75 per cent of their sentence in solitary, cellular confinement with little access to constructive activities.

The research did not support the Inspectorate's observations that 'interactions between staff and the women' were 'relaxed', with staff adopting 'a helpful and constructive approach' (HMCIP, 2003, para. MH.46). Perhaps this was inevitable given that, in contrast to the research, inspectors were in the unit for only a few days in a situation where guards would be determined to impress. A typical comment from a long-termer was that while some staff 'love their job, others are here for the money. The ones who are here for the money just don't care'. Another long-termer agreed:

> The majority simply don't care. They do their job as a means to an end. There's a minority who drive home the fact that you are prisoners, you're the scum of the earth, you're not deemed fit to mix with society.

Occasionally, prison guards were actively abusive in their attitude. A woman recalled an incident regarding the treatment of two Romanian prisoners:

> They [the Romanian women] found it hard enough with the language barrier because their English wasn't that great. The screws [officers] had a pretty nasty attitude to them, not the ones on during the day, mainly at night. I was sitting in the cell one night last week or the week before and wee [baby] was very, very sick. I could hear her vomiting from my cell – she's directly across. They did tell her [the child's mother] to fuck off and everything when she asked to see the doctor.

The one immigration detainee in Mourne House at the time of the research, a young Zimbabwean woman seeking asylum, recounted how guards treated her differently from other prisoners:

> They don't communicate with you the way they do with the white girls. One or two officers have been so nice. Two female officers have been nice but the male officers don't talk to me... No-one takes care about you. I am so depressed. I have never been in such a situation. I just keep crying and there is no-one to help you. I feel inferior here.

I am the only Black girl. The other girls are friendly and help me but I feel left out. The prison officers don't ask me if I have any requests but they ask the other girls.

She described an incident, confirmed by other women:

On Monday a staff lady said, 'Do you want to go for a bath?' I said I had already had a shower. She repeated that I should have a shower. I said, 'Is there something wrong with me?' She said 'You're a wee bit smelly'. This made me feel inferior. Now I'm scared to go near the staff in case they think I smell.

When asked to comment on guards' behaviour, two women who had been in prison for some time stated:

The only form of power in their lives is when they don the uniform and come in here. They're the ones who are playing cards all day or in there [landing office] sleeping off a hangover. They just say 'no' to everything.

They feel threatened by you. It's outrageous that they feel jealous. What of? The fact that you've been handed down a life sentence...How could anyone, if they have a life outside, feel jealous? They just love to take the opportunity to put the boot in.

Trust was a major issue. A long-termer commented: 'You have to be so careful what you say to people. Something innocent can be portrayed in a different way...you have to be careful what staff you speak to'. She continued:

I'm always respectful to them [guards] whether they're nasty to me or not. That's just the way I am. And when you have people who are just respectful back to you and treat you like a person and not like a prisoner it makes a hell of a difference instead of just getting that door slammed on you and telling you to get in. Even a simple thing like somebody opening your door and saying, 'Have you got everything with you?' and then they lock your door. Just wee basic things.

Girls, some as young as 15, were held in Mourne House. At the outset of the research, girls and young women up to 21 years were accommodated on a separate 'Young Offender' (YO) landing, physically identical to adult landings and following an identical regime. Guards working on the YO landing had no training specific to working with children and adolescents. No age-appropriate information about the regime was available. Like adult women, children used the healthcare facilities on the 'male side'. Later the YO unit was removed to create a separate unit for Republican prisoners, so children and young prisoners were integrated on the adult landings in contravention of international rights standards. In interviews, the few women prison guards in Mourne House demonstrated the problems associated with providing appropriate responses to young girls, many of whom had suffered emotional and sexual abuse. While they were acutely aware of girls' vulnerability, the most common response was that they were manipulative, attention-seeking and 'trying it on' through self-harming behaviour.

A clear illustration of how the presumption of manipulation impacted on decision-making was observed during the research. A guard on the landing rang the Principal Officer informing him that a girl had requested to share a cell because, having recently attempted to hang herself, she did not want to be locked up alone. The Principal Officer was dismissive. Over the telephone he told his colleague that she was 'trying it on' so that she could be 'doubled up' with her friend. He instructed she should remain in her cell and, 'if she carries on, clear the cell, make it a bare cell'. He continued, 'If she really misbehaves then put her in C1' (the punishment block). The Principal Officer made his decision without visiting the child.

Three children (below 18 years of age) and one 'young offender' were interviewed. All four were recorded in their profiles as being at risk of suicide or self-harm. One child had made a serious attempt to hang herself and three weeks later the marks on her neck were still evident. The girls criticized the lack of therapeutic support: the 'psychiatric people don't come near you here'; 'you're meant to be on 15 minute watch but you're lucky if you get them here every hour'. They considered that being 'doubled up' would offer some protection from self-harming and suicidal thoughts. One girl expressed unhappiness that her suicidal thoughts were not taken seriously by guards who dismissed her pleas: 'Stop playing on it ... stop playing at hanging yourself'. Her comments were consistent with prison guards' attitudes towards her. They believed she was 'play acting' and attention-seeking. The girls feared the punishment block:

> If you're suicidal they threaten you with the punishment block. 23 hour lock up on punishment block – puts your head away. They don't even look in on you. I'm surprised this whole jail hasn't killed themselves.

Family contact was inadequate: 'your mammy can't phone in and talk to you. You can't talk to your mammy if you have problems unless you have money'. Two Catholic girls alleged that they had been subjected to sectarian intimidation by guards. The allegation was strongly refuted. The girls themselves did not complain about bullying by other young people but a prison guard identified bullying as a significant, persistent issue.

It was evident from interviews with prison managers that they considered the Mourne House regime had stagnated, with most prison guards reluctant or resistant to engage with women prisoners. Managers claimed that a poor industrial relations history at Maghaberry, together with officer redeployment when Long Kesh/Maze closed, had fed a culture of withdrawal. The Principal Governor stated that lack of progress towards meeting the Inspectorate's recommendations was due to industrial relations problems with prison guards and what he judged to be the 'intransigent' Mourne House POA. Another manager commented:

> Mourne House used to be excellent. The male ratio is too high, unhealthily high. In Mourne House older female officers mothered the prisoners. The key element was having older female officers who would have dealt with young prisoners the way they would have dealt with their own children.

The lack of commitment to creating a positive regime had been exacerbated by the 'only thing we've talked about over the last months... the 50 separated [paramilitary male] prisoners' in Maghaberry and 'not the 650 that we lock up every day'. A woman guard confirmed difficulties in realizing the 'rehabilitative ideal':

> When I became a prison officer I thought it would be about rehabilitation. But no rehabilitation is done at all. It's [the job] about trying to keep them alive. The role of prison officer for women is more involved than on the male side.

She considered a key function should be counselling provision to meet individual prisoners' needs yet she noted institutionalized inhibitions in Mourne House to the development of good relationships with women prisoners:

> Caring can be interpreted as a sign of weakness by other officers. Draconian measures don't work with these women we have. A lot of

the male staff love it in here because they see it as an easy option...a different atmosphere has grown over the last few years and a very male environment has been created.

She also criticized male guards 'looking at the women in a state of undress, a bit of flesh showing...the women don't like the men looking at them like that'.

A sharp illustration of the regime's stagnation was the persistent frustration felt by education staff inhibited from operating a full timetable. Plainly angry, a teacher claimed that staff shortages were an excuse to prevent women accessing the education block:

You're always working against a whole lot of things. Laziness, couldn't be botheredness. They [guards] wouldn't give them [prisoners] anything. The women need skills, self-esteem. But you're really working against the system...The education block used to be buzzing. It was a vibrant place but the possible closure of Mourne House has dogged us since September.

The head of education was 'appalled', stating, 'Fifty per cent of the time we have to tell staff to go home because staffing levels of prison officers means the women can't get to education'. All teachers interviewed believed that prison guards did not share their ethos and had no commitment to education, imposing arbitrary rules resulting in an atmosphere 'so rigid' and 'oppressive' that women were often reluctant to attend class. Previously, the learning environment and classrooms had been relaxed but the regime recently imposed, for no apparent reason, inhibited women from leaving the classroom to use the bathroom; 'they even stopped us giving out coffee and biscuits'. The loss was not confined to learning. As a teacher stated, 'we know at times that the girls just want to chat and get stuff off their chests and those conversations are more of use than anything'. The situation had become unworkable and, throughout the previous term, 'if you were open one session [out of 10 scheduled] you were lucky'. On checking the education block attendance book it was clear that this comment was no exaggeration. The head of education concluded:

If the present situation continues I would prefer this place shut. It is a shameful position that we can't plan or project ahead. We have very gifted talented girls going out and we won't have helped them.

Despite the Inspectorate's recommendation (HMCIP, 2003, para. MH.11) that the women's healthcare centre at Mourne House should be reopened and all health care delivered within the unit or in the community, the centre remained closed and women received health care, including overnight stays, in the male prison hospital.

Arrangements for Republican women prisoners created further complications given the physical limitations of the unit. During the research period two Republican women were imprisoned, both members of the same paramilitary organization. They had been held on remand in Mourne House for five months and had demanded separation from 'ordinary prisoners'. This was refused despite male politically-affiliated prisoners securing separation and being housed in discrete units. Both women faced potentially long sentences if convicted. One, known by a pseudonym 'Mary', had refused to disclose her identity to the authorities. To maintain her anonymity she took neither visits nor letters from family or friends. The women acknowledged that the charges against them were serious yet argued that security measures used by the police and prison staff were retributive:

> When we were first arrested and taken to court the cops had the whole place surrounded. You would have thought we were the most wanted people in Ireland. The security was unbelievable. They totally outflanked our families in the dock. There were riot squads the whole way round our families.

Whenever the Republican women were moved within Mourne House they were escorted by several prison officers: 'I was put out on a visit yesterday and there were six staff on the visit for one person. I'm not that high a security risk'. As part of their campaign for separation the women refused association with other prisoners and therefore were confined to their cells for long periods. They argued that their case for separation was to 'feel safe' as they believed that some of the 'ordinary' women prisoners had connections with Loyalist paramilitaries. They were also angry that they had been forbidden to communicate with Republicans held in the male prison, particularly the 'OC' (commanding officer).

The Republican women resented being housed with prisoners they described as 'druggies' and 'ordinary criminals'. Each had complained to guards about drug taking on the landing which they viewed as a 'total insult to Republicans'. Although critical of their location with 'ordinary' prisoners, they also recognized the gravity of problems faced by some women:

We have serious mental health issues in here. When you say to people they laugh but it's no joking matter when you're on a landing with these people... one of the wee girls self harmed the whole way up her arm by taking the razor blade out of a sharpener. They wouldn't open the door until she put out that razor blade. Now that wee girl could have been bleeding to death but they still wouldn't open the door until she put out the razor blade first. I was really shocked. I didn't know what to do because she was next door to me.

During the research, events moved quickly regarding the women's demand for separation. A telephone call was received at the NI Human Rights Commission from one of the Republican women stating she was on hunger strike and wanted to meet the researchers. The researchers went to Maghaberry the following day, Good Friday, where they met the Governor who managed separation in the male prison and the Governor with responsibility for Mourne House. The Governors informed the researchers that separation would be granted the following Monday, but the decision would not be communicated to the woman on hunger strike until she ended her protest as the 'official line' was not to negotiate with hunger strikers. The Republican woman not on hunger strike would be informed of the decision immediately. The researchers expressed concern that the woman's health, possibly her life, was being put at risk, yet the authorities already had decided to accommodate her demands. Why could she not be informed of the intention to grant separation? The reply was that the Prison Service could not be perceived as 'giving in' to a hunger strike. Asked what this implied should she remain on hunger strike, one of the Governors replied, 'She'll die'. His apparent indifference was met with stunned silence.

It was agreed that the researchers would meet the hunger striker in her cell. She expressed determination to continue her protest until separation was achieved. Having talked with her, the researchers met with the other Republican prisoner who had signed a prisoner compact (agreement) on separation thus allowing arrangements for her separation to proceed. Following further negotiation, the Governors informed the researchers that the initial decision had been reversed and 'Mary' would be informed. The Governor in charge of separation conveyed this and issued a compact. 'Mary' refused to sign until she received reassurance from the researchers who confirmed that they would maintain contact with the prison to ensure that separation was operationalized. Separation took place on Easter Monday through the re-designation of the YO landing, resulting in the accommodation of children on the adult landings. Soon after, both Republican prisoners were released from prison, the charges withdrawn.

During the research the Northern Ireland Prison Service announced an 'independent investigation' into 'all aspects of alleged inappropriate behaviour in Mourne House'. The investigation related to circumstances leading to the suspensions and subsequent disciplining of four male guards and one female guard. Its terms of reference were to consider allegations of staff behaviour 'falling short of the Code of Conduct' and allegations of staff having 'improper relations' with female prisoners. While the Northern Ireland Prison Service referred to 'improper relations' local newspapers were not so reticent.

On Sunday 14 March 2004 the *Sunday Life* published a story under the banner headlines, 'Sex-starved Black Widow snares warder; Jailhouse rocked by torrid allegations'. The reporting was unrelenting in its portrayal of a woman prisoner labelled the 'black widow', 'man-eating', 'ruthless', a 'cold-hearted adultress' and 'one of a trio of killer wives in Maghaberry...dubbed the Witches of East Wing'. The other women prisoners in the 'trio' were referred to as the 'Fermanagh blonde' and the 'Ballymena bruiser'. The *Belfast Telegraph*, *Newsletter* and BBC reported that four male guards were under investigation concerning allegations that they had sexual relationships with women prisoners. A female guard had been suspended and subsequently sacked for having an inappropriate relationship with a convicted member of the Loyalist Volunteer Force (LVF).

Despite pleas from the women prisoners named in the newspaper accounts to the Maghaberry Governor to publicly refuted press allegations that the 'inappropriate behaviour' under investigation included sexual relationships, the Prison Service made no intervention to challenge these media representations.

This was not the first time that media allegations had been made about prison officers working in Mourne House. In an interview with the Director General of the Prison Service, a BBC journalist presented allegations made by the POA regarding an investigation in 2002 into allegations of 'inappropriate relationships' between prison guards and prisoners (Media Monitoring Unit). The journalist submitted that

[m]embers of the Prison Officers Association in Mourne House have told us that they are convinced that a file exists that catalogues a number of inappropriate relationships between officers and prisoners

at Mourne House. They have told us the file has become known as the 'dirty dozen' file... these officers believe that two years ago an investigation, either officially or unofficially, was commissioned and that for two years they believe that there have been phones tapped, telephone calls recorded, that information is being gathered on officers working in Mourne House.

The Director General stated he was unaware of the existence of a 'dirty dozen' file and allegations regarding phone tapping were 'all quite extraordinary', but acknowledged that in 2002 the media had carried allegations regarding inappropriate relationships in Mourne House and that 'we took some weeks trying to get to the bottom of the allegations' but 'at that time we weren't able get any evidence that we could act on'. This sequence of events demonstrates the vulnerability of women prisoners and the potential for gendered subjugation in regimes staffed primarily by male guards. It was further evidence of a failing regime in which a coterie of male prison guards enjoyed immense discretion freed from the checks and balances of professional accountability.

Given the violations of human rights evidenced by the research, the Human Rights Commission recommended the initiation of an independent public inquiry focusing on the deterioration in the regime and conditions in which women and girl children were held in Mourne House. Its terms of reference would include: the failure by the Prison Service of Northern Ireland to implement the Inspectorate's recommendations and its consequences for women and girl children prisoners held at Mourne House from 2002 to 2004; the circumstances surrounding the deaths in custody of Annie Kelly in September 2002 and of Roseanne Irvine in March 2004; use of the punishment and segregation unit as a location for the cellular confinement of self harming and suicidal women, including girl children; the circumstances in which prison guards were suspended and dismissed following allegations of inappropriate conduct.

Transfer of women from Mourne House to Hydebank Wood

On 24 April 2004 the Northern Ireland Prison Service announced its decision to relocate all women prisoners from Mourne House, Maghaberry to Ash House, a unit within Hydebank Wood Young Offenders Centre, Belfast. It was clear from the research interviews that women prisoners had no information regarding the proposed move: 'we just know it's going to happen but we don't know when and we don't know what it will mean for us... all the girls [women] are uptight'. Lack of dependable information had provoked rumours that exacerbated their apprehension. The main concern, voiced by all women prisoners, was the move to a predominantly male environment where core facilities would be shared and movement in the grounds of the prison would be tightly restricted: 'They'll [young male prisoners] shout out when you're being moved, on outside recreation or in your cell, whether they can see you or not. That's what they'll do. If they know your name we'll get it all the time'. The women's intimidating experiences of sharing the Maghaberry prison hospital (see Chapter 6) had raised significant fears about sharing healthcare facilities at Hydebank Wood.

Lack of in-cell sanitation and shared ablutions were also major concerns:

> No sanitation in cells... that is a big problem because women need sanitation, like, on their monthly cycle. I know myself I run to the toilet a lot and they're only going to let you out one or two at a time at night. It's demeaning.

> We're all women, yes, but if you're on your period you're not wanting to be standing next to another woman showering.

> They're building cells for the male side where the toilets in cells will have doors... so why are we being pushed back in time when the men are being pushed forward? Where's the equality in that? Is it because there are so few women that we're being pushed back?

Long-termers and lifers considered the 'enhanced' regime to which they were entitled could not be offered in an environment that failed to provide basic facilities. They worried that they would be unable to handle the impact and implications of the transfer:

> It took me [a long time] to settle here... now I'm to be uprooted. How long will it take me to settle there? I'm really used to being here... it's just not fair and they are taking us back in time.

> I'll be honest with you, if this move takes place I don't know how I'll survive because I'm absolutely no good with confrontation. You might think I'm assertive... It's got that way that you don't voice anything and I can't see how I could handle the things we'll face with the move.

The Republican women were emphatic in their opposition to the move, stating their intention to go on hunger strike or dirty protest if they were transferred. Their opposition was based on conditions, safety concerns and their perceptions of a Loyalist bias among prison guards at Hydebank Wood. Eventually, the Prison Service committed to accommodating separated women in Maghaberry rather than at Hydebank Wood but, as discussed in Chapter 9, this arrangement has not succeeded in practice.

While the women were unrelenting in their criticisms of the Mourne House regime, they did not consider that Hydebank Wood could provide a solution to the problems they had faced. The losses, regarding personal hygiene, privacy and dignity, outweighed any gains that might ensue from being in a lower security prison. In May 2004 a staff delegation from Hydebank Wood visited Mourne House to provide information to the women. The opportunity to discuss arrangements was welcomed by the women and they recognized a more positive approach by the Hydebank management. However, the assurances provided – such as more association time and greater access to education than in Mourne House, and that women could decorate their own cells – failed to allay their profound concerns regarding issues of sanitation, privacy and proximity to a young, male population.

In response to the Prison Service's official announcement that women were to be transferred, the Human Rights Commission issued a press statement based on the research findings, demanding the proposed move be abandoned and Mourne House be developed as a discrete, self-contained and lower security unit. Despite the women's fears and the Commission's opposition, all women were transferred from Mourne House to Hydebank Wood on Monday 21 June 2004.

6
Self-Harm and Suicide

'Criminal women' and 'iron therapy'

The marginalization of 'criminal women' is well documented. In contrast to male offenders, the assumed 'exceptional' behaviour of women who offend is often interpreted as irrational, unpredictable and a denial of ascribed servile femininity. Frances Heidensohn (1985, p.74) identifies two 'widely held views about female offenders'. The first centres on assumptions of abnormality and individual pathology. Second, those who commit crimes that carry a prison sentence are considered 'especially...mentally ill or otherwise highly deviant', explaining why there are so few women prisoners. The 'implicit assumption being' that women prisoners are 'less reclaimable, more vile, more "unnatural" than male'.

As discussed in Chapter 1, Pat Carlen's definitive study of women in prison concludes that while most were imprisoned for 'purely punitive purposes' (Carlen, 1983, p.23), a 'high proportion...have been diagnosed as having either "personality disorders" and alcohol and/or other drug-related problems' (p.22). Many women she interviewed had experienced physical abuse by husbands, cohabitees, male relatives or police officers. They were judged, assessed and classified on their capacity for social interaction, on their femininity in terms of appearance, tidiness, motherhood and on their maturity by prison guards, governors and medical staff.

Women prisoners are significantly more likely than men to be defined and treated as predisposed to 'criminal' or 'deviant' behaviour through attributed pathological conditions combining psychological damage and personality disorder. It is an ascription not without historical roots. Also discussed earlier, when prison reformers, such as the former prison governor and government adviser Mary Size, initiated innovative programmes for working constructively with women prisoners they accepted individual pathology as a primary element in women's offending. Unswerving in her commitment to the reformation of 'criminal women', to the improvement 'mentally, physically and morally of every woman and girl who came into our care', Size viewed their 'crimes' as the consequence of 'ignorance, inefficiency, selfishness, jealousy, bad housing, bad family relationships, and lack of Christian teaching, together with a *certain degree of mental abnormality*' (Size, 1957, pp.188–189, emphasis added). The 'mix' of individual and social pathology is clear yet presented in the context of an inherent behavioural deficiency.

Reflecting on 1950s initiatives, a teacher-training college principal turned prison educator, records the establishment of a 'hostel' within prison 'to hold twelve neglectful mothers who were to be given a short, intensive course in home management and the care of children':

> Most of these women are mentally and physically inadequate, slovenly, unhappy and from poor homes... Many women prisoners are emotionally unstable and disturbed... In comparison [to male prisoners] women seem to be apathetic and lacking in initiative, as though living in the pre-machine age.
>
> (Banks, 1958, pp.242–244)

Size and Banks were committed to penal reform that would benefit women prisoners yet they provide a clear illustration of the so-called rehabilitative foundations of contemporary women's imprisonment. Consolidating the reformist ideal, they place aspirations of feminization, motherhood and women's responsibilities to their families and communities alongside mental and physical 'inadequacy'. As Banks observed, women prisoners who resisted a seemingly positive and benevolent intervention self-fulfilled the prophecy of the 'relatively lower mentality of women criminals'.

In the most comprehensive text written on the Prison Medical Service in England and Wales, Joe Sim (1990, pp.129–130) analyses the 'quite different and distinct' experience of 'regulation, discipline and process of normalization' endured by women prisoners since the inception of the modern prison system. It was 'iron therapy', imposed by male 'medical and psychiatric professionals' situating the 'personal and moral life of women... at the centre of the professional's gaze'. He continues:

> Liberal notions of rehabilitation and reform therefore masked a deeper, more fundamental strategy, namely to reshape the very spirit

of the criminal woman back to the role for which she was seen to be biologically and socially suited – that of wife and mother. The concept of femininity built 'around notions of domesticity, sexuality and pathology' was a central element in the relationship between professionals and incarcerated women.

(Sim, 1990, p.130)

This legacy persisted and by 'the late 1960s security and control' were placed alongside 'the psychiatrization of women's behaviour' as the 'dominant pivots in the regimes designed for women prisoners... propell[ing] already damaged women still further into a pit of despair and individualized recrimination' (p.164). Working from contemporaneous policy documents and official discourse, Sim demonstrates how the pathologization of women's offending behaviour became institutionalized in processes and programmes of categorization, classification and treatment within a framework of 'medical surveillance'. As Carol Smart (1976) reveals in her pioneering analysis of women and crime, the core principles adopted in women's prison regimes were informed solely by the domain assumptions within psychiatry. They aimed to deliver modified, corrected and conforming behaviour to those suffering 'individual maladjustment' to the presumed 'well-ordered and consensual society' in which they lived (p.145).

Sim's review of the contemporary history of medical intervention in the lives of women prisoners acknowledges its complexity, but draws out several key themes running through the 'disciplinary matrix' imposed exclusively in women's prisons:

[T]he individualization of women prisoners; the drive to normalize their behaviour; the close interconnection between different, usually male-dominated groups whose activities have been built on the perpetual surveillance of the women's physical and psychological response to imprisonment; the advent of intensive technological control...; the resistance of women to that control and to medical and psychiatric categorization; and the continuing entrapment of women within catch-all psychiatric categories such as behavioural and personality disorder.

(Sim, 1990, p.176)

Carlen's research shows that for the authorities and 'often for the women themselves, each return to prison' represents 'another failure', their recidivism taken as proof of no intention nor motivation to reform. Consequently the 'temporary classification "disorderly", gradually ossifies into the more permanent "disordered"...untreatable...beyond the remit of the treatment agencies, without hope and beyond recognition' (Carlen, 1983, p.194). In her study, over 80 per cent of prison admissions had histories of mental illness yet a prison sentence denied those histories. They were 'clothed instead with the disciplinary needs of the "disordered"...effectively transform[ing] the diagnostic clinical gaze into the disciplinary judicial stare' (p.196). It was a process that provoked a 'compression and dispersion of all those definitional conditions and effects which cluster around the related concepts of personality disorder and anti-social personality disorder'.

Psychiatrists, notes Carlen, possess the 'statutory powers to endow the words "mental illness" with very specific meanings which have institutional effects regardless of laymen's contrary definitions' (pp.205–206). In her study, many women were classified as untreatable and diverted from mental health institutions to a 'discipline setting'. Once in prison, reclassification took place. Those classified 'mentally ill' were prescribed drugs; those classified 'not mentally ill' were subjected to 'normal penal methods of deprivation of liberty and other forms of deprivations' (p.206). Carlen concludes that, in its 'simultaneous identification of "personality disorder" and its refusal to recognise it as a category of "mental illness", psychiatry has succeeded in a masterly stroke of professional imperialism'. Considered neither mentally ill nor treatable, the 'personality disordered' prisoner is cast as a 'residual deviant' beyond treatment's scope. Once the classification is made, the status ascribed, the woman prisoner has 'little chance of having the label removed' and there is 'little hope of change' (p.209). Her rational responses to the conditions of imprisonment to which she is subjected become the grounds for assessing her fulfilment of the ascribed label.

Carlen's primary research lucidly reveals a key dynamic in the imprisonment of women and girls that, regrettably, has prevailed. Three decades on, her words continue to resonate throughout the custom and practice of contemporary women's jails:

Here is the final contradiction: the women are physically located in the prison on the grounds that they are physically (and permanently) located within a psychiatric category whose pathology is always already denied! So, being seen as neither wholly mad nor wholly bad, they are treated to a disciplinary regime where they are actually infantilised at the same time as attempts are made to make them feel guilty about their double, triple, quadruple, or even quintuple refusal of family, work, gender, health and reason. (p.209)

At the most obvious level, women's reproductive cycle, Carlen notes 'little sympathy regarding pre-menstrual tension and even less recognition of their need for increased access to washing facilities during menstruation' (p.104). Twenty years later, Pat Carlen and Anne Worrall (2004, p.61) note that while there had developed a greater acceptance 'that women's healthcare needs in prison – both physical and mental – are more various and complex than men's... the overwhelming experience of women in prison is that their health needs are not consistently dealt with in a respectful and appropriate way'. Unsurprisingly, neglect focused on: 'pregnancy, cervical cytology, breast cancer screening, and miscellaneous hormonally-triggered "women's ailments"... chronic mundane conditions'.

In researching the imprisonment of women drug users in England and Scotland, Margaret Malloch (2000, p.100) notes:

Combined with the emphasis of the prison system on control and security, the boundaries between care and punishment become blurred. For example, the need to monitor the condition of an individual withdrawing from drugs...leads to observation under secure (often strip) conditions...the overall effect is highly punitive. It is a denial of any clinical responsibility for the physical and psychological well being of the person 'in care'.

Malloch concludes that in women's prisons 'informal and discretionary practices are more likely to operate'. Such practices 'are often more pronounced' in the responses to drug users. Despite the 'therapeutic language of rehabilitation', more 'punitive ideologies remain to the fore in the female carceral system (the use of strip and silent cells). Medical care and treatment, or their absence, remain framed in the context of punishment' (p.151).

The regulation of women prisoners experiencing mental ill-health remains a significant issue in contemporary women's prisons, an issue not confined to British or Irish jurisdictions. Researching in Australia, Blanche Hampton (1995, p.107) notes that women 'who attempt suicide or self-mutilate... can expect to be tranquillised and/or isolated... They may or may not be counselled and are seen by custodial staff as attention-seeking'. Also in Australia, Amanda George (1995, p.23) found that women who self-harm were 'put in isolation (solitary), deprived of sensory input and placed in a bare concrete cell with a canvas mattress and a canvas blanket in a canvas nightie'. Research by Tamara Walsh (2004, p.16) in Queensland notes how the identified 'special needs' of mentally ill women are addressed 'by providing for their segregation in the event that they are engaging in self harming behaviour':

> [They] may be removed to a crisis support unit (CSU) under a crisis support order if they exhibit suicidal or self-harming behaviour, or may be placed in a separate cell under a special treatment order if their segregation is considered necessary for their safety and the safety of others. (p.17)

This policy impacted dramatically on women prisoners' willingness to disclose their troubles. In her interviews with ex-prisoners, Walsh notes that 'merely crying may result in their being transferred to an observation cell'. Thus they 'must quickly learn to disengage from their emotions' in the knowledge that any sign of weakness 'will be reported to corrections officers by psychologists' and lead to the isolation unit (pp.22–23).

Experiences of women prisoners placed on observation contrasted starkly to official claims supporting the policy:

> [N]either crisis support units, nor 'observation cells' in which suicidal prisoners are accommodated provide distressed or disturbed prisoners with a therapeutic environment in which they may receive care and treatment... Crisis support units are reportedly used as a 'behaviour management tool' to house difficult as well as disturbed prisoners... [The] unit, 'S4', houses a broad range of prisoners including 17 year old prisoners, prisoners who have received disciplinary breach and women with 'discipline problems', in addition to women with mental illness. (p.25)

Observation cells were 'barren, rubber rooms where prisoners are subjected to 24 hours a day lighting, stripped down and dressed in a suicide gown, and often physically restrained'. One prisoner described how the disorientation of permanent artificial lighting 'plays games with you and it sends you mad. I heard some women kicking and punching the doors and wanting to smash the TV and stuff like that'. Another prisoner talked of being observed on camera, 'having a shower, or having a piss' (p.25). The only concessions to gender in Queensland's penal policy were 'extra visits to maintain a relationship with their [women's] children' and that 'strip searches of women ought only to be conducted and viewed by women staff' (p.16).

Mourne House

Describing the majority of women and girl prisoners accommodated in Mourne House, the Board of Visitors (later renamed the Independent Monitoring Board) used the following words: 'abused'; 'deeply damaged'; 'distressed'; 'depressed; 'vulnerable'; 'self harming'; 'suicidal'. They described the conditions of cellular confinement in which the most troubled women and girls were held as 'ghastly'; 'grim'; 'uncivilised'; 'inhuman'; 'brutal'. As the previous chapter demonstrates, they reflect views universally held by all women and girls interviewed, by many of the non-prison staff and by a minority of prison guards who spoke 'off-the-record'. The locations to which the Board members referred were the punishment block and the prison hospital, each within the male prison. It is instructive that the block's name, initially the 'punishment and segregation unit', was changed to 'special supervision unit' thus softening the representation of a place of profound despair. The male prison hospital was renamed 'healthcare centre'.

As Chapter 5 notes, while the Mourne House regimes and programmes were not overtly gender specific in design or delivery the regulation, control and punishments experienced daily by women prisoners were consistently gendered. Fear, degradation and dehumanization were institutionalized manifestations of this process, most appropriately represented and analysed through their location on a continuum of violence and violation discussed in Chapter 2. This ranged from lack of access to telephones or baths, through lock-ups, to strip searches, personal abuse and transfer to the punishment block. At the sharp end of the continuum women were harmed directly by their subjection to strip searches and physical restraint. At the other, they endured sexual comments, innuendo and insults from guards embedded in the prison's daily routine. Prisoners rarely reported feeling threatened by other prisoners. They expressed feelings of unsafety through threats to the self – self-harm – or threats from prison guards. This was evident particularly in young women's accounts and in the harsh treatments directed towards those labelled unmanageable and/or personality disordered. Ellie's victimization, discussed in Chapter 2, is a clear illustration of the latter.

Built as a 'prison within a prison', the Mourne House unit included a dedicated prison hospital, closed other than for nurse consultations. Following closure, its cells were used for storage. Despite the Inspectorate's recommendations (HMIP, 2003, para. MH.11) that the women's hospital be reopened and health care delivered there or in the community the only hospital facility available was in the male prison. The key monitoring document for prisoners assessed as suicidal was the Referral/Assessment of Suspected Suicide Form (IMR21). This could be initiated by any staff member who was expected to detail their concerns. If considered serious a case was prepared for medical assessment and a healthcare plan formulated. Once 'active' the IMR21 was filed in the prisoner's case notes and held on the appropriate residential landing.

Prison guards expressed concern that IMR21s were simply 'paper exercises'. Care plans often recommended 'optimal personal contact' between guards and prisoners yet, in reality, the 'only contact would be through the [cell door] flap'. Guards felt 'let down an awful lot' by their managers and 'shouldn't have to put up with a lot of what we do'. A female prison guard commented, 'we're not trained to deal with psychiatric cases. All they [managers] do is tell you how to dress, wear your uniform, stick by the book manual'. Another woman guard agreed:

> People [guards] don't have the skills or the knowledge to deal with the complex issues. Females [prisoners] are more problematic and they will put their trust in you. But there's no continuity in personal support. It's the staff on the landing that they have to deal with... There must be some sort of counselling. This should be done by NGOs and there needs to be a structure of programmes. AA [Alcoholics Anonymous] is often turned away at the gates because of lock downs. There are no facilities for personal counselling.

Her colleague agreed: 'These women are ill, mentally ill and we keep saying that this woman isn't well, she's not bad, she's mad'. She continued:

> We had a heroin addict in here. She was on meth outside. They brought her in, the doctor wouldn't write her up and she brought in a tablet. The doctor took it from her. She was five days and couldn't hold water down. She was banging off the wall. She was genuinely hurting. She upset the whole landing... So many women

have come through this system who are ill and it's us looking after them... There's no release for us, we're angry and frustrated. How far gone has someone got to be for something to happen?

A nurse officer (guard) discussed administering a 'healthy' environment in a male dominated context:

We got a call the other night that a female prisoner had stripped herself and was hanging and the prison officer couldn't go in until a female officer came across. The prison officers that came to Mourne House came from the Maze [male prison holding political prisoners]. They weren't used to dealing with prisoners. They didn't know how to talk to prisoners. There needs to be a majority of female officers.

While all prisoners interviewed reported suffering depression while in prison, they recognized that many women – in some cases themselves – had serious mental health conditions. They rejected clinical diagnoses that denied what they considered were serious health problems:

As far as I'm concerned, if a woman's hearing voices, cutting up and bouncing off the walls she is seriously ill and needs hospital treatment. It makes little difference whether a doctor diagnoses that she's got some mental illness or says it's a personality problem.

For women on the committal wing, long hours of lock-up contributed significantly to their parlous state of mind: 'You need communication and you're getting no communication... you think you're being cornered, especially on a Sunday'. Another young woman agreed, 'we might have committed a crime, but we're not animals'. This despair and isolation is illustrated by the following quote:

I tried to hang myself. They wouldn't move me from the cell and it's just provoking. I just wanted to kill myself. There's no hope for me in here. I suffer from depression and phobia. I didn't get my medication for the first week. The doctor wasn't seeing me for a week... I had no medical treatment for that week. They cut down my medication. I was put in a cell and locked down. Nothing given to us, just 'Away to your cell'.

For women serving longer sentences time was a major issue:

> You have too much time. You sit and think about your family...you've nothing to occupy your mind. I have felt real depression and was put on anti-depressants. I needed a bit more support, someone to talk to. It's not like being at home where you have your whole family to explain a problem to. You can't openly talk to anyone in here. They said they'd get the psychiatric nurse to come and see me but she never came so I just had to deal with that in my own way. I have felt like giving up numerous times. It's only my children that give me something to go on for.

A long-term prisoner recalled the admission of a young woman who had a heroin addiction. She had been 'left to lie in her cell and had the sweats and couldn't eat...just left to deal with it herself'. Systemic 'lack of care' contributed to the high level of self-harm among the women:

> I've never self harmed myself but I know a lot of girls who have. They're just trying to find someone to talk to, to give them help. They need a counsellor. Young people cutting themselves. To me that's a cry for help. But instead of having someone to talk to they're just thrown in the punishment unit. It's not on...They're just left in there, there's nothing there for them. Sometimes they'll throw in a magazine...there's nothing. What can you do?

Another long-term prisoner considered that for 'women with mental health problems', Mourne House was 'dreadful, terrifying'. She could not 'believe that people who are in such an unbearable state are treated the way they are'. For longer term prisoners, lack of investment in counselling and creative activities contributed to mental health problems:

> Mourne House simply houses prisoners. Place the prisoner in her cell with a TV and feed until release. TVs are cheaper than allocating more staff to organise constructive activities, but they become a 24 hour substitute. This is a debilitating process and, ultimately, leads to clinical depression over a prolonged period.

Prison guards' treatment of women suffering mental ill-health was condemned universally by women prisoners.

A lot of people hate being locked up, it drives them mental. I've seen it in here. I've seen people trying to drown themselves in the sink. Again that's a lot to do with the screws not being taught how to deal with those sort of prisoners properly. Even showing somebody a bit of compassion goes a long way.

I find in this day and age I can't understand how it is legal. Women who are constantly slashing their arms, legs, throats and trying repeatedly to hang themselves are stripped naked, thrown in a suicide jacket. 'Don't even give her a mattress, let her lie on the floor, let her lie in her own...' Women need help, counselling and therapy but to throw them in a strip cell, take away everything. I would hate to see a poor dog, bedding taken away, treated like that.

One incident, considered typical, was heard by several women:

I often sit in my cell and think, 'I can't believe I'm hearing this'. The week before last a senior officer on nightguard... this woman had twice that day tried to hang herself. One of the other officers said, 'Could you leave the keys? I'm not content just looking through the flap, she could have a ligature around her neck'. 'No, don't be looking in at her. Don't even look at her. Fuck her'. That's the way it was going but it was top volume. 'Fuck the old bitch, let her go.' This was being boomed and everyone on our landing, even the hardened ones, thought it was outrageous. There wasn't an ounce of respect shown to her as a human being.

Another prisoner stated, 'some of the staff treat you like dirt'. She had heard officers telling women 'to shut the fuck up, calling them bastards'. One night she pressed 'the bell' to ask 'if there was a woman I could talk to'. The male guard told her to 'stop ringing the bell and to shut the fuck up. It made me feel worse'.

A teacher reflected a view shared by her colleagues concerning prison guards' responses to women with mental health problems: 'I have never met a girl that officers haven't said was manipulative'. Another teacher stated that the prevailing attitude was, 'I'm going to sort her out. Then they put a self harming woman in the punishment block'. A member of the clergy agreed:

The [Mourne House] environment is unsafe and psychologically poor. Most are vulnerable, fragile women with specific healthcare needs. I really worry about their safety at night, locked up alone for so many hours...a young woman who attempted suicide 10 days ago was unjustly treated.

The most commonly raised healthcare issue was the lack of a discrete facility for women. Although women were visited in their cells or could have routine consultations in Mourne House, more serious conditions or those requiring overnight care were treated in the male prison hospital. Once escorted to the 'male side' women were locked in a holding cell until their consultation and then returned to the holding cell until guards were available to escort them to Mourne House: 'Sometimes you're away for hours and you're in a filthy, smelly cell just for a quick visit'. A long-term prisoner stated:

> Going over to the male prison hospital is a nightmare. We've got our own hospital here. Why it's not used I don't know. We have to go over for the dentist or optician. Say I go over to the dentist. Say it's ten minutes. I have to sit in a cold, smelly, rotten cell for the whole morning until I'm brought back. If we could go to our own hospital we would be dealt with and put straight back on the wing. That's what the men do. They don't have to sit in that cell. It's a cell the men use. There's a toilet in it. There's no toilet roll, no privacy, and it's just awful. You wouldn't even ask a man to use it.

Negative experiences of the male prison hospital were not confined to its physical condition:

> The hospital over the road is just for men. I was over there myself. It is very dirty and the men talk very dirty. It really upset me. There's men over there for rape and some of them men have raped young children. That really upset me. When I heard that I didn't feel safe around them.

This threatening situation was confirmed by a woman nurse and her male colleague:

> Women are very vulnerable in the main hospital. Vulnerable to verbal abuse although they are accompanied by staff...the male hospital is used as a place of safety but it's not appropriate.

> It's obvious that it's not acceptable to lock up women prisoners over here...They're [the men] flirting with them, trying it on...It's just not acceptable that they're housed in this area. There are flaps [in

the cell doors] that can be opened and they're visible from the yards. In the hospital it's a bad mix of prisoners winding each other up.

Members of the Board of Visitors voiced profound concern that the treatment of 'distressed women on the "other side" [the male prison hospital]' was 'totally inhumane'. One member stated: 'There can be a brutality shown to women [who are] at rock bottom', women who were already 'deeply damaged'. Many had 'been abused' and suffered 'domestic violence'.

A prison guard confirmed the abuse endured by women prisoners:

> I've taken women prisoners over to the far side [male prison hospital]. It's very embarrassing for the women because of the remarks and comments made. This shouldn't happen. They're all in separate cubicles. We're transporting 16 year olds to old ladies and they're being bullied and taking abuse.

While transport vehicles have individual cubicles, they are neither sealed nor silent. A woman prisoner recalled the distress that a young woman had experienced using shared transport with male prisoners:

> The men were shouting out of the windows, 'Look at that one. Show us your tits'. They were shouting to the wee girl, 'Would you take it up the arse' and that. They see you getting on the bus and they know the young girls. Some of the girls would sit and cry all the way.

Within hours of beginning the research in Mourne House prisoners, prison staff, members of the Board of Visitors and other professional workers independently had raised the issue of a 17-year-old young woman being held in the punishment block. The block's landing consisted of a standard central corridor with access to cells on either side. It was secured by a barred gate across the corridor, separating the cells from the landing office. There were two types of cell. The 'anti-suicide cell', or strip cell, had bare walls, a thick Perspex lining to the barred window and a metal plated ceiling. There was no bed but a raised plinth built into the floor, a mattress – often removed at officers' discretion – a padded non-destructible sleeping bag and a small potty as a toilet. There was no wash basin. It was classified 'basic'. The other type of cell, classified 'standard', was similar but had a steel-framed bed bolted to the floor, an open metal flush toilet and a hand basin bolted to the wall.

The 17 year old was interviewed in her cell. Her 'standard' regime consisted of 23-hour lock-up in her cell with the possibility of one hour's recreation each day. Throughout the interview she sat on the bed, her legs crossed. She was dressed in a non-destructible, short-sleeved gown. She had extensive and recent wounds to both legs and both arms, consistent with cuts by a sharp implement and scouring with the rough edges of the Velcro. Holding her gown together there were no visible signs of flesh free from injury.

She had just completed a letter, having been given pen and paper by a guard. There was a newspaper, loaned by a guard, and a Bible in her cell. Throughout the interview she was lucid. She clearly understood her situation and the circumstances of her imprisonment and confinement. Her self-harming was compulsive: 'It's how I cope'. She continued:

> I was in a hospital out there [in the community] and I still harmed myself then. I'm not getting the right treatment. They don't understand why I cut myself and I tell them I have to do it. It's my only way of coping. I seen Dr [the psychiatrist] and he gave me medication which helped ... I shouldn't be down here. There's nothing to do. It's worse in the night. I hear voices and see things. But no-one helps me. I should be in the hospital wing. This place needs a women's hospital or a special wing for nurses to control and deal with women with problems. They could have got people in to talk to me. To help me deal with my drink and drugs problems. I've had no counselling since I've been in here.

She refused her allocated one-hour recreation because she would have to go in the exercise yard in a gown and slippers – in winter conditions. A prison guard verified there were no appropriate clothes available for outside exercise. Guards stated that she had completed over two weeks of a 28-day period in cellular confinement. An IMR21 form (Referral/Assessment of Suspected Suicide Risk) was operational as she was considered a 'suicide risk'. Allegedly she had incited other women prisoners to self-harm or take their own lives.

Part of her 'care plan' was 'optimal contact' with staff and other prisoners. Yet she was held in isolation on 23-hour lock-up and experienced minimal staff contact. One guard stated that 15-minute observations of prisoners at risk no longer applied and they were checked 'as frequent as necessary'. This could be 'two or three times an hour' during the day, 'depending on the officer', and 'roughly once an hour at night'. 'Checks' were confined to 'looking into the cell' through a spy-hole.

Contact between staff and prisoner was minimal and entirely at the discretion of individual guards. As noted earlier, prison guards considered themselves inappropriately qualified and under skilled to undertake the responsibilities associated with difficult cases.

The young woman was due to be released, time served, the following week. Following the researchers' intervention, leave for a Judicial Review of the conditions under which she was being held was lodged with the Appeal Court. This was heard the day before her scheduled release. At the hearing it was established that she had been transferred to the punishment block due to disruptive behaviour and failure to conform to prison discipline. She had been classified as 'conduct disordered' rather than 'mentally ill'. It was clear that the conditions under which she was held prevented even partial fulfilment of the agreed care plan. The Judge ordered her immediate removal from the punishment block and transfer to the prison hospital. She spent her final night in isolation in the male prison hospital and was released into the community the following day, with no counselling and no follow-up community-based support.

Within weeks, the young woman was re-arrested following a disturbance in her home town. She was returned to Mourne House and, despite the Judge's previous order, returned to the punishment block, this time on the 'basic' regime. In the strip cell she lay on the raised plinth in the foetal position. There was no mattress and no sleeping bag. She slept on a coarse canvas blanket. She was dressed in a canvas gown from which the Velcro had been removed to prevent self-harm. She was not permitted underwear. There was a potty in the cell corner and no sink or bowl to wash her hands or body:

I was put in the hospital wing for nine days. They brought me over here for one night. That night I tried to hang myself and they wouldn't take me back over.

How did you try?

I ripped up a pillow case.

What was going through your mind?

Everything. I just couldn't cope. Look... [she indicated self-harm]... and on my legs as well.

How did you do that to your legs?

I rubbed this here [the edge of the gown] up against it.

Velcro?

No, not Velcro, just the edge.

Why do you do it?

Because I hear voices and see things. The voices tell me to do them. And I release the pain as well.

When you rub it, and feel the pain, that releases pain from you?

Yes.

Does that make you feel better?

Yes. But I'm not on the right medication. It's an anti-psychotic to stop me from hearing voices. They try to say I haven't a mental illness even though they've got me on anti-psychotic medication.

What's it like at night?

It's terrible, so it is. You sleep and you keep changing positions. I suffer from a bad back 'cos I was in a car accident. And they won't even give me my own clothes...in case I did anything stupid. Just look what they make me go to the toilet in. That's for night time... It's a disgrace.

Are you having any time with anybody? Is anybody talking to you?

No-one at all.

Do the prison officers come in and speak to you?

No.

Do you have any conversation with anybody during the day?

No, not really. Only if I knock the door and ask for something, and that's it.

Do they spend any time with you at all?

No.

Do you think it would help if you had people to talk to?

That's why I want back over the hospital wing, 'cos there's nurses there I can talk to.

> When you were in the hospital wing, did you have any time out of your cell with the men?
>
> On two occasions. But that was for mass.

She had not been provided with underwear: 'None whatsoever'.

> Do they look after you during your periods?
>
> No. They don't give me underwear or nothing.
>
> So how do you manage?
>
> It's hard. They just give you a wee sanitary towel and that's it.
>
> How do you keep that in place?
>
> It's hard.

She had been refused bail and was due to be sentenced but anticipated release as she had served time on remand that would be taken into consideration. She hoped for a place in a 'proper hospital for treatment'. A medical report submitted to a subsequent Judicial Review application at the High Court, confirmed that she required structured, therapeutic intervention and daily practical assistance. It stated that such therapeutic provision was not available in the prison. In fact, it was not available in Northern Ireland. She was diagnosed 'personality disordered'.

Deaths in Mourne House

Phyllis Chesler's classic text on the operational practices of US mental asylums for women echoed Goffman's (1968) work in identifying how the 'degradation and disenfranchisement of the self' was institutionally reinforced by the refusal of access to 'therapy, privacy and self-determination' (Chesler, 1972, pp.34–35). Women's boldness in questioning those in authority and their rejection of imposed expectations of femininity were met with 'punishment programs'. Those who sought support for 'emotional distress' were 'punished for their conditioned and socially approved self-destructive behavior' (p.39). In this punitive context those women who attempted to take their own lives were 'like female tears, constitut[ing] an essential act of resignation and helplessness'. Those who succeeded were 'tragically, outwitting or rejecting their [expected] feminine role, and at the only price possible: their death' (p.49).

On the 22 November 1996 a 20-year-old young woman from Derry took her own life in Mourne House while on remand. Her solicitor recalls a prison Governor commenting: 'You can't watch people all the time as it is a fact that if someone wants to kill themselves or commit suicide they are going to do it. There is nothing anyone can do'. The comment is one made regularly by prison managers and guards, revealing an underlying assumption that suicide is driven by an individual's pathological condition – a force so powerful it defies prevention. For those who have a 'duty of care', however, it provides a convenient rationalization for failure. It suggests inevitability regardless of the quality of support, whatever acts or omissions prevail in the operation of the regime. Implicit is the denial that complacency, negligence or intimidation could contribute to a troubled prisoner's decision to end her life.

Janet Holmes, like many others on her landing, was vulnerable. She had been in care from an early age and had a history of drug and alcohol dependency. A brief marriage had ended in difficult circumstances and she was charged with several petty offences. In prison she was distressed and had been transferred to the prison hospital where, the day before her death, she had attempted to hang herself. While in the hospital she was placed on 15-minute observation. Returned to Mourne House, the observation was stopped and she was allocated a standard prison cell. The ornamental bars inside the cell window offered multiple ligature points. On the day she died a prison doctor considered her sufficiently well to attend a disciplinary hearing. The hearing went against her and her punishment was removal of evening association, access to the gymnasium, radio, cassette and television. A woman known to be suicidal had all basic social contact and amenities removed. Other prisoners reported that she was so upset she was unable to make a cup of tea.

Despite having been on 15-minute observation, Janet was not formally classified a suicide risk, and subsequently, a Governor stated there had been 'no knowledge of any previous suicide attempt'. Governors and prison officers casually remarked that her death was associated with a half bottle of vodka that had been smuggled into the prison by her boyfriend. The pathologist found no alcohol in her blood or urine but noted multiple scars, some of which were recent, on her arms, reflecting a history of self-harm. He also confirmed that information of a previous attempt to take her own life had been available to Governors and guards. Regarding the circumstances of death, the report noted that, on entering the prison cell, prison guards 'found this woman hanging by a shoe-lace from the metal bars of the cell window. She was facing the wall, kneeling with her knees on the cell floor'. Other prisoners stated that at the time of her death they heard Janet banging her radiator. It appears that, having hung herself, she kicked out against the radiator and the ligature slipped, eventually bringing her to her knees. After the alarm was raised, it was 20 minutes before guards opened the cell door and the ligature was cut using nail scissors.

In a written submission to the inquest Janet's solicitor, also appearing as a witness, claimed that she 'was not looked after properly at Maghaberry [Mourne House] during the course of her stay there and in particular there was an inexcusable delay in having the cell door opened once the alarm was raised'. His evidence reflected that given by other women prisoners who stated that, on realizing the situation, they raised the alarm immediately and there was a long delay before guards entered the cell. The solicitor's submission continued:

Furthermore I am particularly concerned at the fact that the prison authorities advised me on the 12th December 1996 that they had no knowledge of any previous suicide attempt with regard to Janet when same is clearly documented in the [pathologist's] report...I am also concerned at the continual allegations made to me by Warders and other members of the prison authorities that 'this all started over a bottle of vodka being smuggled into the prison'. If one is to agree with that view the bottle of vodka should not have got into the prison in the first instance. This did not cause the inordinate delay in the opening of Janet's cell door which in my opinion has cost Janet her life.

The Coroner commented on the 'tragic sequence of events' that preceded Janet's death, focusing on the adjudication procedure earlier in the day. Without legal representation at adjudications it was impossible to know whether Janet had understood the questioning to which she had been subjected. Examination of prison guards' evidence to the inquest considered alarm points and the procedures for the opening of cell doors, the holding and location of keys for accessing cell doors in an emergency, 'suicide watch' and appropriate clothing for those prisoners considered at risk. The inquest also heard evidence questioning the adequacy of prison guards' training to deal with self-harm or suicidal behaviour. A woman guard stated she had not received training for such incidents, before or since Janet's death. The Coroner commented that the response at the time of her death had been 'unacceptable' and it was 'a matter of some concern that officers had received no training'.

Following the inquest the Coroner wrote to the Director General of the Northern Ireland Prison Service. His concerns included the conduct of the prison adjudication process, the training of officers, Janet's medical assessment prior to adjudication and the speed of access to her cell once the alarm had been raised. The inferences were clear: a failure in the duty of care, inadequate training and deficient emergency access procedures. Such serious criticisms from an experienced Coroner required serious consideration and responses from the Prison Service. They went unheeded.

As discussed previously, in 2002 the Prisons Inspectorate visited Mourne House. Its subsequent report (HMIP, 2003) was severely critical of the regime's treatment of suicidal and self-harming women, especially young women. In particular, inspectors were concerned about use of the main male prison hospital for distressed women prisoners and use of the punishment block for those who self-harmed:

> The perception among female prisoners was that, should they declare their vulnerability to self-harm, then there was the possibility that they would be taken over to the observation cells in the healthcare centre [Prison Hospital] in the main prison or to the punishment unit on Mourne. It was not appropriate to accommodate distressed female prisoners in what were little more than strip cells in an environment which essentially centred on the care of male prisoners, many of whom who had mental health problems. This was more likely to increase feelings of vulnerability.
>
> (HMIP, 2003, para.MH 36)

The inspectors also raised the disturbing case of a 15-year-old self-harming child they found in a punishment block strip cell dressed only in a canvas gown. On inquiring about the appropriateness of holding a child in maximum-security strip conditions, 'we were told that staff were not good at recording all the work that had gone into trying alternative strategies with the young person before this action was decided upon'. They questioned whether the child should have been in an adult prison, noting that staff had not been trained in child protection.

At the time of that inspection a young woman, Annie Kelly, was also held in Mourne House. She was the tenth in a family of 12 children and was initially in conflict with the law aged 13 soon after the tragic death of her brother. A year later she received her first conviction. She was sent to training school and then to a Juvenile Justice Centre where she was served with a 'certificate of unruliness'. Aged 15, she was imprisoned in Mourne House. Subsequently she received 28 custodial sentences. Both outside and inside prison her behaviour was challenging, often involving assaults on the police and prison staff. Yet a prison teacher who developed a positive relationship with Annie considered that none of the officers 'knew how to handle her'. She continued:

What happened was dreadful. She responded to the more aggressive staff by hitting out. She was held most of the time in solitary confinement. When I taught her our chairs were bolted to the ground.

Annie was regularly transferred to the male prison hospital. Agitated and disturbed, she 'heard voices' and self-harmed. She lacerated her arms, banged her head, inserted metal objects under her skin and strangled herself with ligatures, often losing consciousness. Between 1997 and 2002 there were numerous assaults on staff, cells wrecked and 40 incidents of self-harm. Her formal psychiatric assessment found no 'organic' impairment or mental illness. She was diagnosed as having attitudinal problems derived within a personality disorder. The diagnosis was offered as an explanation for her antagonistic behaviour towards staff, her self-harm and her 'suicidal ideation'. Outside she drank heavily. Yet her medical assessments record a bright, intelligent young woman suffering from low self-esteem and self-denigration.

In April 2001 Annie, committed to prison over a weekend, was taken directly to the punishment block. Guards claimed she was uncontrollable. She was isolated, unlocked only when three officers were present protected by a full length Perspex shield. She self-harmed and was strip searched. She resisted and a control and restraint team, in riot gear, was deployed. She was restrained, handcuffed and medically examined. Guards alleged that, alone in the cell, she slipped the handcuffs and smashed the spy-hole glass.

Annie's revolving door imprisonment continued and whenever she was inside she was segregated. A slight young woman, depicted as having super-human strength, in June 2002 she wrecked a punishment block cell. According to reports she wrenched the hand basin from the wall, removed the taps and used them to break through the cell wall. She was returned to the basic punishment regime in a 'dry cell'. Dressed in a 'non-destructible' gown, she was given a 'non-destructible' blanket. There was no mattress, no bed and no pillow. She slept on the raised concrete plinth where, according to officers, when awake she lay banging her head on the concrete floor.

She tore ligatures from the supposedly indestructible clothing and blankets. Her repeated acts of self-strangulation were dismissed as attention-seeking or provocative behaviour. A clinical psychologist recorded concern that Annie might unintentionally take her own life. A woman prisoner recalled:

> I talked to Annie. She was a very young girl. She needed a lot of attention and some of the girls upstairs [young prisoners] need the same. But we can't do anything. We know somebody's talking about it [suicide] and we tell staff but we don't know what they do with that. It's not really taken seriously... some of them take it seriously but others will go, 'She's always at it'. That's not the attitude to have.

Annie was transferred to the male prison hospital and later wrote a harrowing account of the transfer to her sister (Personal Letter, dated 13 August 2002, used with consent). It was her last letter home. 'You wouldn't believe the way I'm treated. You would need to see it with your own two eyes'. She described how the 'control and restraint team landed over and told me I had to take off my clothes and put a suicide dress on'. The all male team told her they would hold her down and strip her.

> Then they all held me out in the corridor. I only had the suicide dress on and I was told I could keep my pants cause I'd a s.t. [sanitary towel] on. But when the men were holding me they got a woman screw to pull my pants off. That shouldn't have happened. Then they covered me in celatape to keep the dress closed and handcuffed me and dragged me off to the male hospital.

The male hospital was a 'dirty kip' and she 'stuck it out for 6 days cause they threatened to put me in the male p.s.u. [punishment and segregation unit] if I smashed it'. She 'wrecked' the hospital cell and was returned to the Mourne House punishment block. 'I'm just relieved to be back'. Still in a 'suicide dress', she had 'hung myself a pile of times. I just rip the dress and make a noose. But I am only doing that cause of the way their treating me. The cell floor is covered in phiss cause they took the phiss pot out the other night'.

> They won't let me clean it. I haven't had a shower now in 4 days. I've had no mattress or blanket either the past few nights... At the end

of the day I know that if any thing happens me there'll be an investigation. (I never ripped the mattress or blanket nor did I block the spy). So if I take phenumia it'll all come out... I think you can only last 10–12 days without drinking cause then you dehydrate and your kidneys go. I've no intention of eating or drinking again so their beat there. I know they'd all love me dead but I'd make sure everything is revealed first.

On the day she wrote her letter she was held without basic sanitation or bedding. Refused food and water, she was moved from the strip cell to an intermediate cell in the punishment block. Within a week she had wrecked the cell and strangled herself. She was moved back into strip conditions, ripped her clothing and tried to strangle herself. Days later a member of the Board of Visitors recorded that Annie was refusing to eat; she had 'no ambition except to die'. The Board proposed a 'different approach concerning Annie should be made with some urgency – perhaps a medical approach, assessment and treatment elsewhere' (Internal Review, undated). Yet she was given a further 28-day solitary confinement in the punishment block. Her case was heard in court where she was convicted of attempted robbery and burglary and sentenced to 18 months. Her mental condition, self-harming and suicidal behaviour appear not to have alerted the court to the risk prison posed to her life.

The following day officers stated that Annie had tied ligatures around her neck. She was seen by the prison doctor who noted faint marks. Classified 'at risk', the doctor wrote:

> The whole area of what appears to be an increasing number of young disturbed females needs to be looked at with a view to having a regime in place including specialist help and training for staff in an environment which does not come under the standard application of the prison ethos.
>
> (Internal Review, undated)

Late in the evening a confrontation took place between Annie and night guards. Following the incident a senior guard noted in the incident log: 'A. Kelly Fake Ligatures'. Guards stated she had blocked the spy holes and they could not see into the cell. Minutes later Annie 'was lying on the cell floor with a ligature around her neck tied to the window'. As a control and restraint team was about to be deployed the senior guard 'observed F929 A Kelly get off the floor laughing and get into bed'. He ordered officers to clear the cell 'of anything that could block the spies'. The team returned to the cell twice within five minutes to remove further ligatures from her neck: 'All the ligatures were made from her suicide blanket? [sic] one of them being 9ft long. Lack of female officers made it impossible to search or strip Kelly to prevent this' (Internal Review, undated).

That night a woman prisoner, in a cell directly above Annie, stated that she heard her screaming. The following evening was significantly quieter but in the early hours she heard noises from Annie's cell. A male voice, she assumed a prison guard, was shouting, 'Come on, Annie, come on'. Then all was quiet. During the morning Annie was unlocked, taken to the shower and returned to her cell. There were no other prisoners in the punishment block and guards had minimal contact with her. In the early afternoon through the spy-hole a woman guard saw her at the window, ligatures around her neck and her tongue out. The ligatures were attached to diamond metal mesh through a small gap between the inner window frame and its Perspex cover. Walking from the cell to the office the guard told her colleagues that Annie was again using ligatures. Assuming Annie had staged 'another' incident the alarm was not raised. Having donned riot gear the guards entered the cell. Annie Kelly was dead.

Following Annie's death a case conference was held. It recorded 'the need for...appropriate knowledge to deal with prisoners who suffer from acute personality disorders' and 'for a co-ordinated multi-disciplinary approach' (Internal Review, undated). These conclusions echoed the concerns raised and transmitted by the Belfast Coroner to the Prison Service following the inquest into the death of Janet Holmes discussed above. Of profound and continuing concern was how, given her history and recent behaviour, Annie had the means available to end her life. She was in a strip cell modified specifically for her use. There were two observation windows in the cell door, a cell window protected by metal diamond mesh in a steel frame covered by Perspex. The ceiling was lined with sheet metal with no exposed seams. All conduits, ducting and pipes had been removed. Usually she was dressed in non-destructive, protective clothing, her blanket made from similar material. Yet officers and managers were aware that she was able to tear the blankets and the clothing. Modification to the cell windows, however, enabled access to the metal mesh through a gap sufficiently wide to take ligatures and hold her weight.

The internal inquiry recommended issuing electronic pagers or alternative means of contact to nursing staff for swift emergency response. It called for updating and replacing monitoring equipment and upgrading protective blankets and clothing. It also recommended an inspection of the cell to consider 'modifications that may be necessary as a consequence of this tragedy'. More broadly, the inquiry team 'recognises and endorses the general concern...that an adult institution is an inappropriate place to commit a juvenile female'. The Prison Service 'should consult with all relevant bodies to consider the provision of a secure community based facility for juveniles with personality based disorders within Northern Ireland'. The Prison Service Suicide Working Group's terms of reference 'should be extended to include the management of juveniles with personality disorders' and staff training should be provided 'as a matter of urgency'. Yet, as with Janet Holmes, the warnings went unheeded.

Roseanne Irvine was the youngest in a family of seven children. Although one of her sisters recalls a happy childhood a pre-sentence report stated that as a child she witnessed and was subjected to violence. She left school at 16 and eventually worked in a local factory. Aged 22 she became pregnant, following her daughter's birth she was depressed and drank heavily. Between 1994 and 2001 she was treated on 38 separate occasions for anxiety, depression, alcohol intoxication, drug overdoses, self-harm and attempted suicide. She was admitted to hospital, mental health and psychiatric units on numerous occasions. Roseanne's eventual psychiatric diagnosis was 'chronic psychosocial maladjustment' exacerbated by alcohol abuse, interpreted as 'borderline personality disorder' (Case Notes).

Roseanne was considered a loving and caring mother but her repeated self-harm and alcoholism led to her daughter being placed on the Child Protection Register, cared for within Roseanne's extended family. In February 2002 one of Roseanne's brothers died in a hostel fire and his death had a deep impact. She attempted to take her own life and was admitted to hospital. Immediately after her release she drank heavily and set fire to her home. Despite having no previous criminal record she was charged with arson. Remanded to prison, a 'prisoner at risk' file was opened yet she was not seen by a doctor.

The following month a Prison Officers Association (POA) representative wrote to the Mourne House Governor stating that Roseanne had attempted suicide during the night. She had strangled herself with a ligature and was 'lying face down'. Examined by a doctor her transfer to the male prison hospital was recommended for 'special care'. This did not happen and Roseanne was taken instead to a punishment block strip cell, clothed in a canvas gown without underwear and placed on 15-minute observation. The POA letter noted the criticisms of prison management following Janet Holmes' death. It claimed that the prison hospital management ignored guidelines in the Suicide Awareness Manual, that there was a reluctance to treat women prisoners either in the hospital or in Mourne House. It recorded a significant delay in hospital staff attending Roseanne, failure to admit her to the prison hospital and criticized her admission to the punishment block (Letter, dated 9 April 2002). The POA letter also posed a question: 'Why are the hospital management so reluctant to accept female prisoners and why are those prisoners who are admitted to the Prison Hospital returned to Mourne House after the briefest possible stay?'

Subsequently, the POA reported a further attempt by Roseanne to take her own life: 'To our dismay once again the regulations laid down in the Suicide Awareness Manual were ignored' leaving her 'in her own cell and placed on fifteen minutes observation by the night guard' (POA Letter, undated). The POA considered that 'prisoners deemed to be at risk of self harm' should be 'placed in the Health Care Centre and treated by Nursing Officers'.

Following these incidents, the POA wrote formally to the Governor. The message was clear:

> Hospital management are continuing to ignore the regulations governing the treatment of prisoners who are attempting self-harm. This is placing an intolerable burden on discipline staff by placing these prisoners in residential units instead of the healthcare centre.
> (Notification of Failure to Agree, dated 19 April 2002)

In September 2002 Roseanne was involved in a further incident. Again the POA sent a memorandum, headed 'Treatment of Prisoners deemed to be at risk of Self-Harm' (16 September 2002), noting that Roseanne had 'committed an act of self harm'. It alleged that suicide regulations continued to be ignored by prison managers. She had been placed on 15-minute observations, leaving guards 'untrained in medical procedures... in an intolerable situation'.

The following month, Roseanne was given a two-year probation for her offence and left prison. She was allocated a place in a therapeutic community for women with complex mental health needs. She settled but was returned to prison for breaching her probation order. Again she was assessed as 'at risk'. In November, she was discharged from prison but was unable to return to the therapeutic community. She was allocated a place in a mixed hostel and began taking alcohol, glue, gas and drugs. Transferred to another hostel, she felt seriously intimidated by men living there. She moved to a flat but her substance habit impelled her back to the hostel. A nun who she had met in prison visited her and was concerned that her 'mood became very low and she said she wanted psychiatric help'. One night she slept rough on the streets having been ejected from the hostel and was in clear need of appropriate healthcare.

She was assaulted and made a further attempt on her own life. She was admitted to hospital and although 'withdrawn and depressed' she anticipated she would receive care and treatment. The nun visited her again:

> When I arrived I could see Rosanne was very depressed and did not know what was happening to her. She had seen [the consultant] in a room with many other people, which she found very distressing, and was unable to communicate. I went to see the ward sister who came with me to Roseanne's bedside and told her that she was being discharged under the care of the community health team. Roseanne was very distressed.

Discharged from hospital without medication, Roseanne was taken to the Homeless Advice Centre and allocated a place in a house occupied by men suffering serious alcohol and drugs problems. At the house she was 'very frightened', especially as there was no supervisor on duty throughout the day. The nun continued to visit Roseanne:

> I went to [the house]. I could not get in several times. Then on one occasion a drunk man answered the door and he told me Roseanne was out. I left a message for Roseanne to phone me. I eventually got to see Roseanne. I brought another sister with me as I was afraid to go into this house by myself. Roseanne was in a terrible state of depression, confusion. She said she was frightened 'out of her mind', had taken drugs, drink and glue and no medication.

Concerned that she had not been visited by welfare workers to assess the suitability of the accommodation, the nun telephoned Roseanne's care manager and reported her 'depressed, suicidal and unable to stand, her eyes rolling'. That evening Roseanne telephoned 'drunk and suicidal'. Within a week she was in police custody and 'appeared in court in her pyjamas'. She had set fire to her room at the hostel and again was charged with arson. She was remanded in custody.

At Mourne House Roseanne was 'health screened' by a Nursing Officer. The report noted she had attempted hanging the previous week and had self-harmed her face and arms before setting fire to her room. Incredibly, given this sequence of events, her assessment was: 'No risk indicated at present'. No entry was made on information supplied by the police or other agencies regarding mental or physical health concerns. Yet the police and criminal evidence form accompanying Roseanne to prison was explicit. Under the heading 'May have suicidal tendencies' a police officer had entered three ticks and two bold asterisks. Under 'Physical illness or mental disturbance' it had one tick. In the section 'Supporting Notes' the words SELF HARM were written in capitals, underlined and emphasized with two asterisks. There followed, also underlined with accompanying asterisks, the handwritten comment, 'Informed C.P.N [community psychiatric nurse] that she would cut herself if the opportunity arose'. The asterisks and underlining were in red ink. Yet the prison 'health screening' ignored these comments.

On the committals landing, Roseanne told a guard that she intended to hang herself. A 'prisoner at risk' form was opened. She was put in a canvas gown, her underwear removed. Given a canvas blanket, potty and a container of water she was transferred to the punishment block. Despite the Inspectorate's 2002 recommendations and Annie Kelly's death, women who self-harmed or threatened suicide remained 'managed' by solitary confinement in strip conditions. Her case was discussed the following morning and she was left in the block. A nursing officer stated that Roseanne had threatened to set fire to herself. Her scheduled first meeting with a doctor was cancelled and the healthcare section of her assessment form remained blank. A guard noted her distress in the strip cell. She had torn hair from her scalp. Yet without a doctor's medical assessment she was returned to the committals landing and normal association.

Her cell had multiple ligature points and she had access to a range of ligatures. Still not seen by a doctor, she was visited by the prison Probation Officer who gave Roseanne a note. According to the Probation officer the note stated that Roseanne's social worker had arranged a meeting to plan a visit from her daughter. The note was never found. After the Probation Officer's visit Roseanne was upset and told guards that in fact she had been told she might not see her daughter again. Soon after, during brief evening unlock, Roseanne told guards she had taken '5 Blues' given to her by another prisoner. The guards assumed the tablets to be diazepam. In fact they were Efexor. She was already taking a cocktail of medication including Efexor, Omprazole, Diazepam, Chloral Betaine, Chlorpromazine, Inderal LA and Largactil.

The Mourne House Governor, in another part of the male prison, was informed of the alleged overdose. An immediate cell search was ordered but not carried out. The women were locked in their cells for the night and at approximately 9–15 p.m. Roseanne was observed sitting on her bed writing a note. She asked for the light to be switched off. Just over an hour later she was checked. She was hanging by the neck from the ornate bars of the window – the noose was a draw cord from her pyjama bottoms.

In the immediate aftermath a woman prison guard reflected on Roseanne's death. She stated that two weeks earlier a 17 year old had nearly died by hanging, another 17 year old was being held in the punishment block in strip conditions and an older prisoner, close to Roseanne, had been moved to the male prison hospital in a deeply distressed state. The guard commented: 'After Annie Kelly we felt it couldn't get worse than this – and it has'.

7
Tale of Two Inquests

Introduction

Since the early 1980s, the regularity and circumstances of deaths, including suicides, and self-harm in custody have become matters of profound concern throughout Great Britain and Northern Ireland. Women prisoners have been over-represented in suicide and self-harm statistics. When death occurs in custody, the State has a duty to ensure that it is investigated effectively and expeditiously. In Northern Ireland, deaths in custody are investigated by the office of the Prisoner Ombudsman. Torture, inhuman and degrading treatment are prohibited under Article 3 of the European Convention of Human Rights (ECHR). This is an absolute right and in international human rights law there are no justifications for its breach, regardless of circumstances. It is difficult to successfully progress Article 3 cases as the European Court has consistently set a high bar for defining treatment as inhuman and degrading, until recently equating it closely to torture.

The United Nations Standard Minimum Rules for the Treatment of Prisoners (hereafter 'the Rules'), establishes the underlying principle that detainees and prisoners should not be subjected to unnecessary punishment or degradation:

> [I]mprisonment and other measures which result in cutting off an offender from the outside world are afflictive by the very fact of taking from the person the right of self-determination by depriving him of his liberty. Therefore the prison system shall not, except as incidental to justifiable segregation or the maintenance of discipline, aggravate the suffering inherent in such a situation.
>
> (Guiding Principle 75)

Further, the Rules establish that health care in prison should be linked to the administration of general health within the community. Mental health provision necessary for prisoner rehabilitation should be provided. Medical staff have a duty to inform prison management of circumstances where 'a prisoner's physical or mental health has been or will be injuriously affected by continued imprisonment or by any condition of imprisonment' (Rule 25). They also have a duty to conduct daily consultations with prisoners held in punishment or segregation units and to advise prison management of circumstances where such conditions might be damaging the physical or mental health of prisoners (Rule 32).

Under the United Nations Code of Conduct for Law Enforcement Officials (Article 1), the staff responsible for the care of prisoners have a duty to maintain high standards and 'respect and protect human dignity and maintain and uphold...human rights'. The Rules state that staff should demonstrate 'integrity, humanity, professional capacity and personal suitability for the work' (Article 46). Prison officers are expected to provide positive role models to prisoners in their care, ensuring the protection of prisoners' health. All staff have a duty to report violations or potential violations of human rights against a prisoner.

The Prisons Inspectorate (England and Wales) relies on international human rights standards in setting 'expectations' against which it measures conditions for prisoners (these are used also by the Criminal Justice Inspection Northern Ireland, which inspects prisons in collaboration with the English Inspectorate). The former Chief Inspector, Anne Owers, notes, 'Each expectation is...mapped against domestic and international human rights standards, as set out in various instruments. It is noteworthy that 96 expectations can be derived directly from binding human rights obligations' (HMIP, 2004, p.5). Human rights principles set minimum standards covering all aspects of life in prison: transportation, reception, induction, health care, prisoners' legal rights, education and protection from harm. They extend to the state's responsibility to establish alternatives to custody, including preventative measures and reintegration of prisoners on release. Most principles apply to all prisoners, while some are gender or age specific, and others relate to racism and discrimination.

A body of domestic and European case law has established the State's responsibility to protect the lives of people in custody, and to thoroughly investigate prisoners' deaths. Article 2 of the European

Convention on Human Rights affirms the primacy of the right to life. The State has a particular duty to safeguard the lives of detainees and prisoners. There have been several landmark cases regarding deaths in prison. The *Amin* case concerned the death of teenager Zahid Mubarek in Feltham Young Offenders Institution, England in March 2000 (R (Amin) v Secretary of State for the Home Department (2003) UKHL51). He had been allocated a shared cell with a known racist who battered him to death in the cell. Article 2 was invoked by the Mubarek family to gain a public inquiry.

The earlier *Middleton* case concerned the suicide in prison of Colin Middleton in January 1999 (R (Middleton) v West Somerset Coroner and another (2004) UKHL10). It focused on the State's procedural obligation to investigate a death that might involve a violation of Article 2. The House of Lords ruled that, while an inquest should not attribute criminal or civil liability, it should establish 'how' a person died and 'in what circumstances'. The *Sacker* case was taken by Helen Sacker, mother of 22-year-old Sheena Creamer who was found dead in August 2000 while on remand at New Hall Prison (R (Sacker) v West Yorkshire Coroner (2004) UKHL11). The Coroner instructed the inquest jury that it could not attach a rider of 'neglect' to its verdict of suicide. The House of Lords ruled that this had deprived the inquest of its ability to address the positive obligation of Article 2 to safeguard life.

The cases of Amin, Middleton and Sacker together establish the important principle that deaths of people in custody should be effectively investigated and that the investigation should cover the measures taken to safeguard an individual's life, including the circumstances under which they died. In her review of prisoners' rights, Susan Easton (2011) notes that inquests alone may not constitute sufficient investigation to meet the requirements of Article 2, as established by Jordan v UK (2001) (regarding the killing of Pearse Jordan by the police in Northern Ireland), Edwards v UK (2002) (which related to the killing of Christopher Edwards by a violent fellow prisoner who shared his cell) and Amin (discussed above). To comply with Article 2, an effective investigation 'should be able to give a satisfactory explanation of the death, it should be independent and not conducted by persons implicated in the death, and the next of kin of the deceased should be fully involved' (Easton, 2011, p.72). In Re McKerr (2004) the House of Lords ruled that for deaths which occurred prior to the implementation of the Human Rights Act (1998) there was no requirement to have an Article 2 compliant investigation. However, in 2011, on the basis of the Silih v Slovenia

(2009) decision by the European Court of Human Rights, the Supreme Court (in Re McKerr in In re McGaughey) ruled that inquests held into deaths occurring before that date must as far as possible comply with Article 2 (Dickson, 2011).

Much of the controversy concerning the full and adequate investigation of deaths in custody and detention has focused on the role and function of the Coroner's inquest. It has centred on circumstances in which negligence, lack of care or acts of violence on the part of authorities have been alleged yet not followed by prosecution or disciplinary action. With no recourse to an alternative adversarial procedure, bereaved families, community organizations and campaign groups invariably turn to inquests expecting a thorough inquiry into the circumstances of death. As a court of last resort, the inquest has become the only public hearing through which all relevant evidence can be heard and witnesses examined under oath before a jury.

Such a weight on the inquest, together with the expectations of the bereaved, has been exposed regularly as inappropriate, contradicting the 'popular perception of a court' as 'a place where liability is established, where people are found guilty or innocent, are convicted or acquitted' (Scraton et al., 1995, pp.35–36). The expectation of the bereaved is that 'the court will apportion responsibility'. Yet, inquests remain, 'a complete contrast to the adversarial courts... the coroner's procedure is inquisitorial' – with liability having 'no place in the coroner's inquest... there is no prosecution and no accused' (Scraton and Chadwick, 1987, p.16).

In controversial cases, however, 'liability' is barely disguised. It permeates the atmosphere whatever caveats emanate from the Coroner. Lawyers are well aware of the 'uneasy relationship' between the inquest and courts of liability 'and they attempt to exploit every avenue... to introduce adversarial procedure' (p.44). What results is 'adversarial conflict', often involving several interested parties, 'fought out on the fields of inquisitorial procedure' (Ward, 1984, p.16). Within this context of conflict, the protagonists – often eminent counsel, local authority Coroners (doctors or solicitors by background) conduct affairs with 'a very wide degree of largely unregulated discretion' (Ward, 1983).

In deaths in custody inquests, a jury is a requirement. In Northern Ireland, Coroners and their juries issue 'findings' rather than 'verdicts'. Since the Middleton judgment in 2004, discussed above, when inquests are determining how an individual died they must also 'set out not just the means of death but also the circumstances in which it occurred' (Dickson, 2011, p.123). In determining this, interested parties, the witnesses called and the evidence heard are determined by the Coroner. The procedures, from the order of witnesses and the extent of their examination, through to the summing up of evidence and legal direction of the jury, are laid down exclusively by the Coroner within the broad and permissive parameters of the Coroners' Rules. Within five days of the conclusion of the inquest, the Coroner must inform the Registrar of Deaths about the 'particulars of death'. Although they are prohibited from expressing opinions on questions of criminal liability, where it appears that a criminal offence may have been committed, Coroners 'must also furnish the Public Prosecution Service with a written report of those circumstances' (Dickson, 2011, p.123). When people take their own lives in institutions such as prisons, young offenders' institutions or special hospitals, disputes inevitably focus on whether an established duty of care was compromised.

Routinely, Coroners inform the bereaved that it is 'their' procedure, 'their' time, 'their' right, and that inquests are carefully constructed to establish *who* died, *when*, *where* and *how*. In controversial cases families usually are aware of the first three; their principal objective being *how* they died. Yet over the proceedings 'hangs the denial of their agenda; a spectre'. While the circumstances of death, of *how* the person died, can be discussed, 'it is *how* without liability; *how* without blame' (Scraton, 1999, p.132).

> This is the procedure, an adversarial wolf in inquisitorial sheep's clothing, to which the bereaved have to turn. This is the anachronistic, inadequate and dishonest forum which is left to carry the full weight of responsibility for resolving and revealing the circumstances of death, while giving not so much as a nod towards individual or corporate liability. Coroner's courts are places of illusion; one minute beckoning, the next rejecting.
>
> (pp.132–133)

The rulings in the cases discussed above established the dilemma of the inquest. Clearly, particularly in cases concerning controversial deaths involving state institutions and their employees, inquest juries had to be freed from the rigidity of tightly prescribed and restraining verdicts to provide some indication as to their assessment of the circumstances of death. At the inquests into the deaths of Annie Kelly and Roseanne Irvine, therefore, the juries were invited by the Coroner to provide him with a full narrative in support of their findings.

Inquest into the death of Annie Kelly

The inquest into Annie Kelly's death was held at Belfast Coroner's Court over two weeks in November 2004 – two years and two months after her death. The prison staff view presented at the inquest was that Annie should not have been in prison but in a secure, community-based facility. Governors and guards, supported by others who worked with her in prison, portrayed her as a deeply disturbed and manipulative young woman beyond management or control. It was claimed that she was a danger to herself, to other prisoners and to staff. Her predicament, they argued, although unacceptable to 'normal' people, was of her own making. They stated that the strip cell, 'her' cell, was her choice, that she 'faked' suicide to 'taunt' guards and was capable of formidable violence – wrecking cells, destroying anti-suicide blankets and clothing with her bare hands.

Annie's mother, Ann Kelly, gave evidence. In her signed statement, she recorded how prison visits 'were difficult because of the strict supervision engaged in by Prison Staff who were both very hostile towards Annie and ourselves'. Annie had complained 'on numerous occasions' to her mother 'about the rough treatment she was receiving from Prison Staff and being constantly under control and supervision of male staff'. This was particularly demeaning 'in situations where she was being searched'. Annie also had complained 'that she had been detained in exercise areas which were shared by male prisoners'. This was a reference to Annie's time in the male prison hospital. Ann accepted that it was Annie's intention 'to upset Prison Staff by engaging in mock suicide attempts to create panic and cause staff to feel upset about her and her detention'. Yet she considered that prison guards' persistent hostility had given 'rise to a lack of concern for Annie's safety and led her to be placed in a cell which increased the likelihood of Annie engaging in mock suicide attempts'.

Ann Kelly believed that the 'strong hostility among Prison Staff and Governors towards Annie' had led to complacency. She stated 'I am not satisfied a proper regime was in place to supervise her given that there had been numerous instances of this nature which gave rise to her death prior to it happening'. Following a visit to the cell in which Annie died, Ann concluded that 'nothing had been done by Prison Authorities to ensure that she was placed in a safe environment which would have prevented these mock suicide attempts which were usually in the form of hanging'.

The jury was unimpressed by the proposition that Annie had brought death on herself and the evidence given by prison managers and guards sought to deflect responsibility from prison policy or practice. Detailed and thorough, the jury's narrative based on answers to questions posed by the Coroner was unprecedented in its indictment of the endemic failures prevalent within Mourne House. The jury found the 'main contributor' to her death by hanging had been 'lack of communication and training at all levels'. Its statement continued: 'There was no understanding or clear view of any one person's role in the management and understanding of Annie'. The jury identified a 'major deficiency in communication between Managers, Doctors and the dedicated team' responsible for her health, welfare and safe custody. There were 'no set policies to adhere to', specifically a lack of appropriate management and staff training. Finally, there was 'no consistency in her treatment and regime from one Governor to the next'.

Having established that the Prison Service was institutionally deficient at all levels the jury listed five 'reasonable precautions' that should have been taken to meet minimum standards in securing a duty of care. The anti-suicide blankets were 'deficient' and an 'anti-ligature window should have been installed from the outset'. Given the events immediately prior to Annie's death, 'clearer guidelines on observation and monitoring' might have removed the 'opportunity of making ligatures'. A search on the day would have discovered the ligatures she used and a 'cell inspection should have been carried out frequently and thoroughly especially in regard to the window'.

The jury identified six further 'factors relevant to the circumstances of her death'. They criticized her 'very long periods of isolation' and the lack of appropriate 'female facilities'. They recommended better 'availability of resuscitation equipment within the Prison' and the availability of first aid equipment 'on every landing'. Responding to evidence concerning the paucity of adolescent mental health care in Northern Ireland, the jury called for the provision of a 'therapeutic community'. Failing this, the 'judicial system should strive to provide a like environment'. It concluded: the 'Northern Ireland Mental Health Order needs to be updated to include personality disorders'. Given the failures in broader care provision, the deficiencies in communication and training 'at all levels' and the inadequate and inappropriate treatment of Annie, the inquest decided she did not die 'by her own act'.

The wider context and specific circumstances of Annie Kelly's death provide a partial insight into the abject failure of the criminal justice and penal systems in their handling of children and young people in conflict with the law. It is clear from her case notes that the State had failed in its duty of care from the time of her admission to the adult prison system as a 15-year-old child. As the jury noted, the lack of appropriate adolescent mental health care in Northern Ireland resulted in the imprisonment of vulnerable children and young people who require care and support relevant to their needs. Whatever Annie's mental health diagnosis, the punishment and segregation unit of a high security adult jail, in which she spent much of her life as a young person, was an inappropriate and dangerous location.

Reflecting on Annie Kelly's death, a prison Governor who knew her well stated that prison guards had a 'mind-set' of 'ordering prisoners to do things' rather than 'discussing the issues' with them. A male prison guard working in the punishment block disagreed:

> The prison hospital weren't interested when Annie Kelly was banging her head. It was left to us. I personally don't think I should be dealing with this. I'm not psychiatrically [sic] trained in any way, shape or form. I'm not a counsellor.

Two days after the jury delivered its detailed narrative finding the Coroner wrote to the Secretary of State for Northern Ireland, Paul Murphy. He listed 15 issues arising from the finding: communication problems between management, medical staff and prison officers; inadequate officer training; deficient policies and procedures; inconsistency of approach by successive governors; deficient suicide blankets; failure to provide an anti-ligature and anti-suicide cell; inadequate observations and monitoring; ineffective searches for ligatures; more frequent and thorough cell searches; long periods of isolation; inappropriate facilities in the prison for young female offenders; need for detention in a therapeutic community; availability of resuscitation and first aid equipment; need for legislative change to accommodate people suffering from personality disorders; and the need for the establishment of a therapeutic community in Northern Ireland.

The Coroner considered the Secretary of State was 'in a position to ensure that action is taken to prevent, as far as possible, the recurrence of similar fatalities'. He was concerned, 'that Ann [Annie] was not a unique prisoner and that there are other young offenders held in prisons in Northern Ireland who have personality disorders and would therefore be at risk in a similar manner to her'. Finally, he drew the Secretary of State's attention to the Human Rights Commission report (Scraton and Moore, 2005) on the imprisonment of women and girls stating that its co-authors had given evidence at the inquest. He concluded: 'they expressed concerns that the death of Ann constituted a breach of both Articles 2 and 3 of the European Convention on Human Rights. As the

State's representative in Northern Ireland, I would ask you to consider their views as to non-compliance with Articles 2 and 3'.

In December 2004 the Secretary of State responded at length to the issues raised by the Coroner, affirming that 'it is important to learn lessons from tragic events such as the death in custody of Ms Kelly'. He continued:

> I wish to acknowledge that Prison staff did work closely with Ms Kelly during her periods in custody to ensure she was held in conditions commensurate with the circumstances presenting at the time. It is important that we appreciate that Ms Kelly presented the Prison Service with serious control problems including her threat and use of violence against staff, prisoners and herself.

He listed Annie Kelly's catalogue of resistance within prison: the number of assaults on staff; self-harm incidents; wrecked cells; threats and other adjudications. He made no reference to the issues raised by the jury, particularly the criteria used to assess the appropriateness of 'conditions' under which Annie Kelly was held or their relationship to 'circumstances presenting at the time'. It appeared that the Secretary of State was satisfied that the criteria adopted for such assessments, and the arrangements that followed, were acceptable.

Regarding communication problems between management, medical staff and prison officers, he noted the introduction of a new Prison Service policy for self-harm and suicide following a 'full review'. He referred specifically to the requirement within this policy of 'better co-ordination between staff, Healthcare [sic] and others', the introduction of a 'multi-disciplinary case conference within 72 hours of someone being identified at risk' and the 'new PAR (Prisoner at Risk) process... provid[ing] for residential care plans and Healthcare plans which follow the prisoner wherever they are in the system'. The Secretary of State did not comment on the procedures in place to ensure the accuracy of assessments or records entered in the plans.

Replying to concerns over inadequate training, he noted that the Prison Service recognized the need to improve training. Previously this amounted to a limited number of staff attending a 'half day suicide awareness training seminar' and receiving unspecified refresher training to 'retain their certification' in first aid. He stated that the new policy for self-harm and suicide provided all staff with 'briefing packs', with managers attending one seminar then 'cascad[ing]' the training received at this seminar to their staff. This was to be supported by the 'availability' of a 'half day training pack'. Further, 'staff managing females in custody [had] commenced training on "Working with vulnerable and Personality Disorder Prisoners". Training is ongoing.' No details of this training, its depth or purpose were given.

In terms of deficiencies in the policies and procedures adopted in the management of Annie Kelly, the Secretary of State reassured the Coroner that the Prison Service was committed to the development of new policies for the management of women in custody. These policies 'will be informed by the conclusions of recent unannounced inspections by HCMI [sic] on behalf of the Criminal Justice Inspectorate and by the recent report of the Human Rights Commission'. Provision for 'better procedures, systems and guidance to staff on the management of vulnerable prisoners' were now said to be guaranteed by the self harm and suicide policy, thus addressing many of the deficiencies 'identified at the inquest'. The jury had been concerned that prison Governors managed Annie Kelly differently to other prisoners. In future a Suicide Prevention Co-ordinator at each prison would 'provide greater consistency in managing difficult cases such as this'.

With specific regard to the issue of deficient suicide blankets, the Secretary of State noted that the blanket issued to Annie Kelly 'was supplied by the Prison Service to an approved British standard'. He quoted evidence 'given by male officers to the inquest' that 'they could not tear the blanket'. The Secretary of State did not respond to concerns that she had regularly torn ligatures from blankets and, regardless of what constituted the 'British standard', the material appeared to be not fit for purpose. Blankets and suits, he stated, 'are now supplied by the Scottish Prison Service and are of a higher standard to that [sic] supplied previously'.

On the jury's specific concern regarding the failure to accommodate Annie Kelly in a ligature free cell, the Secretary of State conceded that there 'should not have been any ligature point at the window grille'. He commented that the 'polycarbonate sheet may have been removed for maintenance and in refitting the small gap was left'. This statement was not attributed to any contemporary source and was not evident in the internal prison investigation report into Annie Kelly's death. In a statement of consequence for future prisoners 'identified at risk', the Secretary of State assured the Coroner that '[i]n so far as is practicable anti-ligature windows will be fitted'. Cells at Hydebank Wood (to where women prisoners subsequently had been transferred) for 'vulnerable female prisoners have anti-ligature windows fitted' and 'new buildings will comply with the safer cell design'.

Responding to concerns raised regarding the inadequacy of observation and monitoring of a prisoner locked alone in a cell for long periods of time, the Secretary of State noted that Annie Kelly 'had been observed some 13 minutes before she was found hanging'. He referred to the evidence of a Forensic Psychiatrist who had 'emphasized that where there is an intention to take ones [sic] own life that this can be achieved in 4 minutes'. Further, Annie Kelly 'frequently reacted if staff were overly intrusive in supervising her'. The jury's concern, however, had focused on evidence regarding the adequacy of the observational and monitoring arrangements operational in her management. The Secretary of State noted that it 'is necessary to strike a balance [regarding intrusion] and the case conference arrangements under the self harm and suicide policy will provide clear guidance for staff on observations required in any particular case'.

Further specific concerns concerning the frequency of searches for ligatures, cell inspections and isolation were also considered. The Secretary of State concluded that searches accorded 'with the procedures laid down' but it 'would have been helpful if, given the risk to herself, staff were required to give additional searches'. While stating that 'higher frequency of searches did lead to confrontation' he recorded that 'it is accepted that Ms Kelly should have been subject to additional searches, including her cell and property'. He was reassured that the new policy on suicide and self-harm 'addresses this issue'.

Regarding isolation, the Secretary of State noted, '[i]t is accepted that keeping a prisoner in isolation for long periods is unhealthy but unavoidable where that prisoner is so disruptive and threatening to his/herself and others'. Given she 'was disruptive when located on a normal landing' and 'presented significant control problems' for staff 'when intent on self harm', observation was 'difficult to maintain...when she had the freedom to move through the landing'. Responding to Annie's 'virtual isolation', he reiterated figures on officer assaults and cell wreckings, noting the 'many occasions' that she had 'used debris' to self-harm, the inference being that there was no alternative available other than isolation in a punishment block for such a disturbed young woman.

The Secretary of State did not respond to the jury's concern that the facilities at Mourne House were inappropriate for holding young female offenders other than to state that, following the recent transfer to Hydebank Wood, young women were accommodated in a 'low risk establishment with a relaxed and varied regime'. This would be enhanced as a consequence of the 'recent inspection' through which 'further improvements are planned to deliver more constructive activity including education'.

The jury's final concerns related to the appropriateness of holding Annie Kelly in prison rather than in a 'therapeutic community'. The Secretary of State noted that the 1986 Mental Health Order (NI) 'excludes personality disorder, whereas it is included in English/Welsh legislation, the result being that therapeutic community facilities exist in England and Wales but not here'. Instructively, he added: 'Prison, with its disciplinary approach is "the place of last resort" and could be considered an inappropriate establishment for persons suffering from the disorder'. Despite this, he placed responsibility on Annie Kelly herself for the lack of therapeutic support:

> As one of Ms Kelly's problems was reported to be missing her family, sending her to such a community in England and Wales was deemed geographically inappropriate. Ms Kelly was also required to give her consent to the transfer, but had refused in the past.

The jury had been specific in its criticism of the mental health legislation in Northern Ireland, recommending a change in the law to bring it in line with England and Wales. The Secretary of State did not respond to this important issue. At no point did he seek to explain the significant discrepancy between jurisdictions. Neither did he express any intention to pursue legal reform. The significance of this extensive review of the Secretary of State's response is that it amounted to a comprehensive reversal of the jury's findings, the findings of the independent research and the evidence given to the inquest by the researchers. It was closely aligned with the case presented by authorities at the inquest and, in effect, was a barely disguised dismissal of the Coroner's concerns. It amounted to a reiteration of the Prison Service's case, giving legitimacy to evidence of Governors and guards that had been discredited at the inquest as by the jury.

Inquest into the death of Roseanne Irvine

In its apparent inevitability, the death of Roseanne Irvine was particularly shocking. As a guard stated in interview: 'We have our own list, our own worries as to specific women who might have died ... she displayed the symptoms, the prior attempts. The warning bells were there'. A professional worker within the prison commented that 'everyone realised that Roseanne had great needs but it [the provision] fell short because no-one put their hand up for overall responsibility'.

Given Roseanne's history of vulnerability, self-harm and attempted suicide, the lack of a personal care plan raised immediate concerns about the circumstances of her death. Before discussing the inquest into Roseanne Irvine's death it is important to consider the accounts of the women imprisoned with Rosanne, who were interviewed by the researchers. Deeply distressed, Roseanne was convinced that future access to her daughter was under threat. A woman prisoner recalled:

> She was always talking about her wee daughter. She loved her so much she talked about [her] every day. She hadn't seen her daughter for three weeks and she really missed her. She said to me that she did not think she would see her again because of what her social worker told the prison officer to tell her. She told Roseanne that [her daughter] was happy and it would not be right to bring her up to the prison to see her. That really hurt Roseanne. You could see it in her face when she was telling me. It was Roseanne's child and she had every right to see her.

A prison guard stated that Roseanne 'was not getting to see her daughter' but did not know why. She continued:

> In a letter a week ago she told her daughter that she was not well, but that she really missed her and wanted to see her. She loved her daughter but she was ill and it [the illness] was no fault of her own.

According to other women prisoners, immediately prior to her death Roseanne had suffered intensely in the punishment block. One woman stated that 'she had had to lie on wood' and another commented that she 'was sore on her back after the punishment block'. In fact she had lain not on wood but on a concrete plinth without a mattress or a pillow. Still considered at risk, her return to the committals landing gave her access to several ligatures in a cell with multiple ligature points, not least the patterned metal-work of the window bars. She received no counselling, had little meaningful contact with staff and was locked up, unobserved, for extended periods.

A woman prisoner stated that, on the evening of her death, 'Roseanne told me not long before we got locked up that the staff did not check on the women every hour and she said to me that one of these nights they will find someone hanging and they will be dead. That very night Roseanne was found dead'. She continued:

> If the staff had checked on Roseanne more often that night she might be alive today. They knew she was down...The girl needed help which she did not get. She was so down. This place is like hell on earth.

A woman in a nearby cell heard another woman 'squealing and shouting' to Roseanne but 'no buzzer went off'. She was convinced that guards had turned off the emergency cell buzzers. Another woman stated:

> What happened to Roseanne was frightening. You think you're going to bed safe and you wake up and ask a warder where someone is and they say she hanged herself...All she wanted was to see her child but they didn't listen to her. Roseanne's death could have been prevented.

The impact on the other women prisoners was immediate:

> The next day I just sat and cried. I then had panic attacks. They didn't get the nurse over. I pushed the [emergency] button and they came to the door. I asked to see the nurse and they just said 'No'. They said, 'You're not allowed to push the button. It's for emergencies only'. I said I was having a panic attack. They said, 'Take deep breaths'. It was early evening. I sat up on the bed with a pillow and cried and cried.

Roseanne's closest friend on the landing, Jane (pseudonym), was devastated. Transferred to the male prison hospital, she was interviewed by the researchers several days after Roseanne's death. The interview took place in an office and the constant noise outside was intense. It seemed out of place in a healthcare facility accommodating acutely disturbed and distressed patients:

> While we were talking the daily routine of the prison hospital was happening beyond the door...loud male voices shouting and laughing; jokes and banter between staff; the constant rattling of keys; whistling; telephones ringing; people's names being shouted

down corridors. All interpersonal communications seemed at full pitch.

(Field-notes)

Throughout the interview Jane was agitated and cried. She apologized constantly for her emotional and physical 'state':

> The way that girl was treated, the system let her down. There should be a hospital for women. It was disgusting, dirty in here...I always told her not to do anything to herself. I tried to see her that night but we only got 20 minutes out [of the cells]. I started to write things down myself. I wrote there should be more support for women with mental health problems.

Jane discussed her personal mental health problems: 'You get no support, the staff ignore you'. She had twice received visits from a psychiatric nurse 'then it was stopped'; there was 'no support for women with depression'. In the prison hospital 'you're locked up 23 hours a day'. She continued:

> If you're sitting there [in the cell] for hours there's stuff that goes through your mind. If I don't get out today I'll plan something. They think there's nothing I can do but I can. They think they know everything but they don't. I've got a plan, I know what I'll do. My first cousin hung himself.

She had not wanted to be transfered to the male prison hospital, 'it's filthy'. Jane was held in strip conditions, the bed bolted to the floor and the metal toilet, with fixed wooden seat, open to observation. It was described by a male senior orderly, without a hint of irony, as a 'basic suite' which the staff tried 'to keep as clean and tidy as possible given the circumstances'.

Jane wanted to be returned to Mourne House to resume contact with other women. Initially she thought she would be in the prison hospital just for 'one or two nights'.

> The doctor doesn't want me to go back over there but I can talk better over there. Over here they don't even talk to you and it's supposed to be a hospital. Here, if you feel really down they don't care.

Isolation, particularly from other women, was the most difficult aspect of the 23 hour lock up: 'I've never been in prison before. I hate getting locked up...it brings memories back to me'. She disclosed a history of sexual abuse, 'I'm lying trying to sleep, thinking about these things'. She continued:

> In the hospital they [male prisoners] talk filthy and dirt with the other prisoners. A man exposed himself. Said, 'I'll give her one'. He thought 'I'll pull it [penis] out 'cos there's a woman there'. We were all outside together. One man is in for sexually abusing a child. We have to have association with them. They are crafty, some of them. I told them [staff] about what the man did but they never did anything about it. I did not feel safe around them.

Her account was deeply disturbing. The male senior orderly on duty confirmed that Jane had been on association with male prisoners in the recreation room. He explained:

> There are difficulties housing women prisoners in a male ward. These are acutely disturbed prisoners...Unlock depends if there's sufficient female staff. But they do have association with male prisoners.

On hearing the experiences Jane had endured in the recreation room the orderly stated that a female member of staff was always present but he did not contest Jane's account. The 'situation' in the prison hospital, he stated, was 'acute and volatile'. For Jane, grieving the loss of her friend while struggling with her past memories and current fears, the experience of incarceration was 'like a nightmare and you think it's never going to end'. She said that if 'they'd doubled me up [shared cell with Roseanne] then I could have saved her life. She was worried about whether she would ever see [her daughter] again'. Jane's concern was that 'there'll be more deaths in this prison because people don't get the help they need'. She wrote later:

> I have four kids and four grandkids and I miss them all so much. I keep thinking to myself I will never see mine again. I love them all so much too. But to me time is running out for me. I can't take much more. Every day is like a nightmare.

Roseanne Irvine's family were given no indication by the Prison Service of the circumstances in which she died. The following statement was published in a press release on the Service's website:

The NIPS [Northern Ireland Prison Service] wishes to express its sympathy to the friends and relatives of Roseanne Irvine, a 34 year old female remand prisoner who was found dead in her cell at around 22.15hrs last night in Mourne House, Maghaberry. Her next of kin and the Coroner have been informed.

(Northern Ireland Prison Service, 4 March 2004)

A few weeks later members of the family met with the researchers at the offices of the Northern Ireland Human Rights Commission. For the first time, they received factual information concerning Roseanne's death, how her death would be investigated and what to expect at the inquest. Their grief was compounded by the length of time they would wait for the inquest to be held. In fact, the inquest was held three years later, in February 2007. It was held before the Coroner who had conducted the inquests into the deaths of Janet Holmes and Annie Kelly. Initially, it appeared that the family's barrister considered Roseanne's death had been relatively uncontroversial. To all appearances, a young woman with a track record of alcohol and drug dependency, disturbed behaviour, self-harm and attempts on her own life (including setting fire to her own property) had become so depressed that she took her own life.

Prison guards, prison Governors, nursing officers, doctors and other professional staff who had responsibility for Roseanne's care in prison gave evidence absolving themselves of personal responsibility. Yet it was clear that the night guards on duty had not been passed crucial information from the day guards regarding Roseanne's state of mind. Her claim to have swallowed 'Five Blues' in addition to the cocktail of prescribed drugs she had taken was not investigated. The Governor, who was in the male prison, did not attend Mourne House, merely instructing that a cell search should have been conducted. The search was not carried out and Roseanne was locked down without any special consideration or observation. Under examination, prison guards contradicted each other and the Governors' evidence fell far short of that expected from senior managers responsible for the care of vulnerable prisoners. It was also clear that Roseanne had received no detailed medical assessment prior to, during or after the days she had been held in the punishment block or immediately prior to her death.

As noted in the previous chapter, Roseanne's attempts on her life in Mourne House had been well documented from her previous time in jail. No attention had been given to concerns about her vulnerability that were the subject of several serious complaints by the Prison Officers' Association to prison managers. There was no attempt to explain the abject failure, at the time of Roseanne's admission and 'screening', regarding police warnings of possible suicide. Finally, and crucially, there was no satisfactory explanation given to the jury regarding the information she claimed to have received earlier on the day of her death about withdrawal of access to her daughter. The note said to have been given to her by the prison probation officer had not been found and there was no record of what she had written in her cell when last observed alive.

On 13 February 2007, the inquest jury returned a damning narrative finding. It began: 'The prison system failed Roseanne'. The jury considered that she had taken her own life while the 'balance of her mind was disturbed'. Reflecting on prison guards' and managers' evidence demonstrating a fatal mix of complacency, incompetence and negligence, the jury highlighted the significance of 'the events leading up to her death, ie long history of mental health difficulties specifically the incidents that occurred from 1–3 March'. Clearly, the jury understood that the deep distress of the immediate context was rooted within a prolonged history of despair, depression and self-harm.

Closely resembling the jury narrative at the Annie Kelly inquest, the jury established a series of systemic 'defects' in the treatment afforded to Roseanne. There was a 'severe lack of communication and inadequate recording' between and by staff, including healthcare provision. The 'management of the IMR21', the prisoner at risk document and care plan, was deficient and there had been a 'failure to act'. More broadly the jury was concerned that there was a 'Lack of healthcare and resources for women prisoners' within Mourne House. Each 'defect' in the system had contributed to Roseanne's death. The jury stated that 'all staff were not aware of Roseanne's circumstances and could not act accordingly'. She should have been granted access to a doctor as a 'priority'. Further, the male prison hospital 'was inadequate for female prisoners'. There had been several issues of neglect in taking 'reasonable precautions'. Roseanne 'could have been taken to an outside hospital/out of [hours] call doctor'. There should have been a 'full briefing [between guards] during [shift] handovers'.

The decision to move Roseanne from the punishment block to normal association 'should not have been made by a non-medically trained unqualified staff member'. The jury suggested that Roseanne could have been 'paired up with friend in cell' and that staff should have conducted 'more checks'. Training in 'suicide awareness for prison staff' was emphasized as a priority. The jury's final comments were instructive: 'Prison is not a suitable environment for someone with a personality/mental health disorder'. Yet they also noted that 'no other alternative' existed in Northern Ireland.

The Northern Ireland Prison Service response

Two months after Roseanne Irvine's death the Chief Medical Officer for Northern Ireland and the Director General of the Northern Ireland Prison Service commissioned Professor Roy McClelland to chair and carry out an independent review of non-natural deaths in prison. The decision reflected a growing concern about deaths of male prisoners as well as the recent deaths of two women. Its terms of reference were to review healthcare and mental health provisions to vulnerable prisoners, particularly the cases under scrutiny; to review communications between health care and other areas of the prisons; to examine the nature and effectiveness of healthcare services and to make recommendations. Four members of the Review Group were employed by the prison services of England and Wales, Scotland and Northern Ireland.

McClelland conducted two 'parallel' inquiries. The first was an analysis of the deaths 'with consideration of risk awareness and its management, based on interviews with staff and prisoners' (McClelland, 2005, p.2). The second considered 'the systems, procedures, conditions and culture within the prisons based on visits to all three establishments (Maghaberry, Magilligan and Hydebank Wood) and including observations and interviews with prisoners and staff' (McClelland, 2005, p.2). His report made 28 recommendations for suicide prevention under the headings: Risk Management; Information Sharing; Prison Health (Screening, Health Services, Mental Health Promotion); Raising Standards; Training; Health and Personal Services.

The ethnographic evidence-base for the Review was limited. Only six prisoners and 19 staff were interviewed across three prisons. Each prisoner was under Prisoner at Risk supervision and the semi-structured interviews focused on the Prisoner at Risk process and staff-prisoner interaction. The Review Group visited each prison for one day only and was given a 'walk through' of procedures, conditions and culture regarding vulnerable prisoners. Referred to as one-day 'tours', they provided a 'snap shot of each establishment' through which 'practice, culture and conditions' could be compared and contrasted 'to other prison services, best practice and the relevant national standards'. While accepting that the Review Group was also informed by documentary analysis and literature review, its qualitative evidence-base was severely limited. There was no observation, for example, of Prisoner at Risk meetings and little opportunity to gain any meaningful familiarity with the operation of regimes, staff-prisoner relations or daily activity either in the punishment block or on the landings assigned to 'vulnerable' prisoners.

In the Report's Executive Summary, however, McClelland asserted that the review 'provided an opportunity to examine the whole context of care within the prison system and the various interfaces between the prisons and the wider community including health and social care'. The Review identified 'a need to improve transfer of information from the community into the prisons, within the prison and between prisons and from the prison back into the community' (p.3). It confirmed that, in their interactions with prisoners, prison guards failed to address the priorities established in the care plans for prisoners at risk. The process of assessment 'from reception onwards was somewhat superficial and the system of health care delivery was not joined up' (p.4).

There were deficiencies in health screening on reception, particularly regarding mental health and the suicide indicators, in the provision of adequate and regular suicide risk assessment and in the management of suicide risk. The Review stated that appropriate policies and practices were required 'including sensitive assessment of vulnerable prisoners and the removal of the means to commit suicide... proportionate to the risk' (p.4). It noted a 'fundamental structural weakness in the deployment, management and support of staff delivering healthcare services' to the most vulnerable prisoners, lack of 'a formal health structure' and 'lack of mental health professionals who operate in this capacity' within the prisons. The 'management of vulnerable prisoners is not high enough on the agenda of the NIPS [Northern Ireland Prison Service] at operational and headquarters level'. Such marginalization had 'contributed to the feeling amongst management at an operational level that they are unable to take forward issues themselves to improve the care of the vulnerable' (p.5).

Regimes were 'over-controlled' and the Prison Service, in terms of staffing levels, was not under-resourced. A 'radical change' in staff role, job content and work culture was necessary. 'It is of concern' concluded McClelland, 'that previous recommendations made about NIPS have not been implemented and that similar recommendations are again being made' (p.5). McClelland also questioned the appropriateness of detaining women who presented with complex needs within a prison regime.

The Review made minimal reference to gender. It provided a five-paragraph summary of Annie Kelly's history and a one-paragraph discussion. Roseanne Irvine's history was covered in a nine-sentence paragraph followed by a three-paragraph discussion. The key contextual issues surrounding these deaths, particularly the regimes to which both women had been subjected, were absent from these accounts. That Annie Kelly died in a punishment block strip cell and Roseanne Irvine had been in the punishment block immediately prior to her death were not considered sufficiently significant to warrant a mention. Discussion of Annie Kelly's case simply concluded, 'like that of Roseanne Irvine [it] illustrates that there is a need for a dedicated service for women offenders with personality disorder and complex needs of this kind' (p.5).

Three recommendations emerged from this schematic consideration of the women's deaths. First, as a matter of priority, a multidisciplinary health team approach to the management of offenders suffering from mental health problems should be established. Second, a training programme for prison staff on mental health matters, specifically the recognition, assessment and management of prisoners 'at risk', should be initiated. Finally, it was necessary to provide services outside the prison setting for treating women with personality disorders. For those with 'security needs', treatment should be provided by prison and Health and Personal Social Services in collaboration. 'In-reach' mental health support was also recommended as a priority for women and young men at Hydebank Wood.

On the issue of the diagnosis and treatment of personality disorder, the Review Group commented:

> The review of the two women [sic] deaths highlighted the difficulties inherent in treating people with complex needs in a prison regime. Personality disorder has been designated 'no longer a diagnosis of exclusion'... and therefore consideration needs to be given to the service requirements of people with such disorders... often input is required by several members of the multidisciplinary team. Individual psychotherapeutic provision such as Cognitive Analytical Therapy may be required within a setting where there is consistency of approach and good staff supervision... this is difficult to achieve in a prison setting. The treatment needs of men and women prisoners with personality disorder needs careful review with consideration given to the establishment of hospital based personality disorder services. (p.38)

Further generic recommendations included the improvement of 'activity level, work placements, education for vulnerable prisoners and therapeutic day care regimes', with increased 'attention to detail... into the way that vulnerable prisoners spend their days' (p.38). Governors and their managers 'must display more leadership on suicide and risk management procedures in order to protect the vulnerable' (p.44). Health and Personal Social Services 'should become responsible for the delivery and development of all clinical services' within the prisons (p.46). The Review Group called for an implementation plan to meet the recommendations of all recent reports to secure 'much needed reform of the prisons' duty of care and modernization of mental health services in Northern Ireland prisons' (p.47).

Conclusion

The Northern Ireland Human Rights Commission demanded a strong and thorough response to the deaths of Annie Kelly and Roseanne Irvine, especially as the research had demonstrated that health care for all women prisoners was dire. Condemning distressed and self-harming women and girls to the punishment block represented an egregious breach of their human rights as well as damaging their already parlous health. In this policy, punishment was prioritized over treatment and there was no consideration of the duty of care owed to the prisoners. Holding women prisoners, particularly girl children, for 28 days in bare cells with nothing to read, listen to or look at constituted severe deprivation. The conditions in which they were held contravened Article 3 of the European Convention on Human Rights and Article 3 of the Human Rights Act. The pre-eminent attitude of most prison guards to the women and girl prisoners in their care was, at best, complacent and, at worst, disrespectful and abusive.

In the final analysis, responsibility for providing a positive and constructive environment, adequate and appropriate care, rehabilitative and supportive programmes for women in custody rested with the Director of the Prison Service and the Prison Service Management Board. While the working practices adopted by many, but not all, prison guards demonstrably fell short of minimum professional standards, the Prison Service had failed to resolve a worsening situation at Mourne House. This failure was an indictment of its approach towards the women and girls in its care and had fatal consequences.

The Human Rights Commission recommended an independent inquiry into the Mourne House regime. The proposed terms of reference included failure by the Director General and the Governor of Maghaberry to implement the inspectorate's recommendations and its consequences for women and girl children prisoners held at Mourne House; the circumstances surrounding the deaths in custody of Annie

Kelly and of Roseanne Irvine; use of the punishment and segregation unit as a location for the cellular confinement of self-harming and suicidal women, including girl children. The recommendation for an inquiry, and its terms of reference, were ignored and the Human Rights Commission did not actively pursue the recommendation. Despite a series of highly critical reports, focusing particularly on deaths in custody, by the Prisoner Ombudsman, further independent research into the policies, regimes and conditions of incarcerations in Northern Ireland have not been commissioned.

8
The Prison Within

Introduction

Hydebank Wood is a purpose-built male Young Offenders' Centre close to Belfast's outer ring road. It is a medium-security prison set in a pleasant, wooded environment. The outer, chain-link fence provides a relatively clear view from within and the undulating land gives variation and a feeling of 'openness' to the site. A visitors' centre accommodates family, legal and other professional visits. The five residential houses form a slightly elevated arc across green and well-kept gardens.

In late June 2004 women prisoners were transferred to Ash House in highly controversial and contested circumstances. As stated earlier, the Human Rights Commission publicly opposed the transfer, considering it inappropriate to site a women's prison unit within a male Young Offenders' Centre. The Chief Commissioner wrote to the Director General of the Northern Ireland Prison Service requesting that 'the Commission be granted access to visit female prisoners in Hydebank' (letter, 2 July 2004). The Director General responded that, given the 'unusual amount of interest in the condition of the female prisoners' and the need to 'get new regimes into place without excessive scrutiny', he was 'not prepared for the time being, 'to grant access' (letter, 26 July 2004). The researchers, however, were permitted access to Ash House to meet with an 18-year-old self-harming girl detained in the special supervision unit (SSU). Despite initial barriers to access, the researchers interviewed women prisoners in the legal visits area, or following release from custody. They also interviewed family members, friends and legal representatives.

In late November 2004, the Criminal Justice Inspection Northern Ireland (CJINI) and the Prisons Inspectorate conducted an unannounced inspection of Ash House, publishing their findings the following year (HMCIP/CJINI, 2005). The Inspectorates lamented that 'virtually none' of the recommendations from 2002 had been adopted. The report criticized the inappropriate and 'poorly implemented decision' to move women from the purpose-built centre within Mourne House to a 'much less suitable facility' at Hydebank Wood (HMCIP/CJINI, 2005, foreword).

In Ash House, the Inspectorate found improved staff-prisoner relations noting that most staff and managers 'genuinely wanted to do a good job'. They identified, however, serious concerns about safety, 'principally in relation to the management of vulnerable and damaged women and girls; and about the extent to which Ash House can provide a suitable environment for women'. The 'most acute' problem concerned the management of 'extremely damaged, and sometimes disruptive, young women and girls'. Inspectors found two prisoners, one of whom was a child, held in 'anti-suicide suits' in 'unfurnished and cold cells'. Without appropriate training and 'anxious, by any means available, to prevent another self-inflicted death', guards and managers administered 'very severe' punishments, 'including for children' (p.5).

There was 'not enough for the women to do' (p.6) and boredom was 'likely to compound feelings of depression and anxiety'. The 'underlying and fundamental issues' raised by the previous inspection, and central to the Northern Ireland Human Rights Commission's research findings, remained unaddressed: 'no Northern Ireland Prison Service strategy, policies or procedures to deal with the specific needs of women and girls; and no separate, properly trained, management of the women's prison' (p.6).

The inspection noted that many women felt unsafe, reporting that they had been 'subject to victimisation by other prisoners and staff' (p.10). Its conclusions on safety were severe:

> Procedures for managing suicidal or self-harming women were inadequate, and sometimes unacceptable, and may have increased risk. Prisoners could be disciplined for self-harming; adjudications were unsatisfactory and punishments excessive.

The catalogue of concerns included inadequate help and support prior to and during arrival; poor treatment in reception; no formal first night procedures, little information and no induction programme; victimization by other prisoners and staff; no gender-specific anti-bullying strategy; serious deficiencies in meeting the needs of women and girls, especially regarding histories of sexual abuse; inadequate monitoring and recording procedures for those at risk of self-harm or suicide; no

Listeners' scheme or effective, skilled therapeutic support; lack of clarity of purpose for the use of the segregation unit; unacceptably cold cells in the segregation unit; over-use of severe punishments; disproportionate security including 'full-body' searches following visits; no child protection arrangements.

The Inspectorates published 96 recommendations, reiterating those central to the 2002 Mourne House inspection, particularly the construction of a 'policy and strategic plan for the treatment of women in custody in Northern Ireland based on a full assessment of their specific needs' (p.59). The Prison Service was advised to 'urgently' draw on 'expertise from other jurisdictions' to develop care strategies for women at risk of self-harm and suicide. Second, provision was necessary for women to ensure 'more opportunities for freedom of movement in less restrictive conditions than on a shared site'. Third, girls 'under 18 should not be held in Ash House'. Finally, a Governor with 'sole responsibility for women prisoners' should be appointed. The Prison Service responded to each of the 96 recommendations, claiming that all but two had been met or were in hand.

Also in November 2004 Alvaro Gil-Robles, Commissioner for Human Rights for the Council of Europe, visited Hydebank Wood. His subsequent report (Gil-Robles, 2005) specifically identified the problems for women and young prisoners with mental health problems. While noting the dedication of prison guards working under 'extremely trying circumstances', Gil-Robles concluded that there was 'no possibility for the women to receive appropriate treatment, indeed, the conditions were likely to aggravate their fragile condition still further'. He specified two key issues – the lack of appropriate psychological care available within the prison and the precarious mental health of some women, suggesting they should not be in prison (para. 126). Alongside the Gil-Robles Report, the Committee on the Prevention of Torture (CPT) described 'unacceptable conditions' for women in Hydebank Wood including 'a lack of gender-sensitive facilities, policies, guarding and medical aid, with male guards alleged to constitute 80% of guarding staff and incidents of inappropriate threats and incidents affecting female detainees' (CPT, 2004).

Following the Inspectorates' concern regarding poor resettlement arrangements and reintegration planning, the Prison Service published an internal report based on interviews with 25 women, concerning the 'reintegration needs' of women prisoners. Long-term prisoners 'voiced discomfort at being housed with those serving short sentences' and the in-house researchers concluded that this 'had an adverse psychological impact' (NIPS, 2005, p.14). They noted that 'long-termers experienced little progression through their regime according to the stage of their sentence reached, or flexibility to move'. Conditions were 'fairly secure' with '[l]ong evenings spent alone' in cells limiting interaction thus possibly exacerbating 'psychological problems' (p.21). Of those interviewed, 60 per cent were mothers and 'felt keenly the impact of being separated from their children'.

> A sense of loss, grief and anger is experienced through being imprisoned. Mothers in custody undoubtedly struggle with the separation, and some mothers interviewed were not allowed access to their children either through a court order or by a decision made by the father of their child. It seemed to us much harder for those women with children to cope with their prison sentence. (p.16)

Eighty-eight per cent of women prisoners reported having suffered depression and 76 per cent had experienced bereavement. Sixty per cent were on medication and 68 per cent had been referred for psychiatric assessment. The researchers noted that 'vulnerable young women are often sent to prison despite behavioural problems, personality disorders and mental health problems' (p.20). The report noted that women had provided examples of 'outstanding support in Hydebank Wood'- specifically some 'individual prison officers', the assistant chaplain, the officer in charge of the gardens and the 'gym staff'. A 'good range of activities' was offered but the timetabling 'mitigates against effective delivery'.

Women were 'genuinely fearful of their release' from prison (p.34): 44 per cent did not feel safe in their communities prior to imprisonment and an additional 12 per cent who had previously felt safe in their communities considered it unsafe to return. The researchers concluded that 'addressing the needs of women prisoners in Northern Ireland will always require a delicate balancing act between meeting each and every individual need and the resources for such a small population' (p.36). Recommendations included the separation of long- and short-termers 'wherever possible'; a more flexible regime for long-termers and lifers 'wherever practicable' and a lower security environment with fewer restrictions on movement.

In 2005 the Human Rights Commission supported a Judicial Review taken by Karen Carson, a long-term woman prisoner, concerning conditions in Ash House. She challenged the lack of in-cell sanitation, routine strip searching regime and alleged harassment by male young offenders. Lord Justice Girvan found the policy of random strip searching constituted a breach of human rights law as it failed to 'recognise individual considerations of whether it [a search] is necessary' (para. 26). The Prison Service, he stated, must provide compelling reasons that searches are 'necessary and carried out in a proportionate way and as a proportionate reaction to the relevant mischief' and 'having failed to have proper and explicit regard to the relevant convention rights the current policy of strip searching at Hydebank cannot be demonstrated to be proportionate and necessary' (para. 27). The Prison Service committed to review the policy and practice of strip searching. At the time of the judgement, strip searching had been reduced from every prisoner following every visit, to a random one in five visits, eventually reduced to a random one in ten visits.

Researching the 'prison within'

In December 2004 a new Director General of the Prison Service was appointed. In November 2005 access was negotiated for the Human Rights Commission to carry out research into the human rights of women in Hydebank Wood, following up the Mourne House research. All prison guards and managers, professionals and clergy working with women prisoners were invited to participate. Women prisoners were also invited to be interviewed or join focus groups. Most were keen to be interviewed, including a significant group of immigration detainees. Interviews with prisoners, prison guards and managers, professionals and volunteers took place over four months alongside intensive day-to-day observation of the regime in operation.

At the time of the research, Ash House had a certified capacity of 56 in single cell occupancy. Only three cells had in-cell sanitation, these being for the accommodation of mothers and babies or women with disabilities. Hydebank Wood's houses are on three levels with cell landings on the first and second level. Access to Ash House was via a covered outer area through a barred gate into a spacious ground floor open area housing reception and medical consultation rooms, a classroom, offices and staff toilets. The hub, or 'bubble' as it was known, was located within the central spine giving visibility through windows on each landing from the console control panel. Access to the landings was via the staircase either side of the bubble. Each landing had a barred access gate opening into a spacious area giving access to shared toilets and showers, the entrance to the accommodation corridor, a pay telephone for prisoners' use and a door to the recreation area. Prison guards, two on each landing during unlock, sat at a desk in the entrance area. To be admitted to the landing, visitors stood at the barred gate and shouted to the guards. The accommodation corridor had cells either side and during lock-up was sealed by a further barred gate.

The four landings were used for different purposes and, in theory, operated distinct regimes related to prisoners' assessed needs and classification. The mix of women included those on long-term and life sentences; short sentences; remand; those imprisoned for fine default and immigration detainees. On the first floor, the A1 landing was divided between a Special Supervision Unit (SSU – known as the punishment block) housing women 'undergoing cellular confinement' and a 'vulnerable prisoners unit' (NIPS communication, February 2007). The latter included 'special observation cells' with 'safer type cell furniture'. Those on punishment or 'cellular confinement' had no association and those in the SSU were permitted association in a large, spartan recreation room. A2 was designated a more settled landing accommodating primarily sentenced prisoners on the 'enhanced' regime. It also accommodated some prisoners on the 'standard' regime. A3 was the committal landing on which new arrivals and very short-term admissions were accommodated and A4 accommodated medium and long-termers on the 'enhanced' regime. The A2 and A4 recreation rooms were better equipped than A1 and A3 and had recently introduced sofas. From the outset Ash House was severely limited in adequately providing for the range and complexity of women and young women prisoners. Prison managers made difficult decisions regarding prisoners' allocation and, given the classification system and restrictions on space, the mix of prisoners on landings was often inappropriate.

At the time of the research, management of women prisoners was the operational responsibility of a woman Governor directly responsible to the overall Hydebank Wood Governor. She was recruited from within the Northern Ireland Prison Service and given five days training 'specific to working with females and visited female establishments in England to assist with her development' (NIPS communication, February 2007). Following the Inspectorates' critical report, another woman Governor from England was seconded to assume responsibility 'for the management of women prisoners' and to supervise and mentor a local female Governor who eventually would assume full responsibility for woman prisoners. Staff transferred to Ash House were a mix of those 'widely skilled' and those with 'no experience of working with women'. The Inspectors noted that, following the transfer of women to Hydebank Wood, limited training comprised of a one-day introductory training session on 'understanding and working with women in custody', recommending that more in-depth training was needed (HMCIP, 2005, p.21).

The manager responsible for training agreed that the first priority would be development of a programme ensuring that guards interacted effectively with other staff and with prisoners. The second priority would be to initiate training specific to working with women prisoners. He stated: 'interaction between staff and prisoners must be encouraged and many staff recognise they need help, support and development of their skills'. A senior manager commented that there is a 'struggle to adjust and there's always dinosaurs, always some who are not suited ... in an ideal situation there would be proper selection of staff'.

In most interviews with managers and guards it was acknowledged that, due to the surplus of prison guards following the closure of Long Kesh/Maze, there had been no recruitment of discipline guards. Clearly this was an issue, especially for those guards whose 'mindset' remained locked into regimes that had evolved during the Conflict in response to politically-affiliated prisoners. A Prison Officers' Association (POA) representative commented:

> What we have been through no-one should suffer. These people [guards] are doing a good job despite all they've been through. I had the right to come to work free from fear of intimidation. We did not have the aftercare and there's still a big element of need for support now.

When a senior manager questioned why there was so little interaction between guards and prisoners: 'I always got the same answer – because they're not used to dealing with prisoners but with paramilitaries'. Although many guards more recently had worked with 'ordinary' prisoners, the Conflict invariably was raised in interviews as an issue of lasting significance. A typical response by a manager was: 'You were asking prison officers whose experience was confrontation and personal danger to suddenly switch to working with ordinary prisoners ... and women at that!' Reflecting on the development of prisons since the 1998 Good Friday/Belfast Agreement and the release of politically motivated prisoners, a POA representative stated: 'Anybody who stayed should be prepared for change'. However, it was clear from the research observations that many guards had not made that transition.

Women prisoners' first experience of Hydebank Wood was a journey from court to prison inside a cramped locked cubicle within a white van. Prison managers stated that women shared transport with male prisoners only in exceptional circumstances and on those rare occasions male prisoners were prevented from verbal abuse. Women's accounts, however, contested this official line. Typical responses were:

> They have women and men together in the horsebox. They lock the door sometimes. You have no physical contact with the men but we should have a separate horsebox just for us women. A lot of boys scream abuse at the women going to court.

> The drive to Hydebank is a nightmare. I noticed they had loaded three men onto the prison van...what I had to listen to from those male prisoners was disgusting...I heard one of them asking why the women went to Hydebank now and another prisoner replied, 'Because the screws were riding them in Maghaberry'. They started to laugh and tried to shout in to me but I refused to answer and chose to ignore them. They were saying things like, 'I'll give you one' and 'I'll lick your cunt'. I was terrified.

> They shouted 'smelly pussy'; 'suck my cock'; 'what do you do for relief?'...When we got to court I said to the court guy, 'That was disgraceful'. They say they don't know who it was so they didn't know who to charge. Any strength I had for the court was gone at that stage. You're dreading the bus journey as much as court.

Women reported persistent harassment from young male prisoners and, occasionally, young men received verbal abuse from young women.

> After the Christmas carol service the abuse from the boy's house was appalling...No one attempted to stop them. [They shouted] 'show us your tits'. It was emotional coming out of the service, we didn't need that.

> We had fellas shouting 'get your tits out for the boys'. They know some of the girls who tell them the names. Shout 'me and yous going to party tonight' or 'we're high as kites over here'. A lot of sexual talk from them. But if you tell the Governor, he says it can't happen – says there is no contact with boys.

Prison Service procedure on reception was routine. Forms were completed, photographs taken and, if women arrived during health-centre hours, a nurse was seen. Several women commented that reception staff treated them with consideration.

> They were kind and just telling me that it was their job. I was put in a small room. They said it was procedure and because they were waiting for three other girls to be brought in.

> Staff in the reception were very good, very pleasant and helpful. The only issue was the strip search... They were very good in explaining why the procedure was necessary but that procedure – actually being stripped bare – your dignity and that.

The body search on reception caused significant distress to all women interviewed. Prison Service policy was to strip search prisoners also after each visit, including professional visits. It challenged the depiction of the process as a 'strip search' preferring to name it a 'full body search'. Whatever the official definition, women were required to remove all clothing, using a sheet to cover, in turn, the bottom and top half of their bodies while being closely observed. No woman was exempt from the process, including pregnant women and girls under 18. During interview an older Traveller woman, in prison for non-payment of a fine, cried continually over the degradation she had felt on removing her clothes. The following experiences were typical:

> Two female prison officers were there and they told me I was going to be strip searched. I had to go into a cubicle and was given a torn sheet. I was told to strip off naked and pass out each item of clothing to the officer for inspection. Then I was told to turn around so that the officer could make note of any piercings or tattoos on my body. I was totally humiliated. I never in all my life experienced anything so invading. I was distraught and quite tearful.

> I didn't like the stripping, the way I had to show my body. They were checking me every way. They were counting the spots and they were touching me when they checked. They had an argument about my binding. They put their fingers in my hair. They were feeling if it was mine. I was only wearing a G-string. I asked why they had to do all this. They said they were only doing their job: 'It is the law'. I felt very much humiliated. I was vulnerable and scared.

> When you're on your menstrual cycle you still have to strip. It's very degrading. You have to show them the pants and pad with the blood on it. It's disgusting, you're embarrassed. Their attitude is indifferent. It's their job but it's not a nice thing to do.

> They don't allow us to call it a strip search. They call it a 'full search'. They're standing pondering over your body. Yeuch!... I asked for a wee brown bag to put the sanitary towel in, they asked me to hand it [the s.t.] to them. They make you burl round once so they can look at you. It's downgrading.

Once through reception women were taken to the committals landing. They were not given any written information on the regime or
what to expect. A senior manager stated that the Prison Service was in
the process of developing an induction programme for women. Those
who arrived during lock-up had minimal interaction with staff and were
immediately locked in their cells.

> I was taken to my cell on A3 at 4pm and told we would get unlocked
> in an hour. The cell door was closed and that was it... I sat down
> and looked around the filthy cell and broke down in tears. I felt
> so lonely and devastated, I didn't know when I could ring my fam-
> ily or any routine of the prison. It wasn't until I got out at 5.15pm
> when I met the other women then they told me everything I needed
> to know.

> It was terrible because they wouldn't let me see my parents after I had
> been sentenced and I wasn't expecting to get sentenced and then
> when I got here everybody was locked up and I was just put in the
> cell... It was the afternoon lock-up. It was about 20 past 4... he just
> told me that I would get unlocked again at a quarter past 5... I just
> cried... I just didn't know what was going on because you know the
> other girls were shouting at each other through the cells and I was
> just sitting there I just didn't know what was happening. It was like
> being stuck in the middle of a forest with no one with you... I knew
> I was in Hydebank Prison but I didn't know where that was.

Lack of in-cell sanitation was a serious concern. During periods of
lock-down, toilet access was controlled by an electronic unlock system.
Women pressed a buzzer in their cells registering their request for a toilet
unlock on a panel in the guards' control room. Guards then activated
the system to unlock the cell door. On each landing only one woman
was allowed out of her cell at any one time. Interviews confirmed the
distress caused:

> One night I was dying to go to the toilet for one hour and then
> pushed the emergency button. I was put on report [for discipline]
> and they told me never to push again unless I was dying... I haven't
> used the pot since I was out of nappies and I'm sure not going to use
> one now.

> One night I waited for over an hour. I hit the emergency buzzer and
> two officers came flying down. I said 'Thank goodness, I'm dying to

go to the toilet'. They said, 'Don't push the emergency button unless you're dying'. And you get some officers who tell you to 'Fuck off' and use your potty.

Some officers make our life hell. If you press the buzzer to go to the toilet if that officer is in the bubble who has taken a dislike to you they won't let you out.

I just find it degrading, every time I want to go to the toilet they know. Every time I want to use the toilet they know how long I'm on the toilet. I actually had a member of staff come to me on the 3's and ask me why I was using the toilet so often when I had problems with my stomach and she shouted out in front of the whole landing did I have an infection or anything? Was something wrong with me, did I have an infection, which really embarrassed me. And I couldn't even see her, all I could hear was her voice.

This incident was recounted by another prisoner who overheard the altercation from behind her cell door:

[Name] was picked on because someone asked her the other night, 'Why are you running to the toilet so much?' She said 'because I have a bad bladder and I can't wait'. Like, if you have to go to the toilet you have to go. They shouldn't be questioning how many times you go.

Following the Inspectorates' negative comments on lack of in-cell sanitation the Prison Service finally relented. The boys were decanted from another house, Beech, which had in-cell sanitation, and women moved into Beech while their house, Ash, was refurbished:

Thankfully now we have moved to Beech House and we have in-cell sanitation which is a relief and the cells are much cleaner because the cells in Ash were disgusting.

The building [Beech] is a lot better than Ash. We've got more dignity back because of the toilets.

Despite 'modesty screens' in front of the cell toilets, some women felt vulnerable because of male guards' observations during lock-up.

The officers can see your leg and it's mostly men checking on them at night. I time going to the toilet for when staff won't be checking.

In Ash House, and also in Beech, the daily routine began with unlock at 8 a.m. until 12–30 p.m. Lock-up followed over lunch, 12–30 to 2 p.m., and a second unlock 2 p.m. until 4 p.m. Final unlock was 5–30 until 7–30 p.m. All women were locked up from 7–30 p.m. through to 8 a.m. the following day. The maximum out-of-cell time, therefore, was approximately eight hours but, as had been the case in Mourne House, this was regularly reduced. There was considerable disquiet voiced by all women interviewed that periods of unlock were reduced each day by early lock-up. It was also evident from observing the regime in operation over several months that the majority of women had little to occupy their time. The most disturbing manifestation was on A1 where those women considered most vulnerable or 'at risk' were held. Its association room was bleak and poorly furnished. A few women passed the time, mostly in silence at a table, sitting on hard chairs and smoking. Occasionally they watched television or had brief conversations with guards. There was no structured programme of therapeutic activity. This dull passage of time was replicated on A3, the committals landing. Women in prison for a few days for fine default sat, seemingly lost, in the company of others who had been on the landing for significantly longer periods. The atmosphere was one of resignation to time wasted. It was a malaise shared across all landings:

> The worst thing in here is the monotony, there's very little for us to do. Education is rarely available to us and at that it's very basic. It's hard to cope especially when you were used to a busy life, for it to become the opposite and you end up doing nothing all day long.

> You're just being fed, lying down, locked up and that's it. I did self-assertiveness and anger management at the women's drop-in. There should be more opportunities here.

Senior managers were adamant that guards rejected the 'old days' of Mourne House, when they sat in the 'bubble' and rarely spoke to prisoners. With a few notable exceptions, the research observations contradicted this claim. Women agreed that the quality of their daily experience depended on the guards on duty:

> Some very little [number of] staff will come and ask how you are. 95 per cent won't.

> Most staff are very good. I don't have a problem with staff but some prisoners think they own the place. They call the place 'their wing'.

Well there's some staff just look at you, really treat you like a prisoner, you know...Some of them would just look down their noses
at you as if you're a bit of dirt. Like one of the prison officers
turned around and said [to another prisoner] 'I've cleaned better off
my shoe.'

I've been in jail for all my [adult] life, and this is the only time they've
treated me like dirt...They treat me like a child, like I'm a wee child,
like I'll be good.

Many women felt strongly that, should they clash with a guard or a
particular guard take a dislike to them, the threat of being 'zeroed' and
returned to the 'basic' regime was ever-present.

It's always their word against yours and they're always right. Whenever one officer is on I know I'll get marked down. They don't even
have to tell you why they mark you down.

The staff seemed to close in on me this time. Just being told to do this
and do that. Certain members of staff targeted me. I was told I had
an attitude problem but I'm not going to let strangers tell me what
I'm going to do. If you put in a complaint against a member of staff
then that's you – you're targeted all the time.

An exchange between three women in a focus group illustrated their
collective resentment of treatment by guards:

A. We're afraid to do anything because it's so strict here.
B. There's different rules for different people.
A. I had to get my medication increased because it's doing my
   head in.
C. They don't believe you when you tell them that an officer cursed
   at you. Staff get a buzz out of charging. They say. 'Go ahead. Put in
   a complaint. I've had 21 complaints made against me and I haven't
   lost one yet.
B. I've never heard of a complaint being upheld. People don't put
   complaints in because they [guards] make it obvious they won't lose
   and you'll be dragged down.

A long-term prisoner illustrated how 'rules' were invented to reflect the
immediate needs or moods of guards:

Your confidence is broke all the time. Like you know when you get up in the morning some of the girls will say to you, 'Who's on?' And when you tell them it's, 'Oh no'. Because you know that you can't talk to them or they're going to shout at you for the slightest wee thing.

Guards' discretion was raised in the Education staff focus group:

At times there's a certain lack of humanity [shown by guards] working with the prisoners. Some officers would want them to be kept quiet with minimum exertion. And they don't exert themselves.

Sometimes staff will bend over backwards because they want to do best by the women.

But women frequently and regularly complain to us about their treatment.

Yeh. You get the jobsworth type of officer. Sometimes, because we are there that antagonises them.

Prison chaplains from the main Christian denominations visited Hydebank Wood daily. Their support was acknowledged by the women:

[Chaplain] will give you a big hug. [Another chaplain] comes every morning. You can talk to her about everything. At Christmas they brought presents for everyone. So did the Protestant minister.

Women's access to education was limited by the operation of the regime. Teachers and women complained of 'misunderstandings' leading to delayed arrival of women, while on the landings women were informed by guards that classes had been cancelled. Even on functioning days, class time was lost because women were compelled to wait for escorts between Ash House and the education centre-the reason being that in a male institution it was considered inappropriate for women to move between buildings unescorted.

Teachers agreed that despite the serious limitations on education in Mourne House, they regretted the loss of a women's focus in the Hydebank Wood education centre. Women prisoners' opportunities were inhibited by the shared education building, restrictions on space and the imposition of security measures to guard against women's contact with young male prisoners. This militated against the relaxed atmosphere that teachers considered crucial to successful classes and their engagement with students. They commented that the more vulnerable women were 'scared' to attend classes because they were not confident entering what they perceived to be young men's territory.

Women welcomed the contribution of non-statutory agencies to education and other associated programmes:

> Like I've got a certificate in self esteem, you know. It's learning about yourself, learning to say 'no'. Learning to stand up for yourself in a nice, mannerly way, you know what I mean. She's [the teacher] very, very good.

> [Youth worker] is really, really good and I probably trust her most.

> [NGO worker] and [Youth worker] are brilliant. If it wasn't for these staff in this prison we wouldn't have like the right confidence... I trust them very much and I'm just so relieved that we have them.

Physical education [PE] took place in the 'male part' of the Young Offenders' Centre although women went to classes separately. The PE manager was keen to develop facilities and activities for women:

> I would like my legacy here to be a brand new facility before I go... I know women well but it's a different environment in prison and there are mental health needs.

PE was popular but the most vulnerable women and immigration detainees lacked confidence to walk across the campus to access the facilities, fearing abuse from the male Houses.

Women's visits were held in a large visits room shared with the young men. In the early days at Ash, women were strip searched prior to each personal or professional visit. Following the successful Judicial Review discussed above, strip searching was reduced to random 'one in ten' intrusions. Yet, the possibility of a 'random' strip continued to intimidate women, affecting the atmosphere of the visit:

> It's all power – 'We [prison guards] have the power to do this and we will do it if we feel like it.' I think that's what its all about – to show their power.

Women were conscious of the presence of young men in the visits room and felt self-conscious, especially if their case was well known and had received media coverage. Mothers were concerned about the potential impact on their children of sharing space with male 'young offenders':

> [I]t's us and all the lads all in one room. The alarm's been pulled on the visits maybe three or four times since I've been in, and it's my mother like. It's the first jail she's ever been in and it's quite shocking for her you know 'cos lads would be more prone to fighting and arguing in the visits. So I think if women had separate visits it would be a bit easier.

One pay telephone was located on each landing, operated through an expensive PIN card system. Women submitted phone numbers which were then entered on their phone cards. The busy landings and long periods of lock up led to difficulties gaining telephone access, creating problems in retaining contact with families.

In most women's prisons 'enhanced' prisoners have unsupervised access to prison grounds. The shared site at Hydebank Wood, however, placed severe inhibitions on women:

> Nobody's pretending that it's ideal – it's not ideal at all. There is male offenders in our midst out and about in the grounds, although you know we don't really have much dealings with them – very, very few. But in saying that [Governor] is making the very best of a bad situation.

> Even walking to the house, to the education or even to the gardens it's not very far but you have to be escorted at all times. I know they have to do that because of the lads but it's not very…it's like the women are just all thrown in to this wee corner of this YOC cause there is nowhere else for them.

Women wanted increased access to the grounds:

> Yeah, I'd love to walk around the grounds, even if it was only half an hour or an hour.

> I haven't been offered any fresh air…I would definitely take a walk. I love walking…If I'd the opportunity I'd be out doing a bit of gardening.

A woman on the 'enhanced' regime worked in the administration block and for several months was permitted to walk across from Ash House.

Then it was took off me. They said it was because I could go behind one of the trees with one of the boys. They said it was for my protection. The boys were still able to walk about. Why give it me and then take it off me? It's because I'm a woman I'm not able to walk across. They keep saying 'It's one prison. We can't give you things if we don't give it to the boys'. But it doesn't work the other way round. Personally I think it's sexual discrimination. You're being punished because you're a girl.

The negative impact of the shared site went beyond restricted access to the grounds. Women were also subjected to increased security:

Even if the wee lads are kicking off in Elm [a male YOC house] they lock us up. It takes about 30 of the staff to deal with it. You should see them running.

We're getting punished because the wee boys had a fight and one hit the other with a snooker cue.

Professional workers agreed that the shared site created problems and that in an 'ideal world' women would not be incarcerated within a male prison:

In the first couple of weeks I was here a woman was put in the obs [observation] room in the hospital. If the hospital was in a woman's prison she could wander freely. That can't happen here.

For someone on a long sentence how do you assess risk? By giving them trust and decisions. Here you can't do that. How can you assess the risk of home leave if you can't assess prisoners in the grounds?

Women in prison within a prison will never function fully.

During the research, there was a marked increase in immigration detainees arriving at Hydebank Wood, including women from South Africa, Nigeria, Brazil and China. They had different and complex personal histories yet they shared similar experiences of arrest, police custody and prison transport. Most considered their incarceration a violation of their human rights. Some had recently expired visas and others had been visiting the United Kingdom on holiday or living in England for several years with established family and social connections. As part of the United Kingdom, they had been unaware that there might be problems visiting Northern Ireland. None had received appropriate immigration advice at the airport, the place of arrest or in police custody, although some had been offered duty solicitors: 'They [police officers] were ticking boxes about me without explaining what it meant'. Some women considered immigration officers' attitudes hostile and racist. Strip searches on reception to prison added further upset:

> You have to take off everything and be checked. It was not good. I was very sad. Never in my life would I have thought I would be in prison.

> I was so embarrassed to take off all my clothes. I was choked and embarrassed to be searched. It was just so bad. I have been upset and depressed.

Being locked in cells for long periods felt oppressive:

> We are always being locked in. You cannot even think straight. You keep meditating. The final lock in is seven [pm] until the following day but you can't sleep.

> I am not sleeping: lock-up, lock-up, lock-up. Not all the time but sometimes. I have blood pressure.

Contact with families, friends and legal advisers was difficult and the cost of international phone calls prohibitive:

> The meter is very fast. More than a public phone. Money runs down before you even talk.

Although some detainees spoke little or no English, the Prison Service provided no regime information in languages other than English. Detainees stated that some guards were friendly and helped with information and phone calls:

> Some of them treat us like humans.

> Wardens are good but the system is not good.

Other guards were 'intimidating', unhelpful and 'racist':

> The attitude is racist without saying anything. They talk to us as if we are babies.

> I get the impression it's because we're Black. Even if you say 'Good Morning' she [a guard] replies in a way like it's a trouble.

Detainees found the food difficult to tolerate and there was a lack of appropriate products for Black women's skin and hair:

> The tuck shop list has nothing that a Black person can use. No Vaseline, no shampoo for Black hair or products for skin, no hair food. The toothpaste doesn't clean my mouth. They haven't prepared staff at all about immigration.

A young Chinese woman's experience was particularly bleak. Speaking no English, she had been incarcerated for six weeks, had received no visitors and was lonely and depressed. No arrangements had been made for her to access reading material, magazines or books. Through contact with the Chinese Welfare Association, one of the researchers arranged reading material and visits from local Mandarin speakers. Similarly, it was only through the initiative of another prisoner, who had access to a computer, that details of the prison regime were translated into Portuguese and reproduced for the Brazilian detainees.

Although Ash House was situated within a Young Offenders Centre, there was no age-appropriate regime for girls and young women. Girls as young as 15 years could be held in Prison Service custody (more recently this has ceased and is discussed in Chapter 9). Girl children were also subjected to strip searches on reception. There was no age-appropriate information available about the regime, nor was there an appropriate strategy for helping children to settle on their first night in custody. Several 'young offenders' commented that staff treated them more harshly than older women. A typical comment was:

> Staff seem to close in on you this time. Treating us like shite. When they say jump you're supposed to jump. I don't let my parents tell me what to do so I'm not letting them!

Older women agreed:

> They mess about with the young women. They wind them up over wearing vesty tops or over visits. A wee girl ended up in lock up for wearing a vesty top which she'd borrowed from me.

> They pick on [name] because she's a wee girl. She's not a bad kid, but they wind her up.

If assessed as being in the child's best interests, Prison Service policy allowed babies to stay with their mothers until nine months. At the time of the research there was one baby in prison with his mother. She had been in prison from early pregnancy and prior to this had suffered the tragic death of an older child. Arriving in prison, eight weeks pregnant, the strip search was 'very degrading'. Two days later she was placed on the 'enhanced regime' to accommodate her pregnancy. She stated that other prisoners were 'very nice', but her early days in custody were filled with misery:

> I was grieving bad. I had to grieve on my own. The jail did not help me whatsoever. Because they think I smile but you can put a brave face on. There was many nights I just wanted to kill myself. And that's the truth. But I couldn't tell them ones that because you'd be put down in the block.

Were you afraid of that?

> Aye because the block's not a nice place to be and I didn't want cameras watching me all the time. Because I was pregnant I just had to be strong for the pregnancy. There's many a night I just wanted to bang the doors and scream. Because when you're locked up on your own you do a lot of thinking. There's no-one there to talk to or help you. A member of staff, I says: 'I need to speak to someone'. He says, 'What's wrong?' I says 'I'm not coping very well thinking of my wee boy'. And he sort of laughed at me. And I says, 'What do you find bloody funny?'

Her pregnancy provided a positive focus:

> To be honest like, if I hadn't 've been pregnant ... I probably would've killed myself in jail because I probably couldn't've coped, because I was in a bad way at the very start.

Following the birth of her baby in hospital she was returned to prison. The birth had intensified her feelings of bereavement:

> You know it brought it all back to me and it's just a terrible, terrible feeling, you know. My heart is broke in two and it's never re-healed.

When 'really depressed and down' she had seen a psychiatrist, was diagnosed as suffering from post-natal depression and prescribed antidepressants. Her upbringing in a children's home following her mother's death and her recent history of bereavement were considered key contributors to her depression. As punishment for a failed drug test, a decision later revoked, her television was removed from her cell. It coincided with the first anniversary of her son's death.

> You know, the day of my son's anniversary it was breaking my heart and they took my TV off... You know I could have done myself [committed suicide] then or couldn't have coped. But they didn't seem to care.

Other women on the 'enhanced landing' had received parenting classes from a non-governmental organization (NGO) worker prior to the baby's arrival. Inevitably, having a mother and baby on a landing: had a complex impact. A crying baby kept some women awake and, for some, it was a poignant reminder of their children at home.

Mothers interviewed in a focus group spoke of their sense of loss at being separated from their children.

> I'm a mother and I can't get to see my children because they live too far away. It wouldn't be fair on them. But it drives you mad sometimes when you're in your cell so much and all you do is think and think. You have conversations with yourself. I get worked up sometimes after phone calls to home but then when you're in your cell you get paranoid and upset and you feel useless, especially when you've no control over things in your life. I lost so much when I came in here.

> The first real lesson of being in prison was not to see your daughters for five weeks and then to see them [daughters and husband] expecting one and a half hours on a Sunday and then to be cut short to 45 minutes, 'your time is up'. But I'd been 'enhanced' from the Monday before the visit. They said 'it doesn't state that here'. When I got back on the landing they said it took two weeks for that to go through. Everybody was devastated. My husband tried to say it was alright because he didn't want to make it difficult for me. There were so many personal things I wanted the girls to do for me that I'd left to the end of the visit and suddenly I was away. They just told me I'd have to go and I was completely shocked. Then I knew what being in prison really meant.

A mother whose children had been taken into care said 'You've no-one to talk to'. She intended to keep to myself until I get out and then let it out. The Court said I was like a bomb waiting to explode. I've never been to prison so much as when they took my kids into care. They've ruined my life.

Another mother commented:

Social services came down and told me I would never see my kids again. Said I was a danger to my kids... [I] used shoe laces, attached them to bars on the window... They [social services] say they don't have resources to do supervised visits... They won't give me the telephone number to talk to the children... I'm feeling suicidal about it. It's hard. Knowing the kids need me keeps me alive... If I hadn't kids I'd have been dead weeks ago.

The threat of losing contact with their children was used as a threat by some guards against mothers to gain compliance.

Dealing with women with serious mental health difficulties, who self-harmed or were suicidal, was a major issue in the prison. In late April 2004 the Prison Service introduced the Prisoner at Risk (PAR1) booklet and procedure. The process was initiated when a prisoner was identified as being at risk. A PAR1 booklet was opened and the Residential Unit Manager met the prisoner, checked her records and decided how to proceed in consultation with healthcare staff. Should the prisoner remain on the residential landing, a management plan was initiated. A multidisciplinary case conference (PAR meeting) decided on a personal care plan, helped by residential (discipline) guards and other agencies. Further case reviews were held when considered necessary. Healthcare centre staff were notified in an emergency, particularly following actual self-harm, active suicide risk or possible mental illness. A PAR1 was closed when the prisoner 'appears to be coping satisfactorily' and a multidisciplinary conference was held involving direct or consultative input from the prisoner.

The head of health care, reflecting a view shared by all managers interviewed, stated that many women suffered 'complex behavioural problems' which could 'not be dealt with adequately in prison'. As a prison psychologist stated, 'we deal with those women who have been let down and failed by services in the community where facilities are dire'. She believed the 'damning thing for more vulnerable women is that they have more care, more stability, more interest in them in prison than in the community'.

There were also problems in responding to the needs of women diagnosed 'personality' or 'behaviour' disordered. Legislation reinforced the distinction between mental illness – 'services open' – and personality disorder – 'services restricted'.

Medical provision for women had evolved but female healthcare staff were not available daily. Healthcare professionals agreed that the only model for appropriate health care was a discrete women's facility with fully trained, designated staff on duty day and night. At the time of the research the full staff complement for the male Young Offenders' Centre and Ash House was four registered mental health nurses (RMNs), four state registered nurses (SRNs) and five healthcare officers (prison guards with six-months Home Office training). The head of health care stated that, while staff were committed to good healthcare provision, staffing levels fell considerably short of initial plans and were inadequate to meet prisoners' needs. It was not possible for the healthcare centre to function autonomously because prison regulations and agreements with the Prison Officers' Association had set clearly defined boundaries to working practices.

Women with drug and alcohol dependencies, often a combination of both, arrived at the prison in poor physical health and in highly disturbed, emotional states. They required specialized, coherent and customized medical care sensitive to their social as well as psychological and physiological circumstances. Yet, provision was arbitrary and inadequate. A woman admitted with a known drug dependency stated that on arrival there 'was no prescription waiting for me and they wouldn't give me the prescription I came in with'. She did not see a doctor immediately and had 'a really bad first night, it was a nightmare, I was hot and cold and started withdrawing'. Her main concern was the lack of specialist drug and alcohol training for doctors, nurses and the psychiatrist within the prison. They also lacked communication with doctors and other health providers who previously had treated women in the community. The policy was 'as soon as women come in they want them off drugs and there needs to be some sort of a substitute to help with withdrawals'. Without an out-of-hours general practitioner service women admitted to prison after the prison surgery had closed were refused prescriptions. They were left to withdraw overnight, sometimes for longer periods.

The committal landing, accommodating new arrivals, fine defaulters and others who had received short sentences, denied any possibility of a settled and therapeutic regime for those entering prison distressed and vulnerable. A comment from a remand prisoner provides evidence of the inappropriate environment:

I tried to strangle myself and they brought me to the 1s [Special Support Unit and Segregation Unit]. I still get days like that. My moods are all over the place. I felt as if the staff were against me. They put me into a camera cell and made me wear a canvas dress and took everything off me. The things don't fit you, they're not tight on you. I just felt embarrassed. You need staff who understand and they know what you are talking about. I've started to open up. Some seem genuine.

Other remand prisoners described their confinement to punishment cells during periods of acute mental distress:

First time I tried to hang myself. They took me down the [punishment] block. Took off my underwear and put me in a gown. One blanket. The girl in the cell beside me knew there was something wrong with me, she heard me crying in my cell, putting the shoe laces up. I heard her shouting and jumped off the heater. The door got kicked in...A couple of officers ran up, one male one female. Girls were shouting 'Is she all right?' Staff told them to 'shut up and mind your own business'.

The punishment block is awful – you're not allowed magazines. Just four walls. They forget things – there's a lot you could do [to hurt yourself] in the punishment block. They made me strip in the punishment cell... They put me in a blue dress, mattress, blue pillow, one wee thin blanket. It was freezing. I didn't sleep.

They threw her into a cell and locked the door. She was cracking up, we all were. She banged the door. The ninjas [guards in riot dress] came up. This girl was no bigger than me. Being in a cell with a camera. There's no privacy or nothing. Your whole dignity's taken away from you. The staff sit and watch you get into your stuff [clothes]. But what if a male staff is looking in the camera?

The pain of living in a volatile atmosphere was well illustrated by a settled, sentenced prisoner describing another woman's attempt to hang herself:

We knew something was wrong, she was making funny noises and I pressed the panic button. [Prison guards shouted] 'It's only mad Wilma [not her real name]'; 'She could have at least set it up properly'. They C and R'd [Control and Restraint] at her and put her down the block. You're behind the door and don't know what to do.

I wanted her to be treated with respect. She needed help. It only took a few seconds to treat her as a person, not a piece of scum. A week later she set herself on fire – she was on a PAR1. I asked why she didn't have a suicide suit on. We had to live with the smell. I couldn't stop crying for days and I was moved. I have lost about five friends and it brought it all back. It was the feeling that they didn't want to help her. Even when I didn't want to cry the tears kept coming.

During the research, operation of the A1 regime for vulnerable prisoners was closely observed and up to four repeat interviews were held with women prisoners. As stated previously, within the bare recreation room the floors, walls, furniture and facilities were basic, the antithesis of a warm, therapeutic space. The women sat on hard chairs at canteen-style tables smoking roll-ups. Other than the television there was a marked absence of social engagement or any activities to occupy time constructively. The women had occasional interaction with one of the two guards at the desk on the landing between the recreation room and the cell corridor. Conversation was minimal.

The tension of having the punishment unit located on the same landing as the SSU was raised by women prisoners on another landing. A young woman who had been on A1 for what she termed 'bad' behaviour stated, 'people for punishment shouldn't be put in A1 with vulnerable people'. A professional worker confirmed that A1 was used 'as punishment . . . a punishment wing'. Another woman reflected on her experience:

They punished me for cutting myself. I'm still hearing the voices and I'm not on the right medication. When I'm unlocked I'm doing nothing at all, just sitting here smoking. The nurse comes and gives me tablets but I'm not getting the right medical help in here. The doctor says he can't help me.

The contradictions and tensions between treatment and punishment, between care and coercion, are well illustrated in the following account:

All of us women are vulnerable, we're all vulnerable. Three weeks I was on the 1s [A1] and it did my head in. I was there for punishment and it did my head in. Sometimes I go in [for counselling] but how do we know if she's talking to staff?

Where's the care in healthcare? If I'm feeling down they say there's always someone available and there isn't. If we display a problem they up [increase] the medication. If you start questioning anything or you say you have a problem they up the medication. They've made me dependant on antidepressants and it's not self-sustaining when I leave.

Women suffering mental ill-health and depression expressed fear of isolation on A1 and in the healthcare centre. Their shared concerns were illustrated by a remand prisoner's experience:

They put me in the observation cell from Friday to the Monday. I'd gone through a great loss. I was just out [of her cell] for the shower, no interaction, nobody asking to speak with me. I'm shit scared of going back to the hospital. There's nothing. So I say I'm fine. There's no therapeutic help, nothing.

A woman interviewed in the healthcare centre had been admitted to prison following a period in hospital recovering from serious injuries. Her persistent pain was apparent. She recalled the impact on her life of her partner's death. Having been in hospital in the community, the sudden transition to the prison healthcare centre had been emotionally shattering.

It depends who's on as to how much time you have out of your cell. It's terrible how long you're locked up in your cell. You get breakfast at 8 and you're back in your cell at 8–15. You have supper and medication at 7 and that's lock up until 8 the next morning. You get 10 or 15 minutes association if you're lucky.

The implications were clear. The women who most needed personal support, therapeutic interaction and constructive activity were intimidated and frightened by A1 and the healthcare centre, the two places in the prison designated to respond to mental health needs. As a Hydebank Wood psychologist commented:

Reduced lock up would ease tensions. It's often the quiet of night when there's less activity. People are more reflective and introspective and vulnerability becomes magnified. Yet there's limited access to support. Within the constraints of the prison, therapeutic work is limited.

The researchers observed several Prisoner at Risk (PAR) meetings. A woman held on A1 had a PAR1 open and guards noted her depressed state following the Christmas period and sustained periods of lock-up. Brenda was emphatic that she was driven to self-harm, complaining there was no constructive activity available to deflect her negative thoughts and anxiety. Although permitted to keep her cigarette lighter, she handed it to guards as a precaution against self-harm. Her cognitive behaviour therapy (CBT) sessions had rekindled distressing memories and she had been advised that to move on she would need to face these earlier life experiences and events. She had watched a television programme on self-harm and this had left her deeply upset. She had placed a ligature around her neck, seemingly torn from her gown.

Brenda was encouraged to return to normal association and to become involved in activities. It was considered vital, particularly by the psychologist, that she should have more freedom and be encouraged rather than compelled to have greater interaction with prisoners and guards. While association and a return to work, possibly in the gardens, were desired objectives she needed to feel safe and confident that her mental state was being managed appropriately.

Soon after the PAR meeting had ended it was clear to the guards that Brenda was in danger of taking her own life. She stated openly that she felt unsafe, a threat to herself, and wanted all temptation and opportunity removed. The senior guard decided that the PAR meeting should be reconvened that afternoon, after Brenda had been to her CBT session. It was concluded that increased medication had contributed to her 'dips'. She was assessed as 'impulsive' and at risk of suicide.

Those at the reconvened meeting agreed that the risk to life was significant and imminent. The meeting focused on putting her in an anti-suicide gown and removing her jewellery. A guard stated, '[s]he's crying out for help and she says she'd feel better in the hospital – couple of days in the hospital'. Yet the healthcare centre was shared with young male prisoners, resulting in challenges of 'having both sexes in healthcare at the same time'. A young male prisoner with a history of violence against women, who had threatened a female guard, was being held in the healthcare centre and it 'would not be a good time' to transfer Brenda.

Brenda was then invited into the meeting. She was profoundly distressed, visibly frightened and knew she was at risk of taking her own life. She stated her priority was to be transferred to the healthcare centre for 'just for a couple of days' to be alone. Regardless of male prisoners, she considered it would give her necessary respite.

The psychologist stated that her view should be paramount. It was suggested by guards that while she could be taken to the healthcare centre, 'she'll be behind the door and she should know that'. Brenda was told that, for her protection and not as punishment, she would have to wear the canvas dress. Visibly upset she declined 'because it doesn't fit me'. The nurse was unequivocal and Brenda was admitted wearing the gown and without her jewellery. It was agreed that a further PAR meeting would review her situation the following afternoon.

The researchers visited Brenda in the healthcare centre the following morning. She was unlocked and mopping the floor outside the bare observation cell in which she had been held. Two women guards from Ash House had supervised her exchanging her clothes for the canvas gown. It had been agreed by the Duty Governor that, should she wish for a cigarette during the night, she could knock the cell door for an orderly to provide a light. She had knocked on several occasions throughout the night until her hands hurt. No-one had come. She had no sleep as the young male prisoner, held in the next cell, had played music until late. The bed was hard and uncomfortable. By morning she was desperate to return to A1.

Brenda was told that she had to remain locked in the healthcare centre observation cell wearing the canvas gown until the PAR meeting was reconvened. She had no contact with healthcare centre staff, no activities and no counselling. As she wanted to return to A1, its Principal Officer contacted the healthcare centre to arrange for a guard to collect her. This was refused until after the PAR meeting. This sequence of events revealed profound contradictions in the administration of the Prisoner at Risk policy. While members of staff appeared to be concerned about Brenda's emotional state and personal wishes, the PAR meeting was reactive, confined by stark, intransigent procedures rather than proactively constructing a regime and conditions responsive to her needs. Her threat to take her own life was perceived as real but no strategies were adopted – counselling, therapy or activity – to address the problems underpinning her vulnerability. The formal response was the isolation and desolation of a bare observation cell, dressed in an ill-fitting gown and lying on a hard mattress. Whatever the intention, Brenda was committed to a punitive regime in an inhospitable location where guards were unsympathetic and less-than-appropriately qualified. Overall, the professional practice associated with the PAR process was inadequate and exposed a vulnerable woman to greater risk and long-term damage.

The head of healthcare emphasized the centre's commitment to ensuring a therapeutic environment, particularly for women diagnosed

as personality disordered. Attempts to establish therapeutic initiatives, she stated, were hindered by inadequate staffing and insufficient
resources. A specialized residential unit was under consideration, she
claimed, based on an assumption that 'everybody would buy into
it...commit to it and understand it'.

> It would involve all disciplines, be multidisciplinary...it was about
> treating everybody who came onto the landing as equal, including
> discipline staff. It would be hierarchical in terms of security – but we
> would take away the primary emphasis on security.

A joint initiative, 'Therapeutic Disorders and Therapeutic Accommodation' (Wright and Smyth, 2005), was intended to provide a residential
unit accommodating a maximum of six women. Targeted primarily
at prisoners defined 'vulnerable', 'personality disordered', 'disruptive'
or 'dangerous', it would offer personalized care plans and engagement in therapeutic work. Prisoners' participation would be voluntary.
Proposed activities included: occupational therapy; life skills; therapy
(group, individual, CBT, art, music); education (essential skills and recreational); work; physical activity (indoor and outdoor). Staff would also
be appointed through voluntary application and the unit's 'culture' and
'management' would be secured through 'extensive training' followed
by 'support and supervision'. The intended ethos would generate a 'climate of mutual, therapeutic and social understanding and respect...self
help' promoted by 'group meetings involving staff and prisoners'.
The proposal noted that collective responsibility and decision-making
'involves all staff and users of the unit equally where issues such as
new admissions, rule infractions and discharges are being considered'.
Regarding expectations:

> It would be anticipated that users form appropriate attach-
> ments/relationships with one another and staff. This enables the
> development of a supportive community spirit. By doing so users get
> to emotionally experience a sense of belonging, which is usually what
> has gone wrong in their earlier life experiences.

In setting 'boundaries' for acceptable behaviour within the unit the
proposal shifted the emphasis considerably from established custom
and practice. First it would 'have its own agreed rules'. Second,
'behavioural issues' would 'be addressed through group meetings',
where 'inappropriate behaviour or attitudes of staff or users could be

challenged' in a supportive environment. Third, it invoked a 'culture of enquiry' within which 'neither staff nor users' would be 'immune from their behaviour being challenged'. It was clear, however, that many guards would find their authority undermined by prisoners' challenges.

Following the previous inspection, there had been limited development of resettlement services in Hydebank Wood. The Probation Board had a permanent office within the prison grounds and an NGO, the Northern Ireland Association for the Care and Resettlement of Offenders (NIACRO), had a staff member dedicated solely to working with women prisoners on resettlement. Yet, internal and external deficits remained, including inadequate sentence planning, lack of opportunities for work and employment training and limited appropriate housing on release. Within Hydebank Wood, gardening was the main work experience offered to women prisoners. The gardens were a constant hive of activity. Other work and training opportunities included computing and cookery classes in the education block and working as orderlies in the residential area and laundry. In contrast to young male prisoners, women could not train in the prison kitchens to gain qualifications towards a career in catering, nor could they to train in woodwork and building-related trades.

Lengthy periods on remand created additional difficulties in preparing women prisoners for their return to the community:

I've been on remand for 5 months and I'm in court for my hearing on Thursday so I should be sentenced maybe within six weeks depending on the courts so I won't know until then ... until it really happens at the minute there's nothing. I'm in limbo. I'm just waiting.

There is no resettlement help for prisoners on remand. It is so difficult for girls when they go out because they've had all responsibility taken from them. I'm dreading getting out of here – my strength is just ripped from me. Your integrity is destroyed.

Longer-term prisoners commented on their lack of parity with male prisoners:

Like the men in their last three years [at Maghaberry] are moved over to Martin House ... they don't get locked till 11pm, they have their own room key and they're allowed to make their own meals. Why can they not do something like that for women?

Women prisoners, prison guards and professional workers confirmed the necessity for more effective mental health services for women leaving prison. A healthcare professional stated:

> We know we have got them to a certain stage, and then it's lost when they go out again.... mental health teams need to accept responsibility for prisoners going back to their areas. Child and adolescent mental health is just not there. We have fought on this for years.

Reform priorities generated by the Commission's research were predicated on creating 'viable alternatives to custody' alongside new legislation 'to ensure that prison is a last resort for women'. Further key recommendations included: an end to imprisonment for fine defaulting; the development of a strategic plan and guidelines for policy and practice for women prisoners; the construction of a 'self-contained and separately managed women's custody unit' at Hydebank Wood offering 'site access, discrete healthcare and visiting facilities, kitchens and laundry, education, employment and gymnasium' (Scraton and Moore, 2007, p.128).

9
The Pain of Confinement and Decarceration

Introduction

The focus of the preceding empirical chapters has been qualitative research, case studies and documentary analysis. In this final chapter, recent inspection, monitoring and external reports are considered, their findings and recommendations explored to evaluate progress in the period since completion of the primary research. This is followed by analysis of two recent and, at the time of writing, unresolved cases that raise profound questions about the Northern Ireland Prison Service's commitment to change. In each case the human rights of women prisoners were violated, and the treatment to which they were subjected suggests serious failure regarding the Prison Service's duty of care. They also return the analysis to theoretical and political debate concerning the limits to prisoners' agency and the consequences of prisoners' resistance. Reflecting on the key findings of the empirical research and these recent cases, the human rights implications of the disclosures within this book are considered. The potential and limitations of human rights law as protection for women, and as a catalyst for change, are also discussed. The chapter considers the potential of legislative, policy and operational reform to ensure compliance with international human rights standards.

More broadly the chapter critiques the contradictions inherent within human rights principles regarding imprisonment, identifying the limitations of a human rights framework for initiating change. It considers the significance of transitional justice discourse, noting the marginalization of 'ordinary' prisoners from the transition process in Northern Ireland. Finally, the chapter discusses the limitations of penal reformism, the potential for development community-based initiatives and the case for abolition as an antidote to the continuing global expansion of women's incarceration.

Persistent deficiencies and the barriers to reform

Publication of the in-depth research reports, in 2005 (Mourne House) and 2007 (Hydebank Wood), had an unprecedented impact in Northern Ireland. Exposure of the unacceptable conditions under which women prisoners were held, the problems they faced incarcerated in a male environment, the lack of policies, programmes and appropriate staff training and the marginalization of women's physical and emotional needs were headline news. The *Belfast Telegraph* elevated the revelations to its front page under the banner headline 'PRISON SHAME'. Newspaper editorials were written and television documentaries commissioned noting that, despite the transfer of women prisoners from Mourne House to Hydebank Wood, the fundamental deficiencies of holding women in a male jail and the failure to comprehend and address needs and requirements specific to women amounted to a profound failure in the State's duty of care and an egregious breach of international human rights standards. BBC Radio Ulster broadcast a two-hour investigation, involving the researchers, in which it attempted to hold to account the managers of all the official and non-statutory agencies involved.

The realization that, according to successive inquest juries, the abject failure of the Northern Ireland Prison Service, its management and staff, had contributed significantly to the deaths of two vulnerable women for whom they had a duty of care, had a defining impact on public understanding. While much of the wider debate on the politics of imprisonment in the North focused on the development of separate regimes for the relatively small numbers of politically-affiliated prisoners held in Maghaberry, persistent revelations regarding the plight of ordinary prisoners demonstrated that the prisons in which they were held were not fit for purpose.

As the debate unfolded it became clear that the British Government, at the time still holding responsibility for policing and justice, rejected the evidence placed before it and adopted the Northern Ireland Prison Service's position of refuting its critics through denying responsibility. The Secretary of State's responses to the Coroner's concerns (detailed in Chapter 7) following the devastating indictment of prison policy, management and treatment by the jury in the Annie Kelly case was a classic manifestation of what Stan Cohen (1993) considers to be the State's strategy combining techniques of denial and techniques of neutralization to deny the culpability of its agencies. In a climate of continuing public controversy surrounding the criminal justice and policing deficit and generating severe inhibitions on transition to peace from conflict in the North, further inspections, reviews and reports were conducted and published. The researchers contributed, formally and informally, to these developments.

The cumulative and central element of this more recent body of work is that the profound deficiencies in the incarceration of women exposed by the primary research and its case studies have persisted. As the second research report was published the Inspectorates conducted an announced inspection of Ash House. Hesitatingly, its report noted a *'generally* safe environment' but reiterated its unreserved criticism of accommodating the women's unit within a male Young Offender Centre (CJINI, 2008, emphasis added). It recognized that, while the 'efforts' of some prison guards to 'mitigate the inappropriate location' were 'commendable', the 'inadequacies of the current arrangement remain all too apparent'. It reiterated the recommendation for a 'separate and dedicated women's facility, without which the needs of this vulnerable population are unlikely ever to be properly met' (CJINI, 2008, p.5). This overarching principle was a clear endorsement of the research findings, demonstrating that any gains that might have been made by transferring women prisoners to what was on paper a lower security environment had been lost to the imposition of a high level of security necessary when housing women in a male jail. As stated previously, it was a prison within a prison.

While the Inspectorates continued to criticize lack of appropriate accommodation and care for women prisoners, the Northern Ireland Prison Service persisted in claiming that progress was being made. In fact, modest regime changes with the potential to improve women's daily lives were advanced. The Prison Service (NIPS, 2010a, p.12) noted a series of reforms: the production of a 'first night' DVD; 'less intrusive' search procedures; an extended visits scheme; gender-specific staff training; 'limited unescorted movement' for women within the Hydebank Wood site; the implementation of a new 'Supporting Prisoners at Risk' process. A commitment was made not to hold girls below the age of 18 in the adult women's prison and this was included in the Criminal Justice Order (Northern Ireland) 2008. Since 2009, no girl children have been detained in Ash House. However, no age-appropriate regime for young adults has been developed.

Influenced by Baroness Corston's (2007, p.5) recommendation that strip searching should 'be reduced to the absolute minimum compatible with security', Prison Service policy was revised, requiring the removal of underwear only when 'intelligence or other information' indicates 'reasonable suspicion' of concealment (NIPS, 2010b, p.19). In practice, searches conducted without 'reasonable suspicion' compel women to remove clothing and sanitary towels while retaining their underclothes. Ostensibly to prevent concealment of objects which could be used for self-harm, the procedure for searching self-harming and/or mentally ill women, allows managerial discretion in implementing full body searches (NIPS, 2010b, p.102).

According to the Prison Service, 'the new, less intrusive procedures provided the women with a greater degree of dignity and respect, and were less distressing for those more vulnerable women committed to custody' (NIPS, 2010b, p.101). Women prisoners' evidence to a Prison Service review, however, while accepting that strip searching based on sound and reliable intelligence might be required for safety and security, recorded their continued humiliation in practice. Prisoners' responses contrasted with reassurances given by the Prison Service: 'I was full body searched 6 times during an inter-prison visit. If I am escorted and supervised all the time then why do I need to be searched 6 times?'; 'We were stripped completely naked'; 'I had to part my buttocks'; 'some staff make embarrassing comments' (NIPS, 2010b, p.34).

A self-contained unit for long-term prisoners, 'Ash 5', was opened and according to the Independent Monitoring Board (IMB) its 'benefits...include increased personal responsibility, improved recreational facilities and additional unlocks' (IMB, 2011, p.25). However, negotiations over staffing between the Prison Officers Association (POA) and management resulted in A5's under-utilization. An extended visits facility, enabling imprisoned mothers to have full-day visits with their children in a self-contained mobile unit, has been a further progressive development. Following a satisfactory risk assessment, visits take place without staff supervision and mothers can prepare meals for their children.

Consistent with the research recommendations, responsibility for primary health care in prisons was transferred from the Prison Service to the Department of Health, Social Services and Public Safety. Initial evaluation suggests 'some progress, but also gaps and weaknesses' (PRT, 2011b, p.40). In a thematic review (CJINI, 2010a, p.viii), the Chief Inspector of Criminal Justice observed that

Northern Ireland's prisons hold a number of people with mental health problems who arguably should not be there. Imprisoning them is not always the best response to their offending; it frequently does them no good and risks further harming their mental health, making them more likely to re-offend.

The inspection found a deficit in psychological and psychiatric services throughout the criminal justice system. Probation staff noted the difficulties accessing appropriate accommodation for women with mental health problems. Yet, the inspection found some progress in development of options for the care of women suffering mental ill-health including: improvement of the initial screening process; development of a 'model of care'; consideration of 'other therapeutic interventions'; improved policies and procedures to inform clinical decisions (CJINI, 2010a, p.42).

In 2011 on average 45 women were imprisoned in Hydebank Wood. Typically, 18 were on remand, 25 sentenced and two detained for fine default (NIPS, 2011, pp.97–98). The overall number of women imprisoned in Northern Ireland doubled between 2001 and 2009 (DOJ, 2010b, p.10). The 2011 inspection (CJINI, 2011a) identified some improvement but noted that many of its previous recommendations had been ignored. Control and restraint was used less frequently and the segregation unit had been discontinued. While relationships with staff were 'reasonably good' (CJINI, 2011a, p.v), it criticized the high number of male prison guards working in the women's unit. It considered that the transfer of responsibility for health care to the local health Trust had failed to improve provision, was under-resourced and 'poorly managed'. The needs of women with mental health issues remained a 'particular concern' and the mix of children, young male adults and women in the health centre were significant and unacceptable obstacles to appropriate care provision (CJINI, 2011a, p.v). Inspectors considered that the women's prison had become a safer environment, an ironic observation given the cases of Frances McKeown and Marian Price discussed later in this chapter.

The inspectors reported that women had limited possibilities for exercise, were locked in their cells for long periods and experienced inadequate education, training and work opportunities. Women were still transported to and from court with male prisoners and endured verbal abuse. A reduction in strip searching was noted, but inspectors expressed concern about an incident in which male officers had participated in the strip search of a woman while under restraint (p.4). The site remained 'too restricted', Ash House was 'far from ideal' (p.v) and the previous recommendation for a discrete women's prison unit was reiterated. Some improvement in resettlement provision was acknowledged, but a thematic inspection of resettlement services found that women's needs were a 'bolt-on' to those of young men (manager in Hydebank Wood cited in CJINI, 2011b, p.37). Nine years on from the Prison Inspectorate's scathing report into conditions at Mourne House its key criticisms remained unresolved.

In its 2011 report, the Independent Monitoring Board (IMB) also welcomed changes it considered 'commendable', stating that women prisoners had reported positively regarding 'increasing levels of interaction' with prison staff (IMB, 2011, p.20). Yet, consistent with the Inspectorates, the IMB identified persistent problems. The complex mix of prisoners – adult women, young male adult prisoners (aged 18–23 years) and boy children (aged 15–17) – continued to present 'significant challenges in managing and responding appropriately to the distinct and different needs of this diverse population' (IMB, 2011, p.15). Because of 'fundamental flaws in the shared site at Hydebank Wood', it was 'very difficult to sufficiently focus on the distinct and varied needs of young men, boys and women' (p.9). The IMB stated that poor industrial relations between the prison management and the POA continued to have a deleterious impact including excessive lock-ups and the 'general slowing down of all prisoner-related activity'. It noted 'examples of staff interaction with prisoners which were disrespectful and based on cynicism' (p.8) with guards often using their discretion in ways that had 'negative rather than positive consequences for prisoners' (p.9). There remained a 'tendency for staff to sit at their work stations, at times reading newspapers, or talking to other staff colleagues' and there were 'instances when some staff members behave in a manner which is perceived to be provocative or demeaning' (p.26). Again, such observations from the only independent body with regular access to the jail echoed a decade of previous criticism.

The IMB also concluded that prison guards' resistance remained a fundamental obstacle to reform:

> There are staff who are currently responding positively to the challenge of change; other staff are finding the potential of their changing role a difficult prospect but acknowledge the place of change; another group of staff appear to resist change, at times directly and indirectly appearing obstructive to new initiatives. (p.8)

Work had developed to create physical separation between the women's unit and the Young Offenders' Centre, including the development of gardens, an exercise yard and an education unit within Ash House. Although well intentioned, however, these initiatives were 'square pegging round holes' (p.20). A business case for establishing a discrete women's unit had stalled due to the devolution of policing and justice to the Northern Ireland Assembly. For a fifth consecutive year, the IMB recommended the development of a 'stand-alone, purpose built women's prison' (p.20).

The legacy of the Conflict and its impact on the prison system in Northern Ireland was recognized by the Criminal Justice Inspection (NI) in its review of corporate governance, noting the gulf between Prison Service intentions and the ability of management to deliver: 'a consequence of the past has been the development of a culture, behaviours and working practices that are difficult to change' (CJINI, 2010b, p.v). A 'transformation' was required, incorporating 'changes in values, behaviours and working practices' (p.vi). The Prison Service had developed policies, but 'the difficulties lie in their delivery' (p.x). An example cited demonstrates the impact on women: 'the Governor wanted to move a mother and baby into a larger disabled cell within the Women's Prison but the POA [Prison Officers' Association] objected because the woman was a remand prisoner and the area in which the cell was located was for sentenced prisoners' (p.45).

As explored in Chapter 4, prison guards' culture was shaped by the Northern Ireland Conflict. It reflected a 'static' workforce, with no appointments since 1994, resulting in an assertive yet complacent attitude of, 'this is how we do things around here' (p.39). While operational support staff had been recruited to ensure greater diversity, they were schooled in the traditional methods when they worked alongside experienced guards (p.40). In a despairing tone, the inspectors considered it pointless to make new recommendations as '[t]here is no argument about the "what" – it is the "how" that is crucial in moving the Prison Service from one which is security focussed to one which delivers its purpose, vision and values in an effective and efficient way' (p.xiv).

In 2012 two official policy documents were published: *Strategy for the Management of Women Offenders* (DOJ, 2010a) and *Gender Specific Standards for the Prison Service* (NIPS, 2010c). The Strategy proposed a 'structured, multi-agency approach to developing women-specific interventions designed to address their offending behaviour' (DOJ, p5). It committed the now devolved Department of Justice to a reduction in custodial disposals for women through improved statutory defences for abused women in domestic homicide cases; promotion of the use of electronic monitoring (tagging) as an alternative to custodial remand; improved information on women's circumstances for courts when considering fining women; a multi-agency focus to divert women with mental health problems from the criminal justice system. Although drawing its rationale from the Corston review, the Strategy omitted key elements with no commitment to the provision of residential accommodation for women, scant consideration of the impact of the Conflict on women in Northern Ireland and no assessment of necessary services.

The Strategy established the Inspire Women's Project (Inspire), a Probation-run service to engage with women under Probation supervision, those awaiting pre-sentence reports and a small number on day release from prison. Services are delivered through inter-agency partnerships between Probation and other agencies, including voluntary and community organizations. Inspire's aims are

> to provide a women-centred approach; to provide women offenders with a framework within which they can address their offending behaviour and complex needs; to establish a network of agencies that can provide a holistic multi-agency response for women offenders; and to enable women offenders to desist from crime and reintegrate into society.
>
> (Easton and Matthews, 2011, p.3)

Engagement with Inspire is not voluntary, and 'non-compliance' can be reported to the courts. Provision includes programmes on drug and alcohol addiction, victim awareness, individual counselling, offence-focused work, creative arts, employment and entrepreneurial skills.

Early findings show that most women on the programme had received community rather than custodial sentences (Easton and Matthews, 2011), raising doubts about its significance for decarceration. Good practice with women and practitioners, acknowledging the benefits of a women-only environment, was identified in the initial evaluation. It notes that women were

> grateful for the women-only provision and physical space; the non-judgemental attitude of their probation officers; the flexible but boundaried approach at Inspire; the opportunity for peer support; assistance provided around specific issues such as debt, housing,

attending court etc.; the links that they were making in the community and the range of meaningful activities and interventions provided.

(Easton and Matthews, 2011, p.5)

The majority of women interviewed for the evaluation considered their self-esteem and confidence had improved and their attitude to offending had changed. However, housing, mental health services and the police had not engaged effectively with the project. Women with mental health problems had difficulty achieving consistent participation, and the evaluators' recommendations included provision of greater support for women with histories of violence and abuse, and for those with addictions. Also recommended were increased employment and educational opportunities for women.

Several women had witnessed the murder of relatives or partners but, inexplicably, the evaluation failed to provide information on the context of these deaths, including whether they were Conflict related. While many women were positive about the inspire programme, some mentioned the stigma associated with Probation: 'I don't see myself as a bad person, but coming here makes me feel as if I am a bad person'. Another woman stated, 'Probation is like a stigma. Probation you get a big, black cloud hanging over you and you keep thinking to yourself that people know you're on probation' (Easton and Matthews, 2011, p.25).

The Women's Community Support Project (WCSP), an initiative involving the Probation Service, NGOs and the Prison Service, has also developed. This project links women to the services of over 50 community-based women's organizations across Northern Ireland. The WCSP staff visit Hydebank Wood offering pre-release support on housing, education, training and money management.

While alternatives to imprisonment initiatives have emerged, criminal justice practice continues to increase the quantity and severity of custodial sentences. In October 2010 Pauline Shaw became the first woman in Northern Ireland to be sentenced to an Indeterminate Custody Sentence having pleaded guilty to manslaughter based on diminished responsibility. Speaking in court about her relationship with her husband, who she had stabbed and killed, Pauline stated he had 'battered me many times. I would stand up for myself and hit him back' (para. 5, The Queen v Pauline Shaw and Colin Francis Shaw, Judgment delivered 23 September 2010). The prosecution's consultant forensic psychiatrist assessed her as having a long-standing personality disorder together with a problem with alcohol taken alongside anti-depressant medication and limited 'intellectual functioning'.

The psychiatrist concluded, 'the duration of risk cannot be determined at the point of sentencing' (para. 6, Judgment). A probation officer agreed that 'the likelihood of Mrs. Shaw reverting to past coping mechanisms and destructive relationships is high' (para. 8, Judgment). Indeterminate sentences, based on predictions of dangerousness and risk to public safety, require that the Parole Board is satisfied that a prisoner is safe to release. They have clear potential to increase the long-term incarceration of women with mental health problems. As noted by the Criminal Justice Inspection, 'mentally disordered offenders are adding to the prison population and will increasingly do so with the introduction of extended and indeterminate sentences for offences of "dangerousness"' (CJINI, 2010a, p.viii).

In February 2010, the multi-party Hillsborough Agreement initiated the devolution of policing and justice to the Northern Ireland Assembly. The Agreement also triggered a review of prison conditions, specifically the extent to which women's imprisonment complied with international human rights standards. An independent Prison Review Team (PRT) was headed by Dame Anne Owers, former Chief Inspector of Prisons for England and Wales. It reported in February and October 2011 (PRT, 2011a and PRT, 2011b). Consistent with the research on which this book is based, the PRT concluded the prison system in Northern Ireland had been shaped by experiences of violence and conflict, resulting in an inherent resistance to change. The system was dominated by a 'culture of denial and compromise' (PRT, 2011b, p.6). A change strategy was recommended to include early retirement for prison guards and the recruitment of new staff to establish a balanced workforce in terms of religion, gender and age.

The PRT criticized unacceptably high levels of women's imprisonment for fine default, describing the practice as 'criminalizing poverty' (p.68), and the excessive use of custodial remand. It recommended a strategy of alternatives to custody emphasizing community interventions and the replacement of Ash House with a 'new small prison for the small number of women requiring custody'. This would be 'built, staffed and run around a therapeutic model', supported by an 'acute mental health facility' and drawing on a 'network of staff, services and support in the community' (PRT, 2011b, p.70). In December 2012 the Minister of Justice announced the appointment of an oversight team to monitor progress towards implementation of the PRT's recommendations.

Committed to the construction of a new women's unit by 2018, the Director General of the Prison Service stated:

> What we are proposing to do for women is very different from any-thing that we have ever done before...We have a blank sheet of paper for women offenders and will design something that genuinely meets their needs. What we know is that only a very small number of women need to be in a traditional, prison-type environment, and we have said that.
>
> (*Hansard*, 21 March 2013)

The Director General accepted there had been institutional failure to deliver change. She stated that, although 'we have not been prepared to be radical up to now', a 'once-in-a-lifetime opportunity' had arrived to 'build something from scratch that meets our needs'. These public statements were a tacit acceptance by the Prison Service and the Justice Ministry that for over a decade since the initial research findings were presented – and resisted – women prisoners had been, and continue to be, held in conditions that failed to identify and meet their needs. Equally, the findings and recommendations of official reviews and formal inspections had been denied. There was neither explanation nor apology forthcoming from the Director or the Ministry for egregious and multiple breaches of women prisoners' rights. All women currently in prison, and those sentenced between 2013 and 2018, will endure a further five years of chronic malaise. Two recent cases demonstrate the continuing dire circumstances of women's incarceration in Northern Ireland.

Breaking spirits

The research presented in earlier chapters recounts and analyses the unique circumstances of a prison estate and its associated regimes failing at all levels to make the transition from prioritizing the incarceration of politically-affiliated prisoners to accommodating the complex needs of ordinary prisoners. Two recent cases, one the holding without trial of a political woman prisoner, the other the death in custody of a deeply distressed young woman, demonstrate the profound and disturbing relationship between punishment on the body and the breaking of the self. Despite significant differences in their legal, political and social circumstances, each case demonstrates the pain of confinement, its associated damage and failure of the authorities to acknowledge or effectively address the deficiencies and rights abuses revealed in earlier chapters as endemic within the system. These cases are a troubling extension of the debilitation endured by those women whose testimonies are recounted earlier and an indictment of the so-called reform agenda promised by a Prison Service and criminal justice system trapped in the past, unfit for purpose and resistant to institutional change.

Prominent Irish Republican, Marian Price, has been imprisoned without trial since her detention in May 2011. In 1973 she was given a life sentence for her part in an IRA bombing campaign in London. During their imprisonment in England she, and her sister, Dolours, repeatedly went on hunger strikes in a sustained campaign to gain repatriation to Ireland. They were force fed on more than 400 occasions, a brutal process which led to serious and persistent health problems. Marian described the violence of force-feeding:

> Four male prison officers tie you into the chair so tightly with sheets you can't struggle ... You clench your teeth to try to keep your mouth closed but they push a metal spring device around your jaw to prise it open. They force a wooden clamp with a hole in the middle into your mouth. Then, they insert a big rubber tube down that. They hold your head back. You can't move. They throw whatever they like into the food mixer – orange juice, soup, or cartons of cream if they want to beef up the calories. They take jugs of this gruel from the food mixer and pour it into a funnel attached to the tube. The force-feeding takes 15 minutes but it feels like forever. You're in control of nothing. You're terrified the food will go down the wrong way and you won't be able to let them know because you can't speak or move. You're frightened you'll choke to death.
>
> (Breen, 2004)

As noted previously, the sisters were transferred to Armagh Prison in 1974. In 1980 Marian was released under a Royal Prerogative of Mercy, a form of pardon, due to life-threatening ill-health including anorexia and tuberculosis.

In 2011 at a dissident Republican commemoration Marian, without disguise, held the Real IRA's Easter message read by a masked man. The event was filmed and broadcast worldwide and she was charged with encouraging support for an illegal organization. The judge granted bail, but the Northern Ireland Secretary of State intervened, revoked her licence and returned her to prison. Her lawyers submitted that her 1980 release had been through Royal Pardon and the Secretary of State had no legal power to detain her on licence. The Secretary of State responded that a copy of the Royal Pardon did not exist, having been lost or shredded. In July 2011 Marian was also charged with providing property for the purposes of terrorism. It was alleged that she had purchased a mobile phone used by another party in connection with the killing of two British soldiers in March 2009. She denied the charge. In May 2012, a judge dismissed the Easter commemoration charges but they were later reinstated. Maria's lawyers have stated that her treatment by the Prison Service, including her long detention in solitary confinement, has left her too ill to stand trial.

The context and conditions of Marian's detention illustrate the legacy of the Conflict within the prison system. During a visit to Hydebank Wood by the authors, Marian affirmed her status as a political detainee with a right to separation from 'ordinary' prisoners. She was imprisoned over a year in the high-security male environment of Maghaberry Prison. Her conditions of detention had a significant, negative impact on Marian's mental and physical health. Transferred to Hydebank Wood in February 2012, she was held in an adapted cell within the healthcare centre in conditions of total isolation. Suffering from arthritis, she slept on a dirty, hard mattress exacerbating her weak physical condition. She was disturbed continually by loudspeaker announcements directed towards young men in the Young Offenders' Centre.

In Spring 2012 Marian was visited by two United Nations-appointed doctors who reported to the Minister for Justice. Under Prison Service detention, she was transferred to a hospital in the community, guarded round-the-clock and handcuffed for appointments. The UN Special Rapporteur on Torture, Mr Juan Mendez, stated that solitary confinement beyond 15 days constituted cruel, inhuman or degrading treatment or punishment (UNHR, 18 October 2011). At the time of writing Marian Price had been detained without trial in isolation for more than two years.

On 4 May 2011, 23-year-old Frances McKeown was found hanged in her Hydebank Wood cell. From her early teens she had a well-documented history of mental ill-health, having been referred to community mental health services. Bullied at school, she later gained a diploma in child care. Her marriage ended, her mental ill-health (including post-natal depression), persisted and her two young children were taken into care. She was admitted to a mental health unit on

11 occasions where her diagnosis was 'Emotionally Unstable Personality Disorder'. The Prisoner Ombudsman's report into her death found that, in the year prior to her incarceration, Frances had 'low mood and had self-harmed on a number of occasions by taking overdoses (Paracetamol) and cutting herself; was distressed by the murder of an ex-boyfriend; and was again under the care of a community mental health team' (Prisoner Ombudsman, 2012, p.6).

In September 2010 Frances was remanded in custody and her accompanying records on admission noted she suffered from depression and anxiety: 'Attempted self-harm 6–8 weeks ago' and 'states currently feeling suicidal'. Yet the Prisoner Ombudsman found no evidence that prison committal staff had received this information (Prisoner Ombudsman, 2012, p.12). Experiencing difficulties settling in prison, Frances was referred to a non-governmental organization for crisis intervention support. The support worker recorded that Frances was 'not in a good place. Does not like being locked up' (cited in Prisoner Ombudsman, 2012, p.36). During her time in prison, Frances self-harmed and on five occasions a SPAR (Supporting Prisoners at Risk) booklet was opened. She was considered a suicide risk and was referred for a mental health assessment but this was delayed for six weeks. At her assessment Frances disclosed childhood sexual abuse and domestic violence (Prisoner Ombudsman, 2012, p.43). A request by the mental health nurse for a psychiatric referral was not realized (Prisoner Ombudsman, 2012, p.44).

Frances regularly cut herself and told guards that the pressure of witnessing other women withdrawing from drugs was 'wearing her down' (Prisoner Ombudsman, 2012, p.44). In December 2010 she stated she had overdosed on Paracetamol, was taken to hospital in the community and then returned to the prison. She participated in 'productive activities', learning crafts and working in the gardens, but lock-ups were frequent and lengthy. Coping with isolation was difficult as she felt threatened by 'voices' in her head. Problems identifying the correct prescription for her illness persisted, and, on one occasion, she was deprived of anti-psychotic or anti-depressant medication for 19 days (Prisoner Ombudsman, 2012, p.49). Due to concerns for her safety, Frances was occasionally accommodated in the observation room, a cell that she dreaded and resisted. She was forcibly transferred to the cell by guards using control and restraint (Prisoner Ombudsman, 2012, p.54). A senior guard reported that a nurse was 'very down and upset' by the treatment to which Frances had been subjected (Prisoner Ombudsman, 2012, p.12).

In March 2011, Frances wrote a letter discussing plans to take her own life. Her problems, she wrote, included: 'her childhood, family, marriage, kids and the murder of a previous boyfriend' (Prisoner Ombudsman, 2012, p.11) and additionally the pain of confinement:

> The voices in my head are getting worse and more violent, they run me down and make me so angry. It's like I'm sitting on my own but there is someone in the room with me telling me what to do and to hurt people and I have to fight it's so hard, not to try and listen to it. At night when I am in my cell it is worst because I can't distract myself from it all I can do is listen to it and the horrific things it tells me to do.

> Hell everyday of my life and if I am dead it will all be over for me and I wouldn't have to suffer anymore because I can't put up with it any longer.

> You're evil/your scum
> You deserve to be dead
> You should have been killed the day you were born
> You're a mistake
> You know I'm rite
> Stick to the plan I'll tell you when
> You're pathetic
> You know you're going to hang yourself
> You're going to kill them I'll make sure you do
> I can't do it anymore, I'm done trying, I just want to
> die and end it all.
> I can't put up with it anymore. It's too hard and too tiring.
> JUST LET ME DIE!!!'
> (cited in Prisoner Ombudsman, 2012, pp.53–54).

Frances received Cognitive Behaviour Therapy (CBT) and counselling. A CBT session in April 2011 recorded:

> Frances used humour throughout and couldn't be bothered when trying to demonstrate and talk about the thinking model. Discussed 'roadblocks' – more amenable thereafter...Some understanding of 'just because I think I'm depressed doesn't actually mean that I am'.
> (cited in Prisoner Ombudsman, 2012, p.63)

Despite ongoing concerns for her safety, Frances's first psychiatric assessment was not delivered until April, over six months after her committal and five months after a mental health nurse first prioritized a referral (Prisoner Ombudsman, 2012). At the assessment, Frances stated her intention to kill herself following her release. When asked by the Prisoner Ombudsman why Frances's assessment had been delayed, the psychiatrist replied that she had to divide her time between Maghaberry prison and Hydebank Wood (women's) prison and (male) Young Offender Centre. She stated, 'although the referral may be marked as "urgent" it is not always the case that the person needs to be urgently seen' (Prisoner Ombudsman, 2012, p.59).

On 3 May Frances began a drugs and alcohol programme. Her request for tobacco was refused as 'tuck shop' was the next day (Prisoner Ombudsman, 2012, p.68). Notes from the following day's programme recorded: 'Frances said she was feeling good and realises that she deserves to get her kids back, have a job and is proud of herself for getting off drugs and alcohol' (cited in Prisoner Ombudsman, 2012, p.70.) That evening all units in Hydebank Wood were locked-up because of the death of a young male prisoner. Frances told a fellow women prisoner, 'I can't take any more of these lock-ups' (Prisoner Ombudsman, 2012, p.70). That evening she was found dead in her cell.

The Prisoner Ombudsman identified 18 'matters of concern' relating to Frances's care in prison including: inadequate observation and recording procedures; an overlong delay prior to consideration of her case by the Safer Custody Team; inadequate response to her difficulty sleeping; failure to communicate with her doctor in the community or to obtain her hospital notes; six months delay before Frances was assessed by the psychiatrist; insufficient efforts to avoid the use of control and restraint. Her death had much in common with those of Janet Holmes, Annie Kelly and Roseanne Irvine discussed earlier.

Reflections on agency and resistance

The story of women's incarceration in Northern Ireland, from Armagh, to Maghaberry, to Hydebank Wood, has unique features arising from the context of the Conflict yet it echoes the experiences of women incarcerated in other jurisdictions. The profile of the women interviewed throughout the research was consistent with women incarcerated internationally: poor women who risked imprisonment rather than pay fines they could not afford; Traveller women and immigration detainees; women suffering mental ill-health and addictions, with histories of sexual abuse and experiences of violence; women who feared returning to communities where they would suffer stigma and, in some cases, violent punishments and exclusions by paramilitary organizations.

Conducted over an eight-year period, the research and case studies demonstrate that in prison women were, and are, subjected to conditions and practices that imposed compliance through silencing resistance. Effectively, it was a process that broke their spirits. They were locked in isolation, sometimes in degrading circumstances, strip-searched or forcibly restrained. On a daily basis, they were disciplined for minor infractions, faced hostile attitudes from guards and lengthy lock-ups. They experienced gender discrimination in every aspect of their incarceration; had minimal opportunity for productive activity, education, work or training; and had limited access to fresh air and exercise. Sharing a male jail, they felt exposed, scrutinized and vulnerable, and were constantly intimidated by verbal abuse from boys and young men. Mental health care was dangerously inadequate and lines between care and punishment were often indistinct. Women were reluctant to disclose anxiety or depression to staff – fearful of being locked in isolation, their clothes and possessions removed, and placed under surveillance, whether as punishment or 'for their own good'. In breach of their primary duty of care for vulnerable patients, health professionals participated in the assessment of women's fitness for adjudication and for transfer to isolation cells.

Despite their harsh treatment, women resisted the regime using a variety of means. They showed care and solidarity by supporting women new to prison, informally inducting them and advising on the rules. Many women stated they would not have coped had it not been for the help of other, more experienced prisoners. They maintained their dignity and courtesy against a backdrop of routine provocation. Some women kept diaries or wrote letters to friends and relatives, documenting their experiences and enabling their voices to be heard, even after death – for example, the words of Annie Kelly and Frances McKeown. A few women embarked on legal action or made formal complaints to the Prison Ombudsman challenging treatment they considered unfair. These women were labelled by some managers and guards as troublemakers.

Despite women prisoners' efforts, and attempts by a minority of staff to engage interpersonally and supportively, the power of the prison remained evident and dominant, reflecting 'overt asymmetrical power imbalances between the keepers and the kept' (Zaitzow and Thomas, 2003, p.207). Prisoners who resisted, verbally or physically, risked punishments through removal of 'privileges' or solitary confinement.

Their actions portrayed agency, but they were limited in positive impact and often at significant personal cost. Unsurprisingly, some were resigned to 'doing their time', serving their sentence, and returning to the families and children whom they greatly missed. Yet, their compliance also came at a price. Others were so devastated by their incarceration, especially those on strong prescription drugs for diagnosed mental health conditions, they had very little capacity to fight back. In its daily operation, the regime was not always content to allow women to serve their sentence, as harassment and intimidation were tactics of domination employed by a significant number of hostile guards.

Women who appeared to 'adapt' to imprisonment and navigate the regime, often represented by Governors as 'exemplary' prisoners, spoke of desperately missing loved ones, especially children, of feeling depressed and suffocated. Such adaptation was a strategy of negotiating time until release. Only the politically-affiliated prisoners used organized and collective resistance, but this was increasingly difficult as they were few and isolated. Northern Ireland, unlike other jurisdictions, had no campaigning organization specifically dedicated to the pursuit of prisoners' rights, although some NGOs included prison reform within their remit.

It was clear from the research that those in authority – managers, guards, doctors and other professionals – routinely held women personally responsible for their actions. By attributing the behaviour of prisoners to 'freedom of choice' – a form of personal agency – they deflected responsibility away from failures in their duty of care and their contributions to physical injury, emotional harm or institutional injustice. Women who self-harmed, who were in distress or suicidal were portrayed as making 'choices'. At Annie Kelly's inquest, for example, the jury was told repeatedly by prison managers, guards and those responsible for her health care that she 'chose' to create disturbances and wreck her prison cell because she wanted to be placed in 'her' isolation cell and that ripping her anti-suicide gown and making ligatures were voluntary acts. As discussed in Chapter 7, the jury refuted these claims and, emphasizing the context and circumstances in which she was incarcerated, held the prison authorities responsible for the conditions – of neglect and institutional deficiency – in which Annie died.

The contested terrain of prisoners 'agency' is well illustrated in considering the circumstances of Frances McKeown's death. In her letters and journal, Frances wrote about personal choice and planning her death: 'sometimes I even go far enough to plan a new way to end it all just to stop the pain in my thoughts' (Prisoner Ombudsman, 2012, p.65); 'My plan is not to die in a place like this but if things continue to get bad for me, then I will end up trapping myself in here' (p.67); 'I've got it planned and tonight is the night' (p.71). In Frances' final note to her husband, parents and friend, she acknowledged and accepted responsibility for her actions: 'This is nobody's fault, it is my choice to die' (p.73). On face value, it appears that Frances made a rational decision to take her own life. Yet, the social and institutional context, particularly the relations of power within which her decision and final act took place, are crucial to understanding her death. Katrina Jaworski's (2009) reflections on suicide raise the complex nature of agency and decision-making in this context. As she concludes, suicide is 'never outside power relations' (p.4) and the 'trick of power is to make the doer and the deed look like the deed belongs to the doer as the sole author of the deed' (p.2).

> What might be possible, however, is that someone may no longer literally suffer from unbearable circumstances if they are no longer breathing. This, however, does not curtail the production of truths concerning their deaths, whether true or false. (p.4)

Understanding the deaths of the four women discussed in this book, and the pain endured by so many other women interviewed, can be achieved only through analysis of the context of gendered and class-based power relationships governing women's incarceration. Within this context lie levels of responsibility and culpability. While not denying women's agency and humanity, as discussed in Chapter 2, it is essential to recognize and analyse critically the role of the prison system and its regimes in creating and reproducing the circumstances in which women suffer mental ill-health, self-harm and end their lives.

The significance of human rights protections

Northern Ireland has a reputation, not without foundation, as a socially conservative society that accepts and reproduces punitive attitudes to offending. It is notable, therefore, that the multi-party settlement embodied in the 2010 Hillsborough Agreement included provision for reviews of imprisonment, including specific reference to women's imprisonment and children's and young people's treatment within the criminal justice system. As stated previously, the experience of media and public reaction to the research on which this book is based, surprisingly demonstrated considerable empathy for women prisoners.

Assumptions of public intolerance regarding penal reform proved to be unfounded when the research was published and the harsh conditions under which women were held exposed. The research informed a necessary public debate focusing on the rights of 'ordinary' prisoners in a climate previously and understandably dominated by the rights of politically-affiliated prisoners.

Until the development of the Bangkok Rules (2010), within international human rights instruments the rights of women in prison have been marginal. Previous limited protections existed: the UN Standard Minimum Rules for the Treatment of Prisoners (Standard Minimum Rules); the European Prison Rules and the European Committee for the Prevention of Torture and Inhuman or Degrading Treatment or Punishment Standards. These protections place a duty on member states to ensure women have equality of services and equivalent opportunities to male prisoners and should be imprisoned separately from men, with appropriate and effective health care available. The primary research in Maghaberry and in Hydebank Wood reveals persistent and egregious breaches of women prisoners' rights. These included rights to private and family life, health and health care, education, freedom from inhuman and degrading treatment and the right to life. The culture of denial and impunity, a common characteristic of penal systems, had been reinforced by the special circumstances of the Northern Ireland Conflict. In this context, it became institutionally impossible for women prisoners or community campaigners to gain redress for wrongs done.

Alongside regular inspection reports, annual monitoring and formal reviews, the research established a pressing need for comprehensive reform – from sentencing through to conditions, regime, accommodation, health care and treatment inside prison. Beyond the process of incarceration itself, however, legislative reform necessarily should prioritize a strategy of decarceration that establishes appropriate alternatives to custody. This includes the end of imprisonment for fine default; the elimination of short prison sentences and provision of community alternatives based on restorative principles; alternatives to imprisonment for women with serious mental health difficulties; consideration of children's best interests when sentencing parents of young children and provision of alternatives where possible; an increase in the minimum age of criminal responsibility to address the problem of children's incarceration. These principles are appropriate not only within the Northern Ireland context, although urgently required, but also form the foundation for global initiatives of decarceration, as discussed below.

Given the small population of women incarcerated, the Bangkok Rules (2010) provide a minimum standard for regimes in which women convicted of more serious offences are held. The Rules stipulate that women should be held close to home (Rule 4); their hygiene and health needs should be appropriately met (Rules 5 and 6); their health screening should include female-specific issues including pregnancy, menstruation, reproduction, sexually transmitted diseases, addictions, histories of sexual and violent abuse (Rules 12–18). Therefore, gender and culturally specific health and mental health care should be provided. Strip-searching should be carried out only by appropriately trained female staff (Rule 19) and, whenever possible, alternatives provided (Rule 20). Pregnant women and nursing mothers should not be held in solitary confinement (Rule 22), and physical restraint should not be used during labour or childbirth (Rule 24).

Acknowledging personal histories of abuse and violence experienced by many women prisoners, the rules require provision of appropriate support (Rule 25). 'Open contact' is recommended for mothers and children (Rule 28). All staff working with women prisoners should receive gender-specific training (Rule 33). The Rules recognize that women prisoners present a lower level of risk than male prisoners, noting that high-security measures and use of isolation cells can have a 'particularly harmful' effect on women (Rule 41). Further, women suffering mental ill-health should not be subject to higher levels of security because of their condition (Rule 41). Regimes should provide a 'balanced and comprehensive' range of activities (Rule 42). In terms of resettlement, home leave and other alternatives are encouraged to help with transition from prison (Rule 45) and post-release support should be gender specific (Rule 47).

While reformist in scope and vision, and retaining a commitment to imprisonment as an appropriate and legitimate way of dealing with offending, alongside other international instruments these Rules provide minimum benchmarks for women's treatment thus constituting a means through which prisoners and campaigners can hold states to account. Changes that evolve via human rights campaigns and investigations, as this research demonstrates, offer the potential to improve daily life in prison. As Alison Hosie (2013, p.91) states, 'taking a human rights based approach can improve the working and living environment for those providing a service and those in receipt of that service'. Susan Easton (2011, p.20) also notes that 'rights instruments are increasingly being used internationally and within the UK, to do battle with the principle of less eligibility', although there are significant barriers which may prevent prisoners bringing cases to the courts, including access issues and costs. Easton acknowledges the necessity of stronger mechanisms to enforce compliance. Although critical of an abolitionist approach, which she considers unlikely to succeed in the current punitive climate, she states that 'even if the courts uphold prisoners' rights within prison, they have limited powers in restraining the expansion of prisons as they operate within sentencing parameters' (p.243).

A significant limitation within human rights principles and discourse is an assumption that it is possible to improve the conditions of imprisonment and to bring 'dignity' to the prison experience without fundamentally challenging conceptually the prison as an institution, or analysing the structural conditions which contextualize pathways into prison for millions of people on a global scale. Over a century of research, experiential accounts and prisoner resistance provides compelling evidence that the World Health Organization's commitment to 'healthy' prisons is impossible to deliver for women, young people or men. While international rights standards offer a yardstick against which progress within signatory States can be measured, as Alex Callinicos (1989, pp.31–32) states 'rights based on general standards fail to address people's specific needs', they 'reflect and do not abolish the antagonisms of capitalist society'. As the research demonstrates, these antagonisms are not limited to class but extend to patriarchy, neo-colonialism and age.

Consistent with the principles established within the Bangkok Rules, international research demonstrates the importance of adopting a gender-specific approach to women's imprisonment, without which women's experiences and needs will remain marginalized, overridden by male concerns (Bloom and Covington, 2008). The research clearly demonstrates the consequences of incarcerating women prisoners within predominantly male institutions. Not only are their needs neglected, their treatment inappropriate and their rights breached but also their dignity and humanity debilitated. The Northern Ireland Assembly has given its commitment to developing gender-specific policies and practices. While seemingly progressive, Kelly Hannah-Moffat (2001) and Shoshana Pollack (2008) caution against the potential for net-widening leading to further consolidation of the penal project and the expansion of women's incarceration.

Justice 'in transition'

Conceptually, transition 'implies a journey' (Ní Aoláin and Campbell, 2005, p.173). Northern Ireland remains at the early stages of transition and is regularly misrepresented as being a 'post-conflict' society. The 1998 Good Friday/Belfast Agreement projected policing and criminal justice reforms including 'accelerated' prisoner release. The 'prisoner question' was considered resolved through the early release of politically-affiliated prisoners but, as this research shows, subsequent events challenge this assumption. Failure to deal with institutionalized abuse in prisons has left a legacy of a highly secure and defensive system, until recently staffed entirely by guards who were trained and worked at a time when prisoners were considered the 'enemy' and where guards' lives were under threat from paramilitary organizations.

As Fionnuala Ní Aoláin and Colm Campbell (2005, p.181) observe, in many societies transitioning from conflict there is a

[p]reoccupation with and tension around dealing with the human rights violations (generally serious and systematic) committed by the previous regime. This is allied with general agreement on the need for major change in the institutions of the old state complicit in these violations.

Transition also implies a 'finishing point' to the 'journey' (p.182), the attainment of which requires acknowledgement of prior failures thus preparing for 'significant or "transformative" institutional change' (p.184). Stan Cohen (2001) details how states systemically deny human rights abuses, rejecting responsibility for inhumane treatment, including atrocities. Bill Rolston (2002, p.87) warns that states maintain the power to 'conceal human rights abuses as they occur and to protect those who perpetrate abuses in its name'. For, should the state's institutional power base remain intact, it assures sustainability beyond the 'end of open conflict'. More positively, Rolston notes the strength of communities to 'resist that concealment and protection'. Yet, while communities in the North mobilized in support of politically-affiliated prisoners, prisoners without any such political affiliation, so-called 'ordinary criminals', have not experienced community mobilization in defence of their rights.

Christine Bell and Catherine O'Rourke (2007, p.24) note that women have been marginalized in transitional justice frameworks and mechanisms. They state, '[b]oth the legal standards which transitional justice mechanisms draw on, and the processes by which they have been designed, have tended to be exclusionary of women'. This is unsurprising, they argue, given that 'waging wars and negotiating peace agreements are both predominantly male affairs' (p.25). In Northern Ireland, the exclusionary process is multi-layered. Mary Corcoran (2006, p.218) draws attention to the marginalization of all women prisoners within the transition process:

> the continuous subordination of most prison reforms and conditions to the larger concerns of the political process up to and beyond the Belfast [Good Friday] Agreement meant that the specific problems and needs of women prisoners (political or ordinary) remained as marginal to the prisoner release programme after 1998 as they had been during their imprisonment.

While attempts have been made, most notably by feminists, to include women in transition processes, others have more fundamental criticisms of the narrow parameters of the transitional justice project, based as it is on liberal-democratic conceptions of rights.

In Northern Ireland, transitional justice discourses have been utilized to underline the importance of addressing civil and political rights emphasizing institutional arrangements governing policing, the judicial system and the early release of political prisoners. These were central issues for resolution in securing a political settlement. Yet, reforms and rights protections within the criminal justice system, important though they have been, cannot alone deliver fair and just outcomes while structural inequalities and institutionalized injustices remain the fabric of the social order.

Following the political settlement established by the Good Friday/Belfast Agreement social and economic inequalities remain virtually untouched. In fact, they have worsened in a period of social welfare cutbacks. The over-representation in prison of men, women and young people from communities enduring severe social deprivation, continued violence and conflict, stands as testament to the inadequacy of a transition process locked into the political conflict. While there are few politically-affiliated women prisoners currently imprisoned in the North, women continue to go to jail primarily as a consequence of poverty, mental illness and experiences of violence and abuse. As the evidence throughout this book shows, the transitional process has not offered them justice, nor have their rights been met. As Elizabeth Stanley (2009, p.133) states, 'to be truly effective, transitional institutions have to be connected to wider programmes of social change'. In her defining analysis of Timor-Leste, Stanley argues: 'legacies of violence have intertwined with social conditions of poverty, unemployment, poor housing, limited education, and ill-health' (p.146). This applies to the North of Ireland also, where the Conflict had the greatest impact on people living in poor, working-class areas – the communities of structural disadvantage.

In his powerful study, based on primary research in post-conflict Nepal, Simon Robins (2012, p.27) finds transitional justice discourse predominantly legalistic and elitist. He proposes that neo-liberal human rights frameworks are not only inadequate but constitute a barrier to addressing structural inequalities and injustice: 'Confining transitional justice to a politics of rights under liberal political institutions in which existing power relationships are enshrined ties any process to the system that produced those power relations'. Transitional justice discourse in Northern Ireland and internationally emphasizes the importance of building and promoting a 'rule of law' entwined with a fair and equal criminal justice system and institutional respect for human rights. As explored in the opening chapter, analysis of the history of the penal system within developing democratic states reveals the idealism inherent within this goal. Transitional justice discourse has limited potential in and of itself. Its emphasis on civil and political rights agendas, combined with its neglect of the political-economic necessity of redistribution, has neither the capacity nor the legitimacy to secure the material transition necessary to move from the legacy of conflict to a just and lasting peace.

Reform, decarceration and abolition

'I do not believe, like some campaigners, that no women should ever be held in custody' (Corston, 2007, p.i). While self-professedly not an abolitionist, Baroness Corston concluded that prison is overused for women, proposing an extensive programme of alternatives and the downsizing of women's prison units. Her proposal (p.86) that 'over time' responsibility for women's custodial units should be 'removed from the Prison Service and run by specialists in working with women' is radical and has not been accepted by the Government. The case that too many women go to prison and that imprisonment should not be used for women who are mentally ill, self-harming and suicidal is well established. It extends to those serving short sentences for low-level offences. In 1990 Pat Carlen proposed that to 'reduce the prison population we must first reduce the number of prisoners; to reduce the number of prisons we must first abolish certain categories of imprisonment. Women's imprisonment is, for several reasons, a prime candidate for abolition'. In the decades following her proposal, however, women's imprisonment has increased significantly and on a global scale. Recognizing that prison systems have been 'remarkably effective' in 'neutralizing... liberal critique', David Scott and Helen Codd (2010, pp.162–163) warn that 'unless human rights principles are tied in to penal abolition rather than merely legalism, then security demands and further penal expansion are likely to win out'. They recommend a 'radical rethink of the confinement process itself' coupled with 'profound social change, rooted in a commitment to human rights and social justice' (p.163).

In penal reformism, much is made of international rights standards as foundational to the establishment of a 'fair' and 'just' prison system offering enlightened regimes. This is well illustrated in the England and Wales' Prison Inspectorate's commitment to the four principles adopted from the World Health Organization's criteria for assessing a 'healthy prison'. Prisoners should be held in conditions that ensure personal safety, are human rights compliant, offer purposeful activity and prepare them for community resettlement. In establishing its assessment methodology, the Inspectorate uses international rights standards and its model has been adapted internationally. The recent work of the independent Inspectorate has been groundbreaking in disclosing institutionalized, persistent abuses of discretionary powers in prisons in England and Wales and in Northern Ireland. Inspection recommendations, however, are not necessarily matched by a commitment to implementation. In Northern Ireland, as discussed in the previous chapters, the Inspectorates' persistent and severe criticisms have resulted in minimal policy and practice reform and, in some circumstances, conditions have worsened.

The Inspectorates, alongside regular visits of IMBs and the offices of Prison Ombudsmen, provide a valuable and significant presence in the current penal climate. They raise critical questions about individual cases and institutionalized practices that otherwise would remain hidden from external scrutiny. Yet, reliance on the adoption and implementation of human rights standards and internationally agreed criteria assumes that, through modification, conditions of incarceration in large, diverse institutions can secure and sustain prisoners' good health. While accepting the innovative and committed work of the Inspectorates, the Ombudsmen's offices and independent monitors, the concept of a 'healthy prison' is a contradiction in terms.

As Chapter 1 reveals, its rationale lies at the heart of penal reformism from John Howard and Elizabeth Fry to the present day. Howard's vision of the 'new prison' was the application of a 'just measure of pain' – that the pains of confinement would be balanced against the gains of crime. The contemporary prison system, as noted by Michel Foucault (1979, p.82), originated not in 'punishing less' but in 'punishing better'. Little has changed in the political debate and popular discourse about prisons. It is claimed that prisons 'protect' society by removing the 'dangerous', 'rehabilitate' the prisoner, 'deter' others from wayward paths and 'prevent' crime. 'Rehabilitation', 'reintegration' and 'resettlement' are the watchwords of penal reformism.

Framed posters on the corridors, wings and landings of prisons pronounce evangelical 'mission statements' alongside illustrated key words ('hope', 'motivation', 'commitment' and 'leadership'). They proclaim human rights standards, warn against bullying and extortion and offer procedures for complaints. The message to the uninitiated is that the old regimes have been replaced by institutional acceptance and understanding of a custodial duty of care. In this vision, managers and guards, doctors and nurses, psychiatrists and psychologists, and all who administer the 'healthy prison' are 'rights compliant', transparent in their dealings with prisoners and accountable through inspection and monitoring. Whatever minimal advances have been made by penal reformers the critical issue remains. Year on year in insanitary, infested Victorian prisons recommended for demolition in the 1980s, and in their high-tech, architecturally 'smart' sibling institutions managed by the State or international corporations, emotional and physical abuse, inhuman and degrading treatment are revealed as endemic. As Jude McCulloch and Phil Scraton (2009, p.11) state:

For abolitionists [contemporary] reformism, however well-intentioned, facilitates a politics of incorporation in which places of detention become 'rights-compliant', their managers and staff gain rights, management and protection diplomas and independent monitors annually report their visits and inspections... The violence of incarceration is historically, socially and culturally imprinted on the foundations of the prison. It is moderated or hidden beneath the veneer of mission statements, glossy brochures and internet virtual tours.

Thomas Mathiesen, whose early work set the contemporary agenda for penal abolitionism (Mathiesen, 1973), more recently records the 'denial' and 'negation' of the 'prison fiasco' and its spectacular failure on its own terms (Mathiesen, 1990). There are three spheres, he argues, each of which contribute to the politics of denial and the neutralization of criticism: 'the widest public sphere' and its 'whole range of modern mass media'; the 'narrower public sphere, consisting of institutions directly engaged in crime prevention such as the police, the courts, the prosecuting authorities and the prisons themselves'; the 'even narrower sphere consisting of particular professional groups' (p.139). The latter encompasses independent agencies and professionals whose work claims to underwrite, monitor and guarantee the 'best interests' of prisoners in the context of a collective duty of care within institutions funded by and accountable to wider civic society. Mathiesen concludes, however, not only has the 'fiasco' persisted but its denial has consolidated around the 'pretence' by *all* 'participants' that prisons are 'a success' (p.140).

As Mathiesen established in his earlier work, the rationale and justification for imprisonment is not simply about prisons as institutions. It requires analysis and understanding of the ideological, political and economic construction of 'crime', 'criminality' and 'criminal justice' within democratic societies. Louk Hulsman (1986) challenges traditional notions of 'crime' through which 'criminal events' have been identified and portrayed as 'exceptional'. Within such representations, 'criminal conduct' was considered 'the most important cause of these events' and 'criminals' were perceived as a 'special category of people' (p.63). This ideological construction has dominated 'public debate about the criminal justice system and its possible reform' taking for granted that the system has the potential for fundamental change and 'that the development of the criminal law is one of slowly progressing humanisation' (p.63).

Instructively, Hulsman argues that cooperation between the institutions and agencies within the criminal justice system places it outside the 'control' of the constituency (citizens) in whose name it operates; a 'particularly alarming' situation because 'the typical products of the system are the infliction of suffering and stigmatisation' (p.64). Those stigmatized do not self-identify as a 'special category of people' as 'nothing... distinguishes those criminal events intrinsically from other difficult or unpleasant situations' (p.65). Yet a 'considerable proportion of the events which would be defined as *serious crime*... remains completely outside [the criminal justice] system' (p.66, emphasis added). There exists, he concludes, 'no ontological reality' of crime.

In challenging mainstream analyses within criminology and criminal justice policy, Hulsman (1986, p.67) proposes 'the *abolition* of criminal justice as we know it'. He notes that in any form, a 'criminology which continues to incorporate in its own "language" the concepts which play a key role in this [criminal justice] process, can never take an external view on this reality and is therefore unable to demystify it' (p.71). To be analytically critical it must abandon the 'definitional activities of the system' including the 'notion of "crime" ... [which] is not the *object* but the *product* of criminal policy' (p.71).

As a political and ideological process, criminalization names and outlaws 'a certain occurrence or situation as undesirable'. It attributes responsibility to individuals, responding through the mechanics of 'social control: the style of punishment'. This process requires a 'special organizational setting' – the criminal justice system. Whatever the criminal justice response, its negotiation sidelines the victim and perpetrator, leaving resolution to criminal justice 'professionals, whose main interest is not related to the original event, but their daily work in criminal justice' (Hulsman, 1986, p.72). As Mathiesen argues, it is unsurprising that such professionals operate in denial and, adopting their targets and assessments, proclaim success for *their* system. The evidence presented in the earlier chapters reveals how the process compromises even those whose 'duty of care' should be paramount.

Hulsman notes the all-pervasiveness of the multiple 'problematic' situations and occurrences that constitute the complexity of daily social life. The task, he argues, is not to attempt to eradicate 'problematic situations' (they will always occur in complex societies) but 'to influence societal structures in such a way that people can cope and deal with problems in a way which permits growth and learning and avoids alienation' (Hulsman, 1986, p.73). Decarceration and abolitionism are difficult propositions in political contexts where governments win popularity by adopting a punitive discourse. Yet, as the research throughout the earlier chapters indicates, there are limits to public acceptance of that discourse.

As a perspective within criminology and a movement within democratic societies, abolitionism is not confined to operational contexts of incarceration. Beyond the prison walls, it questions the meaning of 'crime' and 'criminal justice' and the application of criminalizing labels. The dynamics and complexities of social action, interaction and reaction reflect histories, places, cultures, moments and the attribution of meaning within those and associated contexts. While administrative criminology adopts the classical linear relationship between causation and consequence, critical analyses emphasize context – framing interpretation and questioning definition. By identifying and understanding the political-economic and sociocultural contexts of defining, targeting and regulating 'crime', critical analyses challenge the pathological model – both individual and social – that informs correction and punishment. They expose the limitations of the processes of criminalization and emphasize the potential of negotiation, mediation and arbitration.

According to Hulsman (1986, pp.78–79) critical analysis offers the means through which the 'activities of criminal justice and its adverse social effects' can be demystified and understood. To achieve this, the focus on what is defined as 'deviant' or 'criminal' behaviour must shift towards a 'situation-oriented approach, micro and macro'. This requires an investment in alternative strategies and processes 'without having recourse to criminal justice' and the 'control babble' that provides its political and ideological justification.

The 'problematic situations' to which Hulsman refers can be identified, understood and addressed only within the experiential world of everyday life, contextualized within the structural relations of power, authority and legitimacy. Within these determining contexts people do have the capacity and opportunity to be active agents in mapping their destinies. They make choices, think differently, act spontaneously, interact responsively and react on impulse or with considered judgement. As 'agents', they also resist the imposition of controls and regulations. They organize, campaign and collectivize their actions in social movements. There are, however, limits to agency-institutionally and structurally. Structural relations embedded in political economies and their histories, state and private institutions, set boundaries to social interaction and personal opportunity. Nowhere is this more evident than in law enforcement, criminal justice and punishment.

Responding to the immediate consequences of Mathieson's 'prison fiasco' and Hulsman's 'control babble' by arguing for penal reform and prisoners' rights, while not betraying the longer term objective of penal abolition, is demanding. As Angela Davis (2003, p.103) argues, 'frameworks that rely exclusively on reforms help to produce the stultifying idea that nothing lies beyond the prison'. She also recognizes that the 'anti-prison movement' is committed to 'the abolition of the prison as the dominant mode of punishment' while retaining the necessary bond of 'genuine solidarity with the millions of men, women and children who are behind bars'. Actively pursuing 'more humane, habitable environments for people in prison without bolstering the permanence of the prison system' proffers a 'major challenge'. It is a 'balancing act', responding to the immediate, often desperate, 'needs of prisoners' and the privations they endure while working towards the objective of 'alternatives to sentencing altogether, no prison construction, and abolitionist strategies that question the place of prison in our future' (pp.103–104).

Cassandra Shaylor (2009, pp.148–149) considers the limitations of campaigns for the rights of women prisoners based on a discourse of gender specificity or, as she refers to it, gender-responsiveness. It is, she argues, a strategy derived within the 'specious notion that the prison system can at any point meet the complex and changing needs of women', relying on an 'understanding of *woman* that remains encased in a stronghold of gender fixity'. She continues, in 'capitulating to the notion that an acceptable role for the state is to "manage" those it deems women, self-identified feminists end up doing the work of the state to control women, albeit with a plan for "nicer" cells and "better" programs'. This is the fulcrum of Davis's 'balancing act' between reformism and abolitionism. Shaylor argues that gender-responsive incarceration actually strengthens the prison system by affirming the pathology of women prisoners rather than addressing the material circumstances of their 'offending' with a commitment to meeting their needs, not least their health and well-being.

Davis contends that what is required is not a uni-dimensional 'alternative' to custody, but rather a whole 'constellation' of initiatives and institutions, thus generating a 'continuum of alternatives'. Noting the broader context of criminalization and policing, she proposes the 'demilitarization of schools, revitalization of education at all levels, a health system that provides free physical and mental health care to all, and a justice system based on reparation and reconciliation rather than retribution and vengeance' (2003, p.107). In pursuing alternative strategies, the depth and breadth of political and ideological deconstruction necessary to lay the foundations for fundamental, necessary institutional change is neither a straightforward nor short-term endeavour.

As this book shows, the unmet needs of women prisoners in Northern Ireland persist against a backdrop of violence and restraint, strip searching and the systemic denial of bodily integrity, self-harm, segregation, appalling physical and mental health care in facilities shared with men, punitive detox programmes, restricted contact with families and children, bereavement, inadequate preparation for release and authoritarian, poorly trained guards. While there is a compelling humanitarian argument for the abolition of women's incarceration, and certainly political and public empathy for a programme of decarceration incorporating the provision of a 'constellation of alternatives', in the short term the deprivations and immiseration endured by women prisoners cannot be ignored. Discrete accommodation for all women prisoners, gender-appropriate policies, regimes and programmes, humane conditions including those imposed on families constitute immediate objectives. The decade's research on which this book is based establishes the case for immediate reforms, including the development of alternatives to criminalization and criminal justice. In affirming the agenda of decarceration an informed and progressive shift, winning hearts and minds, can be achieved towards abolition. This can be attained without reinforcing, reproducing and perpetuating the compromised history of penal reformism.

Appendix: Campaign Organizations against Women's Imprisonment

While this text is derived primarily from research conducted with women in prison in the North of Ireland, it is important to acknowledge the important intellectual campaign and support work conducted by women's organizations dedicated to the decarceration of women in advanced democratic states. Their work, often involving women with direct experience of jail, has been central to a more profound public understanding of women's incarceration, ensuring that the isolation endured by women and girls in prison is challenged. Their campaigning has continued to provide an oppositional force to punitive state institutions and to liberal reformism that assumes that prisons can be 'healthy' and rehabilitative environments.

Women in Prison (The United Kingdom)

Women in Prison supports and campaigns for women affected by the criminal justice system. It assists women with advice on housing, education, mental health, legal rights, work, benefits, debt, domestic violence and more. Women are often incarcerated miles from their homes and families – they lose their homes, their relationships with their children and their mental health in the process. Better outcomes for women mean a reduced use of prison and an increased use of community alternatives. Prison does not work. The best way to cut women's offending is to deal with its root causes.

Women in Prison
Unit 10, The Ivories
6 Northampton Street
London
N1 2HY
Telephone: 020 7359 6674

INQUEST (England and Wales)

INQUEST was founded in 1981. It is the only organization in England and Wales that provides a specialist; comprehensive advice service to bereaved people; lawyers; other advice and support agencies; the media; MPs; and the wider public on contentious deaths and their investigation.

Its casework priorities are deaths in custody (police, prison, immigration detention and deaths of detained patients) with particular concerns about the deaths of women, black people, young people and people with mental health problems.

This reflects a commitment to challenging discrimination in terms of the treatment and care received by the deceased where they were in custody and the experience of bereaved relatives following the death.

INQUEST develops policy proposals and undertakes research to lobby for changes to the inquest and investigation process, reduce the number of custodial deaths and improve the treatment and care of those within the institutions where deaths occur.

INQUEST
3rd Floor
89–93 Fonthill Road
London
N4 3JH
Telephone: 020 7263 1111

Canadian Association of Elizabeth Fry Societies (Canada)

Canadian Association of Elizabeth Fry Societies (CAEFS) works to

- increase public awareness and promotion of decarceration for women;
- reduce the numbers of women who are criminalized and imprisoned in Canada;
- increase the availability of community-based, publicly funded, social service, health and educational resources available for marginalized, victimized, criminalized and imprisoned women;
- increase collaborative work among Elizabeth Fry Societies and other women's groups working to address poverty, racism and other forms of oppression.

Canadian Association of Elizabeth Fry Societies
701–151 Slater Street
Ottawa
Ontario K1P 5H3
Telephone: 613 238 2422

Sisters Inside (Australia)

Sisters Inside is an independent community organization, which exists to advocate for the human rights of women in the criminal justice system and to address gaps in the services available to them. It works alongside women in prison in determining the best way to fulfil these roles.

Sisters Inside
PO Box 3407
South Brisbane
Queensland
Australia 4101
Telephone: 617 3844 5066

Flat Out Inc. (Australia)

Flat Out is a state-wide advocacy and support service for women who have had contact with the criminal justice and/or prison system in Victoria. Flat Out leads and participates in research and community education, seeking to inform the community and other service providers about the issues that occur for women in the prison system. Through community involvement and education, advocacy and research, Flat Out works towards having a strong voice in the prison abolition movement in Australia, in the hope that eventually prisons will not be seen as a legitimate arm of the justice system, but will be viewed as an antiquated, cruel and ultimately ineffective institution.

Flat Out Inc.
54 Pin Oak Crescent
Flemington
Victoria 3031
Telephone: 03 9372 6155
Email: admin@flatout.org.au

Critical Resistance (The United States)

Critical Resistance seeks to build an international movement to end the prison–industrial complex (PIC) by challenging the belief that caging and controlling people makes us safe. We believe that basic necessities such as food, shelter and freedom are what really make our communities secure. As such, our work is part of global struggles against inequality and powerlessness. The success of the movement requires that it reflects communities most affected by the PIC. Because we seek to abolish the PIC, we cannot support any work that extends its life or scope.

Critical Resistance
1904 Franklin Street, Suite 504
Oakland, CA 94612
Telephone: 510 444 0484
Email: crnational@criticalresistance.org

Bibliography

Agozino, B. (2005) 'Nigerian Women in Prison' in J. Sudbury (ed.) *Global Lockdown: Race, Gender and the Prison-Industrial Complex* (New York and Oxon: Routledge).

Arbour, L. (1996) *Commission of Inquiry into Certain Events at the Prison for Women in Kingston* (Ottawa, Canada: Public Works and Government Service Canada).

Aretxaga, B. (2001) 'The Sexual Games of the Body Politic: Fantasy and State Violence in Northern Ireland'. *Culture, Medicine and Psychiatry* Vol 25, pp.1–27.

Ashdown, J. and James, M. (2010) 'Women in Detention'. *International Review of the Red Cross* Vol 92(877), March 2010. Available at: http://www.icrc.org/eng/assets/files/other/irrc-877-ashdown-james.pdf. Last accessed 26 April 2013.

Bangkok Rules (2010) *United Nations Rules for the Treatment of Women Prisoners and Non-custodial Measures for Women Offenders* 15 October 2010 (New York: United Nations General Assembly)

Banks, F. (1958) *Teaching Them to Live* (London: Max Parrish).

Barry, M. and McIvor, G. (2008) *Chaotic Lives: A Profile of Women in the Criminal Justice System in Lothian and Borders* (Edinburgh: Lothian and Borders Community Justice Authority).

Bastick, M. and Townsend, L. (2008) *Women in Prison: A Commentary on the UN Standard Minimum Rules for the Treatment of Prisoners* (Geneva: Quaker United Nations Office).

Bayour, E. (2005) 'Occupied Territories, Resisting Women: Palestinian Women Political Prisoners' in J. Sudbury (ed.) *Global Lockdown; Race, Gender and the Prison-Industrial Complex* (New York and Oxon: Routledge).

BBC News (5 May 2006) 'What Happened in the Hunger Strike?' Available at: http://news.bbc.co.uk/1/hi/northern_ireland/4941866.stm. Last accessed 12 October 2012.

Becker, H. S. (1967) 'Whose Side Are We On?' *Social Problems*, 14, 3. pp.239–247.

Bell, C. and O'Rourke, C. (2007) 'Does Feminism Need a Theory of Transitional Justice? An Introductory Essay', *The International Journal of Transitional Justice* Vol 1. pp.23–44.

Bloom, B. and Covington, S. (2008) 'Addressing the Mental Health Needs of Women Offenders' in R. Gido and L. Dalley (eds.) *Women's Mental Health Issues Across the Criminal Justice System* (Columbus, OH: Prentice Hall).

Bosworth, M. (1999) *Engendering Resistance: Agency and Power in Women's Prisons* (Dartmouth: Ashgate).

Bosworth, M. (2000) 'Confining Femininity: A History of Gender, Power and Imprisonment', *Theoretical Criminology* Vol 4(3). pp.265–284.

Brady, E., Patterson, E., McKinney, Hamill, R. and P. Jackson (eds.) (2011) *In the Footsteps of Anne: Stories of Republican Women Ex-Prisoners* (Belfast: Shanaway Press).

Breen, S. (2004) 'Old Bailey Bomber Ashamed of Sinn Fein' *The Village*, 7 December. Available at: http://irishfreedomcommittee.net/NEWS/december_2004.htm#Marian_Price_interviewDec04.

CAIN webservice, *Internment: Summary of Main Events*, Available at: http://cain.ulst.ac.uk/events/intern/sum.htm. Last accessed 7 May 2013.

Callinicos, A. (1989) *Making History* (Oxford: Polity Press in association with Basil Blackwell).

Calamati, S. (2002) *Women's Stories from the North of Ireland* (Belfast: Beyond the Pale Publications).

Camp, J. (1974) *Holloway Prison: The Place and the People* (Newton Abbot: David and Charles).

Carlen, P. (1983) *Women's Imprisonment: A Study in Social Control* (London: Routledge and Kegan Paul).

Carlen, P. (1990) *Alternatives to Women's Imprisonment* (Milton Keynes: Open University).

Carlen, P. (1998) *Sledgehammer: Woman's Imprisonment at the Milenium* (Basingstoke: Macmillan).

Carlen, P. and Worrall, A. (2004) *Analysing Women's Imprisonment* (Cullompton: Willan).

Carlton, B. and Segrave, M. (2011) 'Women's Survival Post-imprisonment: Connecting Imprisonment with Pains Past and Present' *Punishment and Society* Vol 13(5). pp.551–570.

Chesler, P. (1972) *Women and Madness* (New York: Avon).

Christie, N. (1994) *Crime Control as Industry* (2nd Edn) (London: Routledge).

CJINI (2008) *Ash House, Hydebank Wood Report of an Announced Inspection by HM Chief Inspoector of Prisons and the Chief Inspector of Criminal Justice in Northern Ireland 29 October–2 November 2007* (London: Her Majesty's Inspector of Prisons).

Cohen, S. (1993) 'Human Rights and Crimes of the State: The Culture of Denial' *Australia and New Zealand Journal of Criminology* Vol. 26, No. 2. pp.97–115

Cohen, S. (2001) *States of Denial: Knowing about Atrocities and Suffering* (Cambridge: Polity Press).

Compton, E. (1971) *Report of the Enquiry into Allegations against the Security Forces of Physical Brutality in Northern Ireland Arising out of Events on the 9th August, 1971* (London: Her Majesty's Stationery Office). Available at: http://cain.ulst.ac.uk/hmso/compton.htm. Last accessed 7 May 2013.

Coogan, T. P. (1980) *On the Blanket: The H Block Story* (Dublin: Ward River Press).

Coogan. T. P. (1984) *The I.R.A.* (Harmondsworth: Penguin).

Corcoran, M. (2006) *Out of Order: The Political Imprisonment of Women in Northern Ireland 1972–1998* (Cullompton: Willan).

Corston, J. (2007) *The Corston Report: A Report by Baroness Jean Corston of a Review of Women with Particular Vulnerabilities in the Criminal Justice System* (London: Home Office).

Covington, S. and Bloom, B. (2003) 'Gendered Justice: Women in the Criminal Justice System' in B. Bloom (ed.) *Gendered Justice: Addressing Female Offenders* (Carolina Academic Press).

CPT (2004) *Conclusions and Recommendations of the Committee against Torture: United Kingdom of Great Britain and Northern Ireland, Crown Dependencies and*

Oversees Territories (CAT/C/CR/33/3) 10th December. Available at: http://www. refworld.org/docid/42cd6d8d4.html.

Craig, S. C. (2009) 'A Historical Review of Mother and Child Programs for Incarcerated Women', *The Prison Journal* 89(1). pp.35S–53S.

Crawford, C. (1999) *Defenders or Criminals? Loyalist Prisoners and Criminalisation* (Belfast: Blackstaff).

Criminal Justice Inspection Northern Ireland (2010a) *Not a Marginal Issue: Mental Health and the Criminal Justice System in Northern Ireland.* March 2010 (Belfast: CJINI).

Criminal Justice Inspection Northern Ireland (2010b) *Northern Ireland Prison Service Corporate Governance Arrangements.* December 2010 (Belfast: CJINI).

Criminal Justice Inspection Northern Ireland (with Her Majesty's Chief Inspector of Prisons England and Wales and the Regulation and Quality Improvement Authority) (2011a) *Report on an Unannounced Short Follow-up Inspection of Hydebank Wood Women's Prison.* 21–25 March 2011 (Belfast: CJINI).

Criminal Justice Inspection Northern Ireland (2011b) *An Inspection of Prisoner Resettlement by the Northern Ireland Prison Service.* October 2011 (Belfast: CJINI).

Davis, A. (1971) *If they Come in the Morning . . .* (London: Orbach & Chambers).

Davis, A. (1990) *Women, Race and Class* (London: The Women's Press).

Davis, A. (2003) *Are Prisons Obsolete?* (New York: Seven Stories).

Davis, M. (2001) 'The Flames of New York', *New Left Review* 12, November–December.

Department of Justice, Northern Ireland Prison Service, Probation Board for Northern Ireland (2010a) *A Strategy to Manage Women Offenders and those Vulnerable to Offending Behaviour 2010–2013.* October 2010 (Belfast: Department of Justice).

Department of Justice (2010b) *The Northern Ireland Prison Population in 2009* (Belfast: DOJ).

Dickson, B. (2011) *Law in Northern Ireland: An Introduction* (Belfast: SLS Publications).

Dodge, J. and Forward, S. (2006) 'Miss Agnes Resbury (1858–1943): The Memoirs of a Warden at Holloway', *Women's History Review* Vol 15(5). pp.783–804.

Donahue, D. (1980) 'Human Rights in Northern Ireland: Ireland v. the United Kingdom', *Boston College International and Comparative Law Review* Vol 3(2), Article 4. Available at: http://lawdigitalcommons.bc.edu/iclr/vol3/iss2/4. Last accessed 7 May 2013.

Eaton, M. (1993) *Women after Prison* (Buckingham: Open University Press).

Easton, H. and Matthews, R. (2011) *Evaluation of the Inspire Women's Project* (London: London South Bank University).

Easton, S. (2011) *Prisoners' Rights: Principles and Practice* (London: Routledge).

European Commission on Human Rights (1976) Ireland v. the United Kingdom, Y.B. EUR. CONY. ON HUMAN RIGHTS 512 (European Commission of Human Rights) (Report of the Commission).

European Court of Human Rights (1978) *Case of Ireland v. the UK*, Application No. 5310/71, Judgment Strasbourg 18 January 1978.

Fairweather, E., McDonough, R. and McFadyean, M. (1984) *Only the Rivers Run Free: Northern Ireland The Women's War* (London: Pluto Press).

Faith, K. (1993) *The Politics of Confinement and Resistance* (Vancouver: Press Gang Publishers).

Fitzduff, M. and O'Hagan, L. (2009) *The Northern Ireland Troubles: INCORE Background Paper*. Available at http://cain.ulst.ac.uk/othelem/incorepaper09.htm. Last accessed 8 October 2012.

Fitzgerald, M. (1974) *Prisoners in Revolt* (Harmondsworth: Penguin).

Foucault, M. (1979) *Discipline and Punish: The Birth of the Modern Prison System* (Harmondsworth: Penguin).

Foucault, M. (1981) *The History of Sexuality: Volume 1* (Harmondsworth: Penguin)

Freedman, E. B. (1984) *Their Sister's Keepers: Women's Prison Reform in America, 1830–1930* (Ann Arbour, MI: University of Michigan Press).

Gardiner Commission (1975) *Report of a Committee to consider, in the Context of Civil Liberties and Human Rights Measures to Deal with Terrorism in Northern Ireland* (London: HMSO).

Gelsthorpe, L. and Morris, A. (2002) 'Women's Imprisonment in England and Wales: a Penal Paradox', *Criminal Justice* Vol 2(3). pp.277–301.

George, A. (1992) 'Strip Searches: Sexual Assault by the State' in Patricia Weiser Easteal (ed.) *Without Consent: Confronting Adult Sexual Violence, Proceedings of a Conference held 27–29 October 1992*, January 1993 (Canberra: Australian Institute of Criminology). Available at: http://www.aic.gov.au/publications/previous%20series/proceedings/1-27/20.html. Last accessed 7 May 2013.

George, A. (1995) 'The Big Prison' in Women in Prison Group (ed.) *Women and Imprisonment* (Melbourne: Fitzroy Legal Service).

Gil-Robles, A (2005) *Report on Visit to the UK, Commissioner for Human Rights*, 4–12 November 2004. (Strasbourg: Office of the Commissioner for Human Rights).

Goffman, E. (1968) *Asylums: Essays on the Social Situation of Mental Patients and Other Inmates* (Harmondsworth: Penguin).

Hampton, B. (1995) *Prisons and Women* (NSW: New South Wales University Press).

Hannah-Moffatt, K. (2001) *Punishment in Disguise: Penal Governance and Federal Imprisonment of Women in Canada* (Toronto: University of Toronto Press).

Hansard, Stormont Assembly, Committee for Justice, 21 March 2013, Review of the Northern Ireland Prison Service Estate Strategy: Final Decisions on Way Forward. Available at: http://www.niassembly.gov.uk/Assembly-Business/Official-Report/Committee-Minutes-of-Evidence/Session-2012-2013/March-2013/Review-of-the-Northern-Ireland-Prison-Service-Estate-Strategy-Final-Decisions-on-Way-Forward. Accessed 23 May 2013.

Harvey, L. (1990) *Critical Social Research* (London: Sage).

Hayman, S. (2007) 'Reforming the Prison: A Canadian Tale' in F. Heidensohn (ed.) *Gender and Justice: New Concepts and Approaches* (Cullompton: Willan).

Heidensohn, F. (1985) *Women and Crime* (London, Macmillan).

Hendrick, H. (2006) 'Histories of Youth Crime and Justice' in B. Goldson and J. Muncie (eds.) *Youth Crime and Justice* (London: Sage).

Hennessy, J. (1984) *Report of Inquiry into the Security Arrangements at H.M. Prison Maze* (London: HMSO).

Her Majesty's Chief Inspector of Prisons (1997) *Women in Prison a Thematic Review* (London: Home Office).

HMCIP (2003) *Report of a Full Announced Inspection of HMP Maghaberry 13–17 May 2002 by HM Chief Inspector of Prisons* (London: Her Majesty's Stationery Office).

HMIP, (2004), *Expectations: Criteria for assessing the conditions in prisons and the treatment of prisoners* Her Majesty's Inspectorate of Prisons (London: Her Majesty's Stationery Office).

Her Majesty's Chief Inspector of Prisons and the Chief Inspector of Criminal Justice in Northern Ireland (HMCIP/CJINI) (2005) *Report on an Unannounced Inspection of the Imprisonment of Women in Northern Ireland, Ash House, Hydebank Wood Prison 28–30 November 2004* (Belfast: HMCIP).

Her Majesty's Chief Inspector of Prisons (2007) *The Mental Health Needs of Prisoners: A Thematic Review of the Care and Support of Prisoners with Mental Health Needs* (London: Home Office).

Her Majesty's Inspectorate of Prisons (2003) *Report of a Full Announced Inspection of HMP Maghaberry 13–17 May 2002 by HM Chief Inspector of Prisons* (London: Her Majesty's Stationery Office).

Hercules, T. (1989) *Labelled a Black Villain* (Fourth Estate Classic House).

Hirst, J. (1998) 'The Australian Experience' in N. Morris and D. Rothman (eds.) *The Oxford History of the Prison System: The Practice of Punishment in Western Society* (Oxford: Oxford University Press).

Hosie, A. (2013) 'Human Rights in an Institutional Setting' in M. Malloch and G. McIvor (eds.) *Women, Punishment and Social Justice* (London: Routledge).

Howard, P. (2006) 'The Long Kesh Hunger Strikers: 25 Years Later' *Social Justice* Vol 33(4). pp.69–91.

Howe, A. (1994) *Punish and Critique: Towards a Feminist Analysis of Penality* (London: Routledge).

Hudson, B. A. (1993) *Penal Policy and Social Justice* (London: Macmillan).

Hudson, B. A. (2000) 'Critical reflection as research methodology', in V. Jupp, P. Davies and P. Francis (eds.) *Doing Criminological Research*, (London: Sage).

Hulsman, L. (1986) 'Critical Criminology and the Concept of Crime', *Contemporary Crises* Vol 10. pp.63–80.

Independent Monitoring Board (2011) *Annual Report 2009–2010* (Belfast: IMB).

Ireland v. The United Kingdom, 5310/71, Council of Europe: European Court of Human Rights, 13 December 1977. Available at: http://www.unhcr.org/refworld/docid/3ae6b7004.html. Last accessed 8 October 2012.

Jaworski, K. (2009) 'Deliberate Taking: The Author, Agency and Suicide', paper delivered at *Foucault: 25 years on, A Conference Hosted by the Centre for Post-colonial and Globalisation Studies*, Adelaide, 25 June 2009. Available at: http://w3.unisa.edu.au/hawkeinstitute/publications/foucault-25-years/default.asp. Last accessed 3 May 2013.

Johnston, N. (2009) 'Evolving Function: Early Use of Imprisonment', *The Prison Journal*, Mar., 2009, 10s–34s.

Jupp, V. R. (1989) *Methods of Criminological Research* (London: Allen & Unwin).

Kathrada, A. and Vassen, R. (1999) *Letters from Robbin Island: A Selection of Ahmed Kathrada's Prison Correspondence, 1964–1989* (Capetown: Zebra Press).

Kelly, L. (1988) *Surviving Sexual Violence* (Cambridge: Polity Press).

King, R. D. (2000) 'Doing Research in Prisons' in R. D. King and E. Wincup (eds.) *Doing Research on Crime and Justice* (Oxford: Oxford University Press, pp.285–314).

King, R. D. and Liebling, A. (2008) 'Doing Research in Prisons' in R. D. King and E. Wincup (eds.) *Doing Research on Crime and Justice* (2nd Edn) (Oxford: Oxford University Press, pp.431–451).

Knepper, P. and Scicluna, S. (2010) 'Historical Criminology and the Imprisonment of Women in 19th Century Malta', *Theoretical Criminology* Vol 14(4). pp.407–424.

Krog, A. (1998) *Country of My Skull* (Johannesburg: Random House).

Law, V. (2009) *Resistance Behind Bars: The Struggles of Incarcerated Women* (Oakland, CA: PM Press).

Lawsten, J. (2013) 'Prisons, Gender Responsive Strategies and Community Sanctions: The Expansion of Punishment in the United States' in M. Malloch and G. McIvor (eds.) *Women, Punishment and Social Justice: Human Rights and Penal Practices* (Oxon: Routledge).

Leder, D. (2004) 'Imprisoned Bodies: The Life-World of the Incarcerated' *Social Justice* Vol 31(1–2). pp.51–66.

Liebling, A. (1999) 'Doing Research in Prison: Breaking the Silence?' *Theoretical Criminology* Vol 3, No. 2, pp.147–173.

Loucks, N., Malloch, M., McIvor, G., and Gelsthorpe, L. (2006) *Evaluation of the 218 Centre* (Edinburgh: Scottish Executive).

Maden, T. (1996) *Women, Prisons and Psychiatry: Mental Disorder Behind Bars* (Oxford: Butterworth-Heinemann).

Malloch, M. (2000) *Women, Drugs and Custody* (Winchester: Waterside Press).

Malloch, H. (2013) 'A Healing Place? Okimaw Ohci and a Canadian Approach to Aboriginal Women' in M. Malloch and G. McIvor (eds.) *Women, Punishment and Social Justice: Human Rights and Penal Practices* (Oxon: Routledge).

Mama, A. et al. (1986) *Breaking the Silence: Women's Imprisonment* (London: Greater London Council).

Mandaraka-Sheppard, A. (1986) *The Dynamics of Aggression in Women's Prisons in England* (Aldershot: Gower).

Martin, C. (2000) 'Doing Research in a Prison Setting' in V. Jupp, P. Davies and P. Francis (eds.) *Doing Criminological Research* (London: Sage) pp.215–233.

Mathiesen, T. (1973) *The Politics of Abolition* (London: Martin Robertson).

Mathiesen, T. (1990) *Prison on Trial* (London: Sage).

McCafferty, N. (1981) *The Armagh Women* (Dublin: Co-op Books Publishing).

McClelland, R. (2005) *A Review of Non-natural Deaths in Northern Ireland Prison Service Establishments June 2002–March 2004.* (Belfast: Northern Ireland Prison Service.)

McCormack, T. (2008) 'Long Bay Prison', *Dictionary of Sydney*, Available at: http://www.dictionaryofsydney.org/entry/entry/long_bay_prison, viewed 26 April 2013.

McCulloch, J. and George, A. (2009) 'Naked Power: Strip Searching Women in Prison' in P. Scraton and J. McCulloch (eds.) *The Violence of Incarceration* (Oxon: Routledge).

McEvoy, K. (1998) 'Prisoner Release and Conflict Resolution: International Lessons for Northern Ireland', *International Criminal Justice Review* Vol. 8. pp.33–59.

McEvoy, K. (2001) *Paramilitary Imprisonment in Northern Ireland: Resistance, Management and Release* (Oxford: Oxford University Press).

McEvoy, K., McConnachie, K. and Jamieson, R. (2007) 'Political Imprisonment and the "War on Terror"' in Y. Jewkes (ed.) *Handbook on Prisons* (Cullompton: Willan).

McGowan, R. (1998) 'The Well-Ordered Prison: England, 1780–1865' in N. Morris and D. Rothman (eds.) *The Oxford History of the Prison System: The Practice of Punishment in Western Society* (Oxford: Oxford University Press).

McGuffin, J. (1973) *Internment* (Dublin: Anvil Books).

McIvor, G. and Burman, M. (2011) *Understanding the Drivers of Female Imprisonment in Scotland. Report number 02.2011* (Universities of Stirling and Glasgow, Scottish Centre for Crime and Justice Research).

McKeown, L. (2001) *Out of Time: Irish Republican Prisoners Long Kesh 1972–2000* (Belfast: Beyond the Pale Publications).

McKeown, L. (2009) 'An Afternoon in September' in P. Scraton and J. McCulloch (eds.) *The Violence of Incarceration* (Oxon: Routledge).

McKittrick, D., Kelters, S., Feeney, B., Thornton, C. and McVea, D. (2004) *Lost Lives:the Stories of the Men, Women and Children Who Died as a Result of the Northern Ireland Troubles* (Edinburgh and London: Mainstream Publishing).

McMullan, S., Mamelin, K. and Willis, M. (2004) 'The Northern Ireland Prison Population in 2003', *Research and Statistical Bulletin* 2/2004 (Northern Ireland Office).

Medlicott, D. (2007) 'Women in Prison', in Y. Jewkes (ed.) *Handbook on Prisons* (Cullompton: Willan).

Ministry of Justice (2007) The Government's Response to the Report by Baroness Corston of a Review of women with particular Vulnerabilities in the criminal Justice System. London: Ministry of Justice.

Ministry of Justice (2012a) 'Population and Capacity Briefing for Friday 23/11/12'. Available at: http://www.justice.gov.uk/statistics/prisons-and-probation/prison-population-figures. Last accessed 27 November 2012.

Ministry of Justice (2012b) 'Types of Offender: Foreign National Prisoners' Available at: http://www.justice.gov.uk/offenders/types-of-offender/foreign. Last accessed 28 November 2012.

Neufeld, Roger. (1998) 'Cabals, Quarrels, Strikes, and Impudence: Kingston Penitentiary, 1890–1914.' *Social History/Histoire Sociale* 31.61.

Ní Aoláin, F. and Campbell, C. (2005) 'The Paradox of Transition in Conflicted Democracies' *Human Rights Quarterly*, 27. pp.172–213.

NIPS (2005) *The Re-integration Needs of Women Prisoners in Northern Ireland* (Belfast: Northern Ireland Prison Service).

NIPS (2010a) *Annual Report and Accounts 2009–2010* (Belfast: Northern Ireland Prison Service).

NIPS (2010b) *A Review of the Searching of Prisoners in the Northern Ireland Prison Service (NIPS). 30* September 2010 (Belfast: Northern Ireland Prison Service).

NIPS (2010c) *Gender-Specific Standards for Working with Women Prisoners.* November 2010 (Belfast: Northern Ireland Prison Service).

NIPS (2011) *Annual Report and Accounts*: 2010–11 (Belfast: Northern Ireland Prison Service).

O'Hearn, D. (2006) *Nothing but an Unfinished Song: Bobby Sands, the Irish Hunger Striker Who Ignited a Generation* (London: Pluto Books).

O'Keefe, T. (2006) 'Menstrual Blood as a Weapon of Resistance', *International Feminist Journal of Politics* Vol 8(4). pp.535–556.

O'Toole, S. (2006) *The History of Australian Corrections* (New South Wales: New South Wales University Press).

Parvaz, N. (2003) 'Beneath the Narcissus: A Woman's Experience of Iranian Prisons and Beyond', *Feminist Review* Vol 73. pp.71–85.

Peckham, A. (1985) *A Women in Custody* (London: Fontana).

Pickering, S. (2002) *Women, Policing and Resistance in Northern Ireland* (Belfast: Beyond the Pale Publications).

Pollack, S. (2008) *Locked in and Locked out: Imprisoning Women in the Shrinking and Punitive Welfare State* (Waterloo: Wilfred Laurier University).

Prison Review Team (2011a) *Review of the Northern Ireland Prison Service: Conditions, Management and Oversight of all Prisons, Interim Report February 2011* (Belfast: PRT).

Prison Review Team (2011b) *Review of the Northern Ireland Prison Service: Conditions, Management and Oversight of all Prisons.* Final Report October 2011 (Belfast: PRT).

Prisoner Ombudsman (2012) *Report by the Prisoner Ombudsman into the Circumstances Surrounding the Death of Frances McKeown who Died whilst in the Custody of Hydebank Wood Women's Prison on 4 May 2011 Aged 23* (Belfast: The Prisoner Ombudsman for Northern Ireland).

Quinney, R. (2006) 'The Life Inside: Abolishing the Prison', *Contemporary Justice Review* Vol 9(3). pp.269–275.

Radford, J., Harne, L. and Friedberg, M. (2000) 'Introduction', in J. Radford, M. Friedberg and L. Harne (eds.) *Women, Violence and Strategies for Action: Feminist Research, Policy and Practice* (Buckingham: Open University Press).

Rafter, N. (1985) *Partial Justice Women in State Prisons, 1800–1935* (Boston, MA: Northeastern University Press).

Rafter, N. (1990) *Partial Justice: Women, Prisons and Social Control* (2nd Edn) (New Brunswick: Transaction Publishers).

Robins, S. (2012) 'Transitional Justice as an Elite Discourse', *Critical Asian Studies* Vol 44(1). pp.3–30.

Rolston, B. (2002) 'Assembling the Jigsaw: Truth, Justice and Transition in the North of Ireland', *Race and Class* Vol 44(1). pp.87–105.

Rothman, D. (1998) 'Perfecting the Prison: United States, 1789–1865' in N. Morris and D. Rothman (eds.) *The Oxford History of the Prison: The Practice of Punishment in Western Society* (Oxford: Oxford University Press).

Rotman, E. (1998) 'The Failure of Reform: United States, 1865–1965' in N. Morris and D. Rothman (eds.) *The Oxford History of the Prison: The Practice of Punishment in Western Society* (Oxford: Oxford University Press).

Ryder, C. (2000) *Inside the Maze: The Untold Story of the Northern Ireland Prison Service* (London: Methuen).

Sandler, M. and Coles, D. (2008) *Dying on the Inside: Examining Women's Deaths in Prison* (London: INQUEST).

Scraton, P. (1999/ 2009) *Hillsborough: The Truth* (Edinburgh: Mainstream).

Scraton, P. (2004) 'Speaking Truth to Power: Experiencing Critical Research' in M. Smyth and E. Williamson (eds.) *Researchers and their 'Subjects': Ethics, Power, Knowledge and Consent* (Bristol: The Policy Press).

Scraton, P. and Chadwick, K. (1987) *In the Arms of the Law: Coroners' Inquests and Deaths in Custody* (London: Pluto).

Scraton, P. and Haydon, D. (2002) 'Challenging the Criminalization of Children and Young People: Securing a Rights-based Agenda' in J. Muncie, G. Hughes and E. McLaughlin (eds.) *Youth Justice: Critical Readings* (London: Sage/The Open University).

Scraton, P. and McCulloch, J. (eds.) (2009) *The Violence of Incarceration* (Oxon: Taylor and Francis).

Scraton, P. and Moore, L. (2005) *The Hurt Inside* (Belfast: Northern Ireland Human Rights Commission).

Scraton, P. and Moore, L. (2007) *The Prison Within: The Imprisonment of Women at Hydebank Wood 2004–2006* (Belfast: Northern Ireland Human Rights Commission).

Scraton, P., Jemphrey, A. and Coleman, S. (1995) *No Last Rights: The Denial of Justice and the Promotion of Myth in the Aftermath of the Hillsborough Disaster* (Oxford: LCC/Alden Press).

Senior, J. and Shaw, J. (2007) 'Prison Healthcare' in Y. Jewkes (ed.) *Handbook on Prisons* (Cullompton: Willan).

Sharoni, S. (1999) 'Gendering Resistance within an Irish Republican Prisoner Community: A Conversation with Laurence McKeown' *International Feminist Journal of Politics* Vol 1(2). Available at: https://www.researchgate.net/publication/233200382_Gendering_Resistance_within_an_Irish_Republican_Prisoner_Community_A_Conversation_with_Laurence_McKeown. Last accessed 11 May 2013.

Shaw, H. and Coles, D. (2007) *Unlocking the Truth: Families' Experiences of the Investigation of Deaths in Custody* (London: INQUEST).

Shaylor, C. (1998) 'It's Like Living in a Black Hole: Women of Color and Solitary Confinement in the Prison Industrial Complex', *Criminal and Civil Confinement* Vol 24. pp.385–416.

Shaylor, C. (2009) 'Neither Kind Nor Gentle: The Perils of Gender Responsive Justice' in P. Scraton and J. McCulloch (eds.) *The Violence of Incarceration* (New York/ London: Routledge).

Sheehan, R., McIvor, G and Trotter, C. (eds.) (2011) *Working with Women Offenders in the Community* (Cullompton: Willan Publishing).

Shoemaker, R. (1991) *Prosecution and Punishment: Petty Crime and the Law in London and Rural Middlesex, c. 1660–1725* (Cambridge: Cambridge University Press).

Sim, J. (1990) *Medical Power in Prisons* (Milton Keynes: The Open University Press).

Sim, J. (2003) 'Whose Side Are We Not On? Researching Medical Power in Prisons' in S. Tombs and D. Whyte (eds.) *Unmasking the Crimes of the Powerful: Scrutinizing States and Corporations* (New York: Peter Lang) pp.219–238.

Singleton, N., Meltzer, H., Gatward, R. and Coid, J. (1998) Office for National Statistics, *Psychiatric Morbidity among Prisoners: Summary Report* (London: ONS).

Size, M. (1957) *Prisons I Have Known* (London: George Allen and Unwin).

Sjoberg, L. (2007) 'Agency, Militarized Femininity and Enemy Others: Observations from the War in Iraq', *Feminist Journal of Politics* Vol 9(1). pp.82–101.

Smart, C. (1976) *Women, Crime and Criminology* (London, Routledge and Kegan Paul).

Smith, C. (2009) 'A Period in Custody: Menstruation and the Imprisoned Body', *Internet Journal of Criminology.* pp.1–25.

Sontag, S. (2003) *Regarding the Pain of Others* (New York: Picador).

Spierenburg, P. (1998) 'The Body and the State: Early Modern Europe' in N. Morris and D. Rothman (eds.) *The Oxford History of the Prison: The Practice of Punishment in Western Society* (Oxford: Oxford University Press).

Stanko, E. A. (1985) *Intimate Intrusions: Women's Experience of Male Violence* (London: Routledge and Kegan Paul).

Stanko, E. A. (1990) *Everyday Violence: How Women and Men Experience Sexual and Physical Danger* (London: Pandora Press).

Stanley, E. (2009) *Torture, Truth and Justice: The Case of Timor-Leste* (London: Routledge).

Steele, J. (2003) *Review of Safety at HMP Maghaberry* Safety Review Team Review to the Secretary od State for Northern Ireland.

Stop the Strip-Searches Campaign (undated circa 1987) *Stop Strip Searching* (Dublin: Stop the Strip-Searches Campaign).

Sudbury, J. (2004) 'A World without Prisons: Resisting Militarism, Globalized Punishment, and Empire' *Social Justice* Vol 31(1–2). pp.9–30.

Sudbury, J. (ed.) (2005) *Global Lockdown; Race, Gender and the Prison-Industrial Complex* (New York and Oxon: Routledge).

Sykes, G. (1958) *The Society of Captives: A Study of a Maximum Security Prison* (Princeton, NJ: Princeton University Press).

Target, G. (1975) *Bernadette: The Story of Bernadette Devlin* (London: Hodder and Stoughton).

The Billy Wright Inquiry Team (2010) *The Billy Wright Inquiry – Report.* HC431 (London: The Stationery Office). Available at: http://cain.ulst.ac.uk/issues/collusion/docs/wright_140910.pdf. Last accessed 9th October 2012.

United Nations Office on Drugs and Crime (UNODC) and World Health Organization (WHO) (2009) *Women's Health in Prison: Correcting Gender Inequity in Prison Health* (Copenhagen: WHO).

United Nations Women (UN Entity for Gender Equality and the Empowerment of Women) (2011) 'Suspended Lives: Palestinian Female Prisoners in Israeli prisons'.

Vetten, L. and Bhana, K. (2005) 'The Justice for Women Campaign: Incarcerated Domestic Violence Survivors in Post-Apartheid South Africa' in J. Sudbury (ed.) *Global Lockdown: Race, Gender, and the Prison-Industrial Complex* (London: Routledge).

Walsh, T. (2004) *Incorrections: Investigation Prison Release Practice and Policy in Queensland and its Impact on Community Safety* (Queensland: QUT).

Ward, T. (1983) 'Coroners Inquests 1: Before the Inquest' *Legal Action Bulletin* December 1983.

Ward, T. (1984) 'Coroners Inquests 2: The Inquest' *Legal Action Bulletin* February 1984.

Welch, M. (1997) 'Regulating the Reproduction and Morality of Women', *Women & Criminal Justice* Vol 9(1). pp.17–38.

Whyte, D. (2000) 'Researching the Powerful: Towards a Political Economy of Method?' in R. King and E. Winchup (eds.) *Doing Research on Crime and Justice* (Oxford: Oxford University Press).

Wright Mills, C. (1959) *The Sociological Imagination* (New York: Oxford University Press).

Wright, M. and Smyth, V. (2005) *Personality Disorders and Therapeutic Accommodation*, Unpublished Proposal, December 2005.

Wybron, D. and Dicker, K. (2009) *ACT Women and Prisons: Invisible Bars: The Story Behind the Stats* (ACT, Australia: Women's Centre for Health Matters).

Zaitzow, B. and Thomas, J. (eds.) (2003) *Women in Prison: Gender and Social Control* (London: Lynne Reiner publishers).

Zedner, L. (1998) 'Wayward Sisters: The Prison for Women' in N. Morris and D. Rothman (eds.) *The Oxford History of the Prison: The Practice of Punishment in Western Society* (Oxford: Oxford University Press).

Zedner, L. (2006) 'Women, Crime and Custody in Victorian England' in Y. Jewkes and H. Johnston (eds.) *Prison Readings: A Critical Introduction to Prisons and Imprisonment* (Cullompton: Willan).

Cases

In the High Court of Justice in Northern Ireland, Queen's Bench Division (Judicial Review) An Application by Brendan Conway for Judicial Review and in the Matter of an Adjudication at HMP Maghaberry on 25 October 2010. Neutral Citation No.: [2011] NIQB 40.

McKerr (2004) House of Lords Judgment re McKerr (AP) (Respondent) (Northern Ireland) UKHL 12, 11th March.

Silih v. Slovenia (2009) European Court of Human Rights Judgment (Application No. 71463/01) ECHR, 9th April.

Index

Names Index

Agozino, B., 96
Anderson, Martina, 47, 89
Arafa, Fairouz, 93
Arbour, L., 8
Aretxaga, B., 89, 90
Ashdown, J., 15

Banks, F., 121
Barry, M., 21
Bastick, M., 17
Bayour, E., 92, 93, 94
Becker, H.S., 66
Bell, C., 225
Bhana, K., 52
Black, David, 73
Bloom, B., 16, 17, 21, 224
Bosworth, M., 1, 4, 5, 9, 10, 35, 36, 37
Brady, E., 80, 82, 83, 86, 95
Breen, S., 214
Burman, M., 15, 16

Calamati, S., 90, 91
Callinicos, A., 224
Camp, J., 12, 13, 14
Campbell, C., 225
Carlen, P., 11, 14, 15, 17, 18, 20, 36,
    47, 48, 49, 50, 51, 120, 122, 123,
    124, 227
Carlton, B., 20
Carpenter, Mary
    and the reformatory movement, 9
Carson, Karen
    judicial review of conditions in Ash
        House, 175–6
Chadwick, K., 152
Chesler, P., 136
Christie, N., 60, 61
Cohen, S., 61, 205, 225
Coles, D., 57
Coogan, T.P., 73, 76, 84, 86

Corcoran, M., 47, 80, 81, 82, 83, 85,
    86, 87, 88, 91, 226
Corston, J. (Baroness)
    the 'Corston Report' (2007), 23–4
Covington, S., 16, 17, 21, 224
Craig, S.C., 5, 6, 9
Crawford, C., 74, 75, 76
Creamer, Sheena
    death in New Hall Prison, 151

Davis, A., 43, 44, 48, 95, 96, 232, 233
Davis, M., 56
Devlin, Bernadette, 81
Dicker, K., 20
Dickson, B., 152, 153
Dillon, Pacelli, 75
Dodge, J., 12, 13
Donahue, D., 74

Eaton, M., 20
Easton, H., 210, 211
Easton, S., 151, 224

Fairweather, E., 82, 84, 85, 86
Faith, K., 35, 41, 42
Farrell, Mairead, 87
Fitzduff, M., 72
Fitzgerald, M., 38
Foucault, M., 4, 33, 58, 229
Freedman, E.B., 6, 7, 10, 11
Friedberg, M., 52
Fry, Elizabeth, 5–6, 229, 236

Gatt, Margaret, 82
Gelsthorpe, L., 15, 16
George, A., 17, 56, 94, 124
Gibson, Maureen, 84

Gil-Robles, Alvaro
 visit to Hydebank Wood Women's
  Prison and Young Offenders
  Centre, 174
Goffman, E., 38, 39, 40, 41, 50, 136

Hampton, B., 44, 124
Hannah-Moffat, K., 26, 224
Harne, L., 52
Harvey, L., 62
Haydon, D., 32
Hayman, S., 21, 22
Heidensohn, E., 120
Hendrick, H., 9
Hercules, T., 37, 38
Hirst, J., 4
Holmes, Janet, 137–8, 144, 218
 inquest into the death of in Mourne
  House, 138–9, 143, 165
Howard, P., 77
Howard, John, 5, 229
Howe, A., 49, 50
Hudson, B.A., 62, 63
Hulsman, L., 230, 231, 232

Irvine, Roseanne, 99, 117, 168, 169,
  170, 171, 218
 detention in Mourne House, 144–8
 inquest into the death of in Mourne
  House, 153, 160–7

James, M., 15
Jaworski, K., 221
Johnston, N., 2, 12
Jupp, V.R., 63, 64

Kathrada, A., 45, 47
Keenan, Mary, 80
Kelly, Annie, 98, 117, 147, 148, 165,
  166, 168, 169, 170, 204, 218,
  219, 220
 detention in Mourne House, 139–43
 inquest into the death of in Mourne
  House, 153, 154–60
Kelly, L., 52
King, R. D., 59, 61
Knepper, P., 1
Krog, A., 46

Lagrua, Liz, 85, 86
Law, V., 41, 42
Lawsten, J., 26
Leder, D., 38, 40
Liebling, A., 59, 61, 64, 65, 66
Loucks, N., 23

Maden, T., 14
Malloch, M., 22, 23, 26, 124
Mama, A., 47
Mandaraka-Sheppard, A., 19, 20
Matthews, R., 210, 211
Martin, C., 60
Mathiesen, T., 63, 229, 230, 231
McAllister, Rose, 82, 83
McCafferty, N., 82, 83, 85, 86
McClelland, R., 167, 168
McConville, Madge, 80
McCormack, T., 12
McCulloch, J., 17, 91, 229
McEvoy, K., 73, 78
McGowan, R., 4, 5
McGuffin, J., 80, 81
McIvor, G., 15, 16, 21, 26
McKee, Elizabeth, 81
McKeown, Frances, 207, 219, 220
 death in Ash House/Hydebank
  Wood, 215–18
McKeown, Laurence, 47, 75, 77, 87, 94
McKittrick, D., 72
McLoughlin, Pauline, 86
McMullan, S., 102
McWilliams, Anne-Marie, 82
Medlicott, D., 1, 15, 17
Middleton, Colin, 151, 152
Moore, L., 17, 156, 202
Morris, A., 15, 16
Mowlam, Mo, 79
Mubarek, Zahid
 death in Feltham Young Offenders
  Institution, 151

Neufeld, R., 8
Ní Aoláin, F., 225
Nugent, Kieran, 75

O'Connor, Eilish, 84, 86
O'Dwyer, Ella, 47, 89
ÓFiaich, Cardinal Tomás, 76

O'Hagan, L., 72
O'Hearn, D., 76, 87
O'Keefe, T., 86
O'Neill, Ann, 83
O'Neill, Bridie, 81
O'Toole, S., 2, 3

Parvaz, Nasrin, 92
Peckham, A., 18, 19
Pickering, S., 88
Pollack, S., 20, 224
Price, Dolours, 95
Price, Marian, 95, 207
    imprisonment without trial from
        2011, 214–15

Quinn, Anne-Marie, 84
Quinn, Karen, 90
Quinney, R., 56, 57

Radford, J., 52
Rafter, N., 1, 7, 8, 9, 10
Robins, S., 227
Rolston, B., 79, 225
Rothman, D., 7
Rotman, E., 11
Ryder, C., 73, 75, 83

Sandler, M., 57
Sands, Bobby, 77, 87
Scicluna, S., 1
Scraton, P., 17, 32, 67, 91, 152, 153,
    156, 202, 229
Segrave, M., 20
Senior, J., 10, 11
Shaw, H., 57
Shaw, J., 10, 11
Sharoni, S., 75, 88, 94
Shaylor, C., 42, 233

Sheehan, R., 21
Sheehy-Skeffington, Hanna, 80
Shoemaker, R., 2
Sim, J., 26, 58, 121, 122
Singleton, N., 17
Size, Mary, 13
Sjoberg, L., 92
Smart, C., 122
Smith, C., 36, 37
Smyth, V., 200
Sontag, S., 57, 58
Spierenburg, P., 2, 3, 4
Stanko, E.A., 52
Stanley, E., 226, 227
Steele, J., 79
Sudbury, J., 15, 16, 53
Sykes, G., 17

Thomas, J., 63, 219
Townsend, L., 17
Trotter, C., 21

Vassen, R., 45
Vetten, L., 52

Walsh, T., 42, 43, 125
Ward, T., 152
Welch, M., 2
Whyte, D., 63
Worrall, A., 36, 124
Wright, Billy, 78
    inquiry into the death of in Long
        Kesh/Maze Prison, 79
Wright, M., 200
Wright Mills, C., 62
Wybron, D., 20

Zamel, Ghoufran, 93
Zedner, L., 3, 5, 6, 8, 9, 10, 11, 12, 13

Thematic Index

abolitionism, 229–30, 231, 233
'agency', 21
    choice, autonomy and
        responsibility, 35–6
    the concept of, 28
    contextualising 'agency', 30

denial of, 221
diverse and contrasting forms of, 33
limits to, 27, 203, 232
and prison, 30, 33
and relationship dynamics in
    prisons, 35

'agency' – *continued*
  and resistance, 35, 41–8, 218
Armagh Gaol, 80
  campaign for political status,
    75–6, 83
  the closure of, 79, 89
  'dirt' protest, 84–7
  hunger strike, 87
  politically affiliated prisoners in,
    80–2

Bangkok Rules 2010, 222–3, 224
Belfast/Good Friday Agreement 1998,
    91, 178, 226
  early release of politically affiliated
    prisoners, 72, 79
bridewells, 2
  see also workhouses
Brixton Prison, 6, 47, 89
Brown Royal Commission of Inquiry
    1849, 8

children, 2, 3, 5, 29, 32
  contact with during imprisonment,
    16, 42, 43, 103, 105, 126
  incarcerated, 6, 102, 111, 116, 117,
    155–6
  the pain of separation from, 44, 51,
    105–7
confinement, 2, 9, 54, 65, 133
  challenge to the conditions of, 41
  institutions of, 2
  pains of, 56, 203–24, 229
  solitary, 7, 8, 19, 41, 42, 103, 140,
    142, 147, 215, 219, 223
  the use of, 4
  of women, 4, 25; *see also*
    incarceration, of women;
    women's prisons
conflict in Northern Ireland, 72, 178,
    209, 222, 227
  and the imprisonment of women,
    72, 80–91, 218
  the legacy of for prison policy and
    practice, 73–80, 178, 209,
    210, 215
  transition from, 72, 205, 225–6
Cornton Vale Prison, 18, 50

criminalization, 234
  the policy of in Northern Ireland,
    75–7, 85
  the processes of, 88
criminal justice, 22, 205, 225
  alternatives, 204
  institutions of, 63
  politics and practices of, 62–3, 72,
    91, 96, 211, 231
  system, 6, 21, 25, 49, 96, 103, 207,
    210, 214, 221, 226, 230, 232
Criminal Justice Inspection Northern
    Ireland, 150, 158, 172, 209, 212
critical analysis, 32, 56–9, 62, 231–2
  the potential for challenging and
    affecting change, 63

deaths in custody, 117, 149, 170
  inquests, 149, 152, 165
  McClelland Review of non-natural
    deaths in prisons in Northern
    Ireland, 167
  principles for investigation, 151–3
Department of Justice (Northern
    Ireland), 209

European Committee for the
    Prevention of Torture (CPT), 222
European Convention on Human
    Rights (ECHR), 67, 74, 98, 149,
    156, 170
European Court of Human Rights, 74,
    149, 152

Gardiner Commission, 75
gender, 1, 10, 25, 29, 45, 47
  gendered construction of
    imprisonment, 1, 80, 88, 221
  gendered forms of discipline and
    control, 26, 30, 48
  gendered prison experiences, 16–20,
    92–4
  gendered violence, 48, 52
  gender-specific initiatives, 2, 20, 26,
    126, 173, 205, 223–4
  gender-specific offences, 7
  and identity, 50–1
  mixed-gender prisons, 6

segregation; in the 19th century,
5–6, 8
and sexuality, 32, 51

Hennessy Inquiry, 77–8
Holloway Prison
changes to the women's regime in,
12–14
the founding, development and
consolidation of, 12
the 'New Holloway', 14
redevelopment as a secure hospital
for women prisoners, 14
Human Rights Act 1998, 151, 170
Hydebank Wood Women's Prison and
Young Offenders Centre, 29, 67,
68, 69, 70, 71, 99, 158, 167, 169,
172–6, 178, 185, 187, 197, 201,
202, 205, 207, 211, 215, 218, 222
access to education, 183, 185–6, 207
Ash House, 70, 172, 173, 183, 185,
187, 199, 205, 208, 209, 212
conditions in, 118–19, 175–7, 187–8
healthcare provision in, 118, 194,
197–8, 202
immigration detainees in, 186,
188–90
the impact of research in, 222
imprisonment of mothers, 191–3
incarceration of children in,
174, 190
Independent Monitoring Board for,
71, 208
relationship between prisoners and
staff, 173, 183–5
shared facilities with male prisoners,
186–7
the transfer of women prisoners
from Mourne House to
Hydebank Wood, 68, 69,
117–19, 159, 172, 177, 204
treatment of self-harming and
suicidal women prisoners, 173,
174, 183, 193, 195–201

imprisonment, 1, 3, 17, 18, 24, 30, 53,
63, 68, 78, 100, 123, 156, 175,
203, 221, 227
'culture' of, 4
impact on communities, 73
increased levels of women's
imprisonment, 14–16, 23
of politically motivated women, 72,
80; in an international context,
91–5; in Northern Ireland,
80–91
the pains of, 17
of suffragettes between 1905 and
1914, 13
women's experiences of, 2, 4, 7,
12–13, 16–20, 25, 49, 50–1
incarceration, 31, 33, 38, 65, 188, 219,
222, 233
histories of, 1, 24–5
regimes of, 30, 231
of those awaiting trial, 3
the violence of, 229
of women, 3, 8–9, 18, 20, 25, 27, 29,
46, 57, 82, 103, 204, 205, 212,
213, 218, 221, 224, 233; *see also*
women's prisons
inhuman and degrading treatment,
22, 31, 67, 74, 149, 215, 222, 229
Inspire Women's Project (Inspire), 210
internment, 73, 74–5
see also reactive containment

Ladies' Association for the
Reformation of Female
Prisoners, 5
lifers, 64, 108, 109, 118, 175
Long Kesh/Maze Prison, 74, 79, 83,
87, 98, 112, 178
'blanketmen', 75–6
'dirt' protest, 76
escape from, 77–8
hunger strikes, 76–7
internment camp at, 74–5
and special category status, 74,
75, 77

managerialism, 91
the policy of in Northern Ireland,
73, 78; gendered dimension, 88
Maghaberry Prison, 34, 67, 69, 99,
100, 112, 167, 215, 218
the development of, 78, 89

Maghaberry Prison – *continued*
separation of politically affiliated
prisoners in, 79, 119, 204
Ministry of Justice (England and
Wales), 15, 24
Mourne House, 34, 67, 68, 70, 98,
102, 185
access to education, 100, 103, 106,
109, 113
allegations of 'improper relations'
between male staff and female
prisoners, 116–17
Branch of the Prison Officers'
Association (MHPOA), 69, 99,
112, 116
conditions in, 108, 112
deaths in custody in, 136–48; *see
also* Holmes, Janet; Irvine,
Roseanne; Kelly, Annie
immigration detainees in, 109
the impact of research in, 204–5
incarceration of children in, 110–11,
116, 117, 170
regime in, 99, 103, 119, 126
relationship between prisoners and
staff, 112–13
reports of the Prisons Inspectorate
on, 67, 98, 100–1, 174
separation of politically affiliated
prisoners in, 114–15
treatment of self-harming and
suicidal women prisoners,
127–36, 163
the use of male hospital to treat
women prisoners, 118, 127,
131, 166
the use of punishment cells, 132,
139, 140, 142

Northern Ireland Assembly, 72, 209,
212, 224
devolution of policing and justice
powers to, 72
Hillsborough Agreement 2010,
212, 221
Northern Ireland Human Rights
Commission, 61, 67, 69, 71, 98,
115, 119, 156, 158, 165, 170, 171,
173, 175
investigations of the treatment of
women in prison, 117, 176
opposition to the transfer of women
prisoners from Mourne House
to Ash House, 69, 119, 172
Northern Ireland Office, 84
Northern Ireland Prison Service, 68,
69, 70, 73, 79, 89, 91, 99, 101,
103, 115, 116, 119, 139, 143, 155,
157, 158, 160, 164, 165, 167, 168,
170, 172, 174, 175, 177, 179, 180,
182, 189, 190, 193, 203, 204, 205,
209, 211, 213–15, 227

penal system, 1, 4, 24, 155, 222, 227
penitentiaries, 4, 7–9, 12
physical brutality, 2, 74
and sexual abuse, 7, 11, 24, 25, 41,
46, 51, 93
assaults, 6, 29, 39, 93, 96, 140, 159
power, 21, 40, 51, 52, 62–4, 92, 186,
219, 221, 225, 227
and authority, 32, 65, 232
differentials in prisons, 25, 29, 35,
37, 55, 228
medical, 58
opposition to, 31, 94; *see also*
resistance
structural relations of power,
authority and legitimacy,
30–2, 47
prison(s)
architecture, 4
discipline, 3, 7, 11, 25, 27, 29, 53,
99, 123, 134, 149, 219
histories, 1, 7, 53
regimes, 6
security, 17, 18, 20, 26, 54, 61, 91,
119, 169, 206, 228
as sites of political struggle, 45–6,
72, 92, 94, 95
time, 38
for women, 3, 5, 6, 10, 42; *see also*
women's prisons
prison guards, 34, 44, 47, 68, 70, 74,
76, 100, 109, 120, 126, 165, 166,
168, 178, 184, 194, 212, 233

'culture': in Northern Ireland
    prisons, 209
deaths: in Northern Ireland, 73,
    75, 77
female officers, 25, 84, 89, 90, 98,
    111, 116, 199
indifference, 78, 98, 105, 170, 199
male officers, 24, 37, 73, 92, 113,
    116, 174, 207
relationship with prison
    management, 37
and the use of discretionary powers,
    25, 29, 35, 54, 55, 103–4, 134,
    185, 208
views of self-harm by prisoners, 111,
    112, 127, 130, 137, 140, 154,
    170, 220
in women's prisons, 41, 42, 81
prison research, 42, 57, 66
access and funding for, 59–60, 63
critical approaches to, 32, 56,
    57–9
dissemination of findings, 61, 64
feminist, 37
independent, 66
limitations of state-commissioned
    research, 65
Prison Review Team (PRT), 212
Prisons Inspectorate (England and
    Wales), 16, 67, 71, 100, 139, 150,
    172, 208
prisoner(s)
'at-risk', 55, 70, 111, 133, 138,
    142, 144–5, 147, 157, 166–7,
    169, 173–4, 183, 193, 198,
    205, 216
Catholic/Nationalist/Republican,
    47, 74, 75, 76, 77, 79, 80, 82,
    83, 84, 87, 89, 91, 94, 95, 100,
    102, 111, 114, 115–16, 119, 214
long-term, 65, 73, 98, 105–10, 129,
    131, 174, 175, 177, 206
'ordinary', 30, 44, 48, 74, 78, 79, 80,
    82, 88, 89, 91, 95, 96, 114, 178,
    203, 204, 213, 215, 222, 225
'personality disordered'; the
    treatment of, 18, 123, 126, 134,
    136, 193, 200, 212

political; politically motivated;
    politically affiliated, 47, 72, 73,
    79, 80, 82, 83, 86, 88, 89, 91,
    92, 94, 95, 96, 97, 98, 100, 114,
    178, 204, 213, 220, 222,
    225, 226
Protestant/Unionist/Loyalist, 74, 75,
    78, 79, 82, 83, 91, 95
remand, 17, 83, 88, 102, 103, 165,
    194–5, 207, 209
women, 1, 5, 6, 7, 8, 13, 14, 17, 20,
    23, 25, 26, 36, 41, 42, 44, 46,
    47, 50, 51, 52, 53, 67, 68, 71,
    75, 82, 84, 86, 87, 89, 91, 92,
    95, 98, 99, 101, 102, 112, 114,
    116, 117, 118, 120, 121, 122,
    124, 125, 132, 138, 145, 149,
    158, 164, 166, 169, 170, 174,
    175, 177, 202, 203, 205, 208,
    213, 219, 221, 222, 223,
    226, 233
Prisoner Ombudsman for Northern
    Ireland, 149, 171, 216, 217, 218,
    219, 221
punishment, 4, 8, 18, 26, 32, 39, 62,
    63, 124, 149, 173, 174, 192, 213,
    219, 232
alternative form(s) of, 3, 43
Block/Cell, 17, 29, 34, 35, 45, 55,
    67, 68, 98, 100, 101, 111, 117,
    126, 130, 132, 134, 139, 140,
    141, 142, 143, 144, 147, 148,
    150, 156, 161, 165, 166, 168,
    169, 170, 177, 195, 196
histories of, 1
physicality of, 2, 3, 8, 58
places of, 3, 24; *see also* prison(s)
public agencies of, 7, 53
regimes of, 25

racism, 25, 32, 96, 150
institutional, 37, 49
reactive containment, 73–4
resistance, 31, 36, 41, 47, 157
collective, 33, 42, 45, 47, 73, 80, 94,
    95, 220
and compliance, 41
punishment for acts of, 29, 43,
    50, 219

resistance – *continued*
of women prisoners to medical and
psychiatric categorisation,
35, 122
reformatories, 9–10

sectarianism, 32, 73
self-harm and suicide, 14, 16, 17, 22,
120–48, 157–9, 172–4, 206, 233
care plans, 55, 127, 168, 200
inadequate staff training, 111,
138–9, 142, 144, 156, 157–8,
166, 169
the use of 'strip cells' and
'punishment cells', 26, 42, 117,
124–5, 130, 147
Spinhuis (Amsterdam), 3
strip-searching, 13, 17, 20, 24, 39, 42,
175–6, 180–1, 189, 190, 206, 208,
219, 223, 233
in the context of self-harm, 19, 43,
101, 130, 140
of men prisoners: politically
affiliated, 76
of women prisoners: politically
affiliated, 46, 47, 82, 88–90, 126
Styal Prison, 18–19
surveillance, 4, 10, 11, 18, 20, 25, 26,
42, 88, 106, 122, 219

torture, 47, 67, 74, 93, 149
transportation, 3

United Nations Code of Conduct for
Law Enforcement Officials, 150

United Nations Standard Minimum
Rules for the Treatment of
Prisoners, 149, 222

violence, 48, 102, 154, 214, 218,
223, 233
'continuum of violence', 52–3,
126, 211
inflicted by prison officers, 84,
92, 152
in prisons, 14, 19, 24, 29, 44, 52,
53, 65
politically motivated, 72, 73, 75,
78, 212

women prisoners
as 'criminal women', 53, 120–1
distinct/gendered needs of, 1,
177, 208
healthcare needs in prisons, 16, 17,
21, 25, 44, 93, 101, 115, 124,
128, 130, 146, 150, 166, 174,
193, 194, 197
resettlement in Northern Ireland,
101, 174–5, 202–2, 208,
223, 228
see also prisoner(s), women
Women's Community Support Project
(WCSP), 211
women's prisons, 12, 16, 19, 23, 24,
25, 50, 51, 122, 124, 187
see also prison(s), for women
workhouses, 2, 4
see also bridewells